UFOs in the New Age

CRI *Books*

UFOs
in the New Age

Extraterrestrial Messages
and the Truth of Scripture

William M. Alnor

A **CRI** *Book*

BAKER BOOK HOUSE
Grand Rapids, Michigan 49516

Copyright 1992 by
Baker Book House Company
P.O. Box 6287
Grand Rapids, MI 49516-6287

ISBN: 0-8010-0226-5

Second printing, December 1992

Printed in the United States of America

Library of Congress Cataloging-in-Publication Data

Alnor, William M.
UFOs in the New Age: extraterrestrial messages and the truth of Scripture /
William M. Alnor.
    p.   cm.
Includes bibliographical references.
ISBN 0-8010-0226-5
1. New Age movement. 2. Unidentified flying objects—Religious aspects. 3.
Channeling (Spiritualism) 4. Eschatology. 5. Bible—Prophecies. I. Title.
BP605.N48A49   1992
239—dc20
92-482

To
Jacqueline
my wife
and partner

Contents

Foreword

There was a time when talk of flying saucers and meetings with "space brothers" was considered to be news not fit to be printed in respectable periodicals and certainly it was not a topic of serious discussion among sane people. This book demonstrates how times have changed. The literature and lore of UFOlogy are receiving increased attention from all sectors of society. Our culture is fascinated with the lure of the occult, especially as it is represented in the New Age movement.

In many circles, New Age thinking is not only trendy, it is also seen as a legitimate form of spirituality, an alternative religion. That which was once relegated to the realm of the fantastic is now viewed by many as plausible, and worthy of belief. Enter the resurgence of interest in UFOs, aliens, and "channeled" information. As this book ably demonstrates, our culture has been prepared for the "new religion" and that religion does not appear to be a passing fad. William Alnor clearly establishes the many linkages between New Age thought and UFO phenomena. Some of his conclusions may surprise you.

Alnor has written what social scientists would call an ethnography of the UFO subculture. It is an in-depth analysis of a topic which easily lends itself to sensationalism, yet he demonstrates the kind of balanced, careful approach so often missing in evaluations by evangelical Christian observers. His writing is based on extensive field research coupled with a comprehensive review of the relevant literature, past and present. He has done his homework. This is not a superficial treatment of an exotic subject, but a thought-provoking excursion into the nature of "the power out there." Whether or not you agree with all of his conclusions, you will be challenged to rethink the UFO enigma.

What strikes me most powerfully about this book is the illustration of how God's adversary is capable of deceiving a wide spectrum of people—from sophisticated science fiction writers to ordinary farmers and housewives. In dramatic and convincing fashion, Alnor informs and warns us about the cosmic gospel of the UFO enthusiasts, or what he terms "the gospel according to extraterrestrials." As you will discover, this "gospel" is as old as the Garden of Eden, yet as "new" as the latest Hollywood movie or TV sitcom.

Ronald Enroth
Department of Sociology
Westmont College

Acknowledgments

Many people assisted me in the completion of this book. They were Keith Tolbert of the American Religions Center, Tal Brooke of the Spiritual Counterfeits Project, and author/professor James Bjornstad. They went over the manuscript and offered constructive criticism. Friends Michael Ponente and Camille Obnamia also critiqued the manuscript. Dr. J. Gordon Melton opened his files at the University of California, Santa Barbara, and gave me interesting insights on the UFO movement.

Walt Andrus, director of the Mutual UFO Network, provided tips and data on the Eduard "Billy" Meier UFO case. Brad and Sherry Steiger spent some time with me in both New York and San Diego giving me fascinating insights on the topic, and Bud Press of Watchman Fellowship, and Janet Mayfield of Southern California provided some interesting documentation. Rich Pyle also helped dig out some documentation. Pierre Dubreuil and Stuart Goldman helped with the background information.

Thanks also go to author/cult apologist Robert Bowman for his insights on Star Trek and to Judy McMahon for helping me research the pagan Baal worship systems. Former UFO contactees turned Christians, Lawrence Gianguzzi and Barbara Schutte, helped me understand the abduction phenomena.

Many thanks also to my colleagues at the Christian Research Institute, Irvine, California. Among them were resource manager Rich Poll, who opened CRI's UFO files. New Age experts/

authors Elliot Miller and Ron Rhodes answered questions and provided additional documentation.

I also thank the staff of Calvary Chapel of Philadelphia, most notably Pastor Joe Focht, who not only helped gather information, but also helped undergird me financially during this difficult project.

Thanks also to board members at Eastern Christian Outreach for their support. Special mention goes to Frank Gianni and Rod Rafetto. And last, I especially thank my wife Jacqueline who was by my side all the way in research, writing, and editing.

Introduction

My phone rang one hot summer afternoon in July. The Associated Press was calling.

"What do you have on the army desertion case?" a reporter asked me.

Dumbfounded, I didn't know what he was talking about.

"You mean you didn't hear about it? Well, you will!"

He was right. Because of a religious-trend story I had just written in the *Christian Research Journal* detailing how religious belief in unidentified flying objects (UFOs) was rapidly growing in New Age circles, I received several other media inquiries. Reporters wanted to know my thoughts on why six United States soldiers—all intelligence analysts with top-secret security clearances—went AWOL from their posts in West Germany at the same time, came back to America, and were trying to make it to an alleged rendezvous point with a flying saucer in Florida.

The *Philadelphia Inquirer's* story the next day said the six were arrested near Gulf Breeze, Florida, a town famous for its UFO sightings. What was most bizarre about the story was its religious flavor. They claimed that they were chosen through "psychic messages" to greet alien spaceships commanded by "Jesus," an alien, and would lead a group of people "to a science fiction-style heaven."

"They were apparently convinced that the aliens had chosen them as the chosen few to be on hand when they reclaimed the Earth," said Stan Johnson, a friend of the group's apparent leader.

The six, who are being held at Fort Benning, Ga., adhered to an offshoot Christian belief called the "rapture," said Johnson.

According to the belief, the rapture is the second coming of Jesus Christ, who will return to Earth to take the believers with him seven years before the Earth is destroyed. The group of soldiers, though, is said to believe that Jesus was an alien and would return in a spaceship for the chosen.[1]

As weird as the story sounded, it didn't surprise me. By that time I was well into my research for this book, in which I found that stranger things have happened. It turned out that the Army decided the six had not compromised security. They were promptly fined and discharged, according to an Associated Press story filed ten days later.

What I discovered during the next year as I traveled more than twenty thousand miles, attended various UFO and New Age conferences, read hundreds of books and interviewed many experts on UFOs, talked with many contactees and abductees (people who claim they are regularly contacted and kidnapped by aliens from outer space), and even attended several sessions during which aliens were allegedly giving messages to crowds, is that the UFO "movement" around the globe has blossomed into a powerful religious movement. It has an apocalyptic bent; the aliens usually say they have something to do with the end times referred to in the Bible, and many talk about a "second coming." Believers of these extraterrestrial messengers often call them space brothers. I also refer to them as UFOnauts.

In short, this new religion is intent on changing the world. It wants us to reject traditional Judeo-Christian ideas about God, morality, and even reality itself in favor of a new world order and an occult-based spirituality.

Others, of course, have noted this. But what has caused it? Carl Sagan, the famed astronomer from Cornell University who hosted television's *Cosmos,* suggested that "unfulfilled religious needs" may be partly responsible.[2] I agree with Sagan, but that's only part of the answer.

The answer I will give you in these pages is that UFOs are real, that thousands of people around the world are receiving messages from them, and that these messages are forming the backbone of a new, powerful New Age religion of universalism and fellowship with entities many identify as aliens. Everyone is welcome in this powerful new movement, they say. But their messages make apparent that not everyone is welcome but only those who go along with their New Age plan.

"Man is on the brink of tremendous changes and breakthrough," according to longtime contactee and UFO enthusiast Wayne Aho of Washington State. "And *ONLY* New Age Man, transformed man, can make it through to a new world and a spiritually sane existence."[3]

Said the space being OX-HO who allegedly speaks to those associated with a British Columbian UFO contact group: "People of Earth, you are becoming fourth dimensional [meaning that humanity is evolving into a new species] whether you are ready or not. Leave the old to those who cling to the old. Don't let the New Age leave you behind."[4]

Popular New Age-UFO writer Brad Steiger has been following these messages from alleged-aliens, often called space brothers, for decades. He thinks these messages are so important that he has included many of them in a book called *The Fellowship*, which is part of his attempt to codify them into a new bible of sorts. He wants these ideas to supplant many of the old traditional ideas of Christianity, in favor of a new world occultic faith. He summarizes what the space brothers' job appears to be as we near the twenty-first century:

> Contactees have been told that the Space Beings hope to guide Earth to a period of great unification, when all races will shun discriminatory separations and all of humankind will recognize its responsibility to every other life form existing on the planet. The Space Beings also seek to bring about a single, solidified government, which will conduct itself on spiritual principles and permit all of its citizens to grow constructively in love.[5]

Lest you object to my premise that UFOs are real and that thousands of people worldwide receive messages from them, let me add that I know of very few people in UFOlogy today who don't believe that. As Temple University history professor and UFO expert David Jacobs puts it, UFOs' existence is so well established that it is not a matter to prove anymore as was the tendency in the 1950s and 1960s.[6]

At the same time, I have not affirmed that these messages come from extraterrestrial beings (although UFO believers say they do), and I do not affirm that there is life on any other planet. Without getting into an extended theological discussion, I also do not affirm that there is not life on other planets, either. As a Bible-believing evangelical I have carefully listened to brothers and sisters argue both sides of the issue. My position at this time is to have no position at all on the topic, because we don't have all the facts. But as a result of my research for this book, my sympathies have clearly swung to the side of those who do not believe life exists elsewhere. (This in spite of the fact I grew up a certified science-fiction addict who was almost certain of the opposite.)

If you wonder how I can believe in flying saucers and that thousands of people receive detailed messages from them without my believing in the extraterrestrial-beings hypothesis, this book will tell you why. My conclusions may surprise you; they date back to the dawn of humankind. Other people who have honestly researched this topic, not all of them Christians, have reached similar conclusions, though they are not popular within the UFOlogical subculture.

I came to my conclusions based on the evidence. I have carefully gathered from around the world the messages from the alleged extraterrestrial beings and have read them by the thousands. I spent quality time with people in the movement. I laughed with them, ate with them, and asked them hard questions. Even though in this book I will take the gloves off some of them (I believe some of them are deceived and pushing dangerous doctrines), I personally like most of them. Brad and Sherry Steiger are among them. They were friendly, warm people, eager to answer questions and help me out, even though they knew I had serious problems with their views.

My rationale in taking this direct reporting approach was that since no one can come up with real, live aliens I can talk to (rumors of various saucer crashes and government conspiracies abound, with there being little proof for any of them), the next best thing is to examine, with an open mind, the testimonies of the contactees. The direct reporting approach was also the most honest for me as a Christian. I didn't want to take the approach many would be tempted to take of bashing away at the New Age-UFO movement without spending some time at the conferences and talking to many of its key figures.

I also compared the aliens' messages with God's Word, the Bible, to see if there is any common ground. Are the space brothers really demonic, as some Christians charge?

Many of these messages have come through occultic means like channeling and automatic writing, while others came through first-person testimonies of contactees. The results of these messages were in many ways frightening to me. Although the many different messages have come from many different alien sources, almost all of them say essentially the same thing. They are unified to the point that a person could believe an alien conspiracy had been unleashed against humanity.

Similarly, I believe the beings, whoever they are—and this book reveals who they are—are up to no good, and their motives are far from helping us to usher in the New Age. I also warn the reader to try to avoid having anything to do with UFOs and channeled messages, no matter how fascinating the subject is. The intrigue and spiritual dangers surrounding even small amounts of fooling around in this field are great. Long time UFO researcher John Keel notes a high number of fatalities among those dabbling in UFO contacts.[7]

While discovering that the phenomenon is real, I also found that the UFO arena is loaded with fakery, hoaxes, and people so paranoid they probably belong in mental institutions. It is also true that many people exploit the UFO phenomenon for financial gain. In reading these extraterrestrial messages it is obvious many of them cannot be taken seriously.

Am I to take the Reverend June Young from Milwaukee seriously, for example? Using the name Bright Star, she sold channeled messages from Elvis Presley, whom she claims was aboard a flying saucer somewhere still writing songs. For $3.95 you could order Young's book containing her talks with Elvis Presley "since he made his transition, August 16, 1977." In one message "Elvis" says that he is "no longer flesh, I have an Electronic Body . . . I can go back to my true IDENTITY before the world was made—one of God's many sons."

I also did not delve too deeply into speculative theories on themes many UFO buffs love to talk about: an alleged government conspiracy (actually, many government conspiracy theories) to keep "the truth" about UFOs away from the public; alleged genetic experiments the "grey" aliens carry on that involve cattle mutilations, etc.; or speculative theories on the identity of the Nephalim of Genesis 6. Although some of these—the cattle mutilation mystery in particular—warrant further investigation, many of these theories are unprovable.

I also thought it unwise to dig too deeply into certain occult themes that seem to be intertwined with the UFO phenomenon. I only mention in passing the hollow-earth theory, the imminent-pole-shift theory, the "prophecies" of Nostradamus, and certain other related themes.

This book is also about belief, one of the central points in understanding the UFO phenomenon. Something about human nature wants to believe in flying saucers and extraterrestrial life. But it often doesn't matter if some UFO theory (such as the theory of the United States government's secret MJ-12) has been decisively shot down; people will still believe it.[8]

Perhaps Percival Lowell so wanted to believe there was life on Mars that his eyes played tricks on him, causing him to draw canals on his diagrams of the Martian surface in the late 1800s. As John Wiley wrote in *The Smithsonian*:

Many people, I suspect, want the aliens to arrive for the sheer excitement and for the disruption of the routine of daily life. . . . We have a history of yearning for alien life. The popular response today to movies about lovable, or at least benign, aliens seems little different from the excitement of newspaper readers in 1835 over a phony report that Sir John F. W. Herschel had "discovered" batlike people living on the moon. . . . The hoax could not have lasted as long as it did unless people wanted to believe it.[9]

I also recall the story of a young man in Scranton, Pennsylvania, who had quite a reputation of being a prankster. He staged an elaborate UFO landing illusion and called various reporters. One by one he told them the same story about a UFO. Later, even after this story, one of the many hoaxes he had pulled on the public, unraveled and he laughed with glee over how he had fooled everyone, and even after he talked about it to the media, many people in his region were still convinced it was a real UFO.[10]

But this is also a story of deception. The key to the UFO enigma is partly answered in 1 John 4:1–3:

Dear friends, do not believe every spirit, but test the spirits to see whether they are from God, because many false prophets have gone out into the world. This is how you can recognize the Spirit of God: Every spirit that acknowledges that Jesus Christ has come in the flesh is from God, but every spirit that does not acknowledge Jesus is not from God. This is the spirit of the antichrist, which you have heard is coming and even now is already in the world.

1

Armageddon and the 144,000

Haifa is a beautiful, working-class city situated in northern Israel on the Mediterranean coast. The Jewish state's third-largest city, it strikes a picturesque pose from atop nearby Mount Carmel, with its harbor forming a rounded half-bowl shape in the distance. Occasionally gray American warships are anchored there, floating purposefully in the blue water in the glistening sun.

Mount Carmel has seen a lot of history. Perhaps its best-known tourist site is a small area on the side of the mountain called Elijah's Cave. The site is not the real cave where Elijah, the mighty Hebrew prophet of old, hid from Queen Jezebel after he successfully invoked the Almighty to rain down fire on a water-soaked altar. That's considerably south of here, but traditions die hard. Here on Mount Carmel Elijah slew 450 prophets of a false god named Baal on a day around 870 B.C. after they failed to induce their god to shower down fire from heaven to consume their sacrifice. Bible scholars still speculate as to why Elijah hid from Jezebel following his greatest moment.[1]

But these days strange new things are going on in the same area. During 1990 and 1991 more than two hundred UFOs were sighted, and reports of strange fire and of saucer-craft landings are on the rise.

According to Hadassah Arbel, a social welfare worker from Haifa, these sightings may signal the soon return of Elijah. They may be an omen of what the Old Testament refers to as "the great and terrible day of the Lord," she surmised in an interview in the December 15, 1990, *Jerusalem Post*.

For, as Arbel pointed out, the Bible (in what comprises the last two verses in the Old Testament) contains a promise that God will send Elijah back to earth just before a future time period in which God will judge the world. "Behold, I will send you Elijah the prophet before the coming of the great and dreadful day of the Lord" (Mal. 4:5 KJV).

Arbel reasons that Elijah was an extraterrestrial being because many of the region's "encounters of the second kind" (physical evidence of an actual spaceship landing[2]) have occurred in the vicinity of Elijah's cave. She also pointed out that, according to the Bible, Elijah was taken up by "a chariot of fire," which she thinks could have been a UFO, and that he did not die but "went up to heaven in a whirlwind" (2 Kings 2:11). Arbel wondered out loud to the *Jerusalem Post* if we are receiving "a signal of some sort" that the day of the Lord is near.

A Biblical View of the End

On the other side of Mount Carmel, a mere twenty miles southeast of Haifa, is a large mound of dirt that has kept archaeologists busy almost since the birth of Israel in 1948. It is the ruins of the ancient, historic city of Megiddo. Today tourists walk through some of the reconstructed ruins and climb through an underground tunnel in a fantastic tour of past history. But what really makes the area noteworthy to many is the picturesque vast valley in which Megiddo sets.

It is the Valley of Armageddon, a strategic flat, lush valley that has been the setting of many battles dating back to antiquity.

When Napoleon brought his army into the valley in the early nineteenth century, he reportedly was amazed by its vastness and remarked that all the armies of the world could maneuver in it for battle.[3] And according to a literal reading of the last book of the New Testament, the armies of the world will do battle at Armageddon. It will be the bloodiest battle mankind will ever see, according to the Book of Revelation, so bloody that it will result in the return of Christ to save Israel and to usher in one thousand years of peace and tranquility on earth. When Jesus spoke of his return in Matthew 24 he said that those days will be a time of "great distress, unequaled from the beginning of the world until now. . . . If those days had not been cut short, no one would survive" (Matt. 24:21, 22).

According to the Book of Revelation (also called the Apocalypse of John, because it was revealed to the last surviving apostle in a vision when he was exiled on the Island of Patmos), the final (seventh) and most terrifying bowl of wrath God will pour out on the world during a seven-year period called the great tribulation will take place when "they gathered the kings together to the place that in Hebrew is called Armageddon." John continues to describe "flashes of lightning, rumblings, peals of thunder and a severe earthquake. No earthquake like it has ever occurred since man has been on earth. . . . The great city [which many scholars believe to be Jerusalem] split into three parts, and the cities of the nations collapsed. . . . Every island fled away and the mountains could not be found. From the sky huge hailstones of about a hundred pounds each fell upon men. And they cursed God on account of the plague" (Rev. 16:16, 18, 20, 21).

Revelation describes many other horrifying scenes on earth for that time. Vast plagues will be unleashed on humankind, such as scorching heat that will burn many with fire (Rev. 16:8, 9), sores breaking out on people throughout the world, the destruction of all life in the seas (Rev. 16:3), and the poisoning of the earth's rivers and springs (Rev. 16:4). And it prophesies the world coming under the control of a "beast" during this time, a worldwide leader often called the Antichrist, who will declare himself to be God and demand worship.[4]

Is there a connection between the "great and terrible day of the LORD" that was continually referred to by the Old Testament Hebrew prophets[5] and the battle of Armageddon and the great tribulation referred to in the New Testament? I, along with many scholars throughout the centuries, believe there is. And the key to unlocking the connection is the apparent fulfillment of specific Bible prophecies in 1948 when a remnant of the

Jews, long nonexistent as a nation when its people were dispersed throughout the world, came back to their land and became the nation of Israel again. And I believe that if this is a true fulfillment of prophecy, we could be living in the time of the destruction of the old order, the start of a new world order, and the dawn of a new age that will begin when Christ returns to Planet Earth.

If true this will demonstrate that the Hebrew prophets spoke of future events with 100 percent accuracy. For throughout the Old Testament they stated that the Jews, the priest-nation chosen by God to spread his word to all the nations, would be dispersed throughout the world for a long period of time before being brought back in the "latter days" to form a single nation again. They identified that as the period during which the Messiah would return to earth. The psalmist wrote: "For the LORD will rebuild Zion and appear in his glory" (102:16). The prophet Daniel, writing in Babylonia (modern Iraq) at about 600 B.C., also saw a vision of the end times and the coming of the Messiah to usher in a new age:

> In my vision at night I looked, and there before me was one like a son of man, coming with the clouds of heaven. He approached The Ancient of Days and was led into his presence. He was given authority, glory and sovereign power; all peoples, nations and men of every language worshiped him. His dominion is an everlasting dominion that will not pass away, and his kingdom is one that will never be destroyed (Dan. 7:13, 14).

But the Old Testament makes it clear that during this same time, when a remnant of the Jewish people return to the Promised Land, there will be great distress and unrest in the Middle East. The prophet Zechariah, writing in about 520 B.C., stated that in those days Jerusalem will become "a cup that sends all the surrounding peoples reeling. Judah will be besieged as well as Jerusalem. On that day, when all the nations of the earth are gathered against her, I will make Jerusalem an immovable rock for all the nations. All who try to move it will injure themselves" (Zech. 12:2, 3).

In the same chapter Zechariah alluded to a coming multinational invasion of Israel when God will "set out to destroy all the nations that attack Jerusalem" (v. 9). Nevertheless, it will be a time of terrible hardships for the Jews. "How awful that day will be!" declared the prophet Jeremiah when he talked of the restoration of the Jews in the latter days. "None will be like it. It will be a time of trouble for Jacob [Israel], but he will be saved out of it" (Jer. 30:7). The prophet also noted, several verses further, that David their king, the Jewish Messiah, will be raised up during that time.

The Book of Revelation teaches that although God will pour out judgment on the world during this time, he will also have a number of his true followers in those days. Revelation, chapters 7 and 14, talks about the Messiah having 144,000 witnesses, 12,000 from each of the twelve tribes of Israel, who will remain pure to the truth during the tribulation (an element totally overlooked by New Agers who subscribe to a literal 144,000 prophecy.)

Today many people are baptized into a New Age religion who claim to be members of the 144,000, say that the second coming of Christ is near, and who talk about a battle of Armageddon (which they sometimes refer to as the "cleansing") that they believe soon will take place. Many of these people, who are scattered throughout the world, claim to be visionaries. Some of them talk about an imminent "rapture"— the removal of God's people from the earth during a time of tribulation. Others talk about having visions of God's city, the new Jerusalem, descending to earth in the near future, another theme from the Book of Revelation. A number of these new believers claim to hear from Jesus himself, and they distribute these messages throughout the world in lectures, tapes, and videos, and through various publications.

Most intriguing of all, these new 144,000 claim that UFOs form the central foundation of their faith. Virtually all these new believers embrace New Age occultic beliefs and mix them with Christian terminology and their own brand of prophecy that parallels Bible prophecies. Many of them (indications are that their numbers are swelling and becoming a mainstream part of the burgeoning New Age movement)[6] claim to be in direct contact with aliens—extraterrestrial messengers or space brothers—who have arrived to help humankind weather the coming storm and then to help usher in the second coming of Christ and a time of peace and brotherhood.

Virtually all such believers reject the traditional, evangelical, "old-time" Christian religion, and many bitterly talk of centuries-old misunderstandings and coverups which they claim have caused the church (both Catholic and Protestant) to miss Christ's "true" message and plan for the world. Most of them also attack the church's guardianship of God's Word, the Bible. Almost all of the new believers teach that the Bible has been tampered with in places or that it is incomplete and other books should be added to it, and they charge that because of this many Christians don't clearly understand the nature of God himself.

Could it be that these new believers are on to something? Has the Christian church been deceived for centuries? Is God about to bring a new age to the planet through the help of the gospel of the extraterrestrial messengers? Is he about to put a new twist on the fulfillment of end-time prophecies in ways the church has never dreamed?

Doorway to the New Age

The scene is a large conference room on an upper floor of New York City's chic Penta Hotel in late October 1990. There, several hundred followers of a charismatic, dark-haired woman adorned in a sparkling, sequin-studded robe stand in a large circle with eyes closed and faces turned upward. The hall resonates with a soft humming noise, a sound they mouthed in unison as they concentrate on something otherworldly.

These people are being led in an "empowerment" ceremony by an up-and-coming New Age leader, a woman who calls herself Solara. Hours earlier many of them had listened intently as Solara told a packed meeting room at the Whole Life Expo, one of the largest New Age conferences ever held on the East Coast, that she was going to empower them to become part of the 144,000 people needed to help bring a new age to mankind.

Increasingly Solara is gaining influence and followers in New Age circles, and her conference workshop was one of the best attended. She has not been around long. She founded her movement, called Star-Borne Unlimited, in the mountainous wilderness of southeastern Arizona, about forty miles north of the Mexican border, in the 1980s. At first she lived a hermitlike existence as, so she said, she received messages from space. But in early 1990, directed by a literal message from the stars, she moved her religious movement to a new communal headquarters in Charlottesville, Virginia, where she would begin to increase her visibility and outreach.[7]

Solara, who refuses to give out information on her birth name ("That's not me anymore," she says, adding that her new full name is Solara Antara Amaa-ra), has written three books outlining her beliefs. She holds to an unusual New Age twist: She claims she is an angel and that human beings are part of and come from different individual stars. Perhaps one reason her movement grew so rapidly was that she said she had until January 11, 1992, to gather 144,000 followers. That date was a "doorway" to mark the best opportunity mankind would ever have to reach a new golden era (one thousand years of peace), that is, if 144,000 persons would "unite together in conscious Oneness all over the planet."[8]

Solara meant that if 144,000 united in meditation on that date, humankind would reach a "mass ascension into new realms of consciousness" and would become united with the God-force for a new golden era. She added that if the earth missed the date—and it did—a "doorway" would be left open until December 31, 2011, for mankind to keep trying to move into the new age. After that there may not be another chance.[9]

"We are in the time of the great awakening of the Star-borne," she told the gathering. "God moves to a higher level, and we are the propulsion."

Solara's message is not unlike that of the "harmonic convergence," a large worldwide event that garnered a lot of press coverage and was coordinated by New Age author José Argüelles. According to Argüelles's paperback cult book, *The Mayan Factor* (Santa Fe: Bear and Co., 1987) if 144,000 people went to places such as the Pyramids, Mount Shasta, Peru, and elsewhere on August 16–17, 1987, and "resonated" (meditated, chanted, hummed mantras, had good vibrations), Armageddon could be averted, UFOs would land throughout the world, and a new age would come to earth. In Argüelles's scenario highly intelligent aliens came to earth centuries ago, dwelt with the Mayans in South America, then left behind a "galactic calling card" in the Mayan calendar that would give clues as to how Earth could join the galactic federation after the calendar concludes in 2012.[10]

Many pundits slammed the harmonic convergence,[11] including some of the followers of the New Age, but the idea of mankind taking a quantum leap (after enough humans simultaneously meditate on it to achieve "critical mass") into the golden age has remained a popular New Age theme that is almost universally accepted.

But unlike the harmonic convergence, Solara says, her movement is not about aliens making contact with humankind and imparting ancient wisdom. "UFOs might come and take you somewhere," she said in her speech, "but they're not going to take you all the way" as her movement will.[12] But an overview of her own writings indicates that UFOs were an important early step in her own initiation into the occult and later in her development as a New Age leader. In an account of how she discovered that she was an "angel," Solara writes:

> I had the good fortune of being brought up in a conscious, though highly eccentric and unbalanced, family. My mother was very aware of the spiritual realms. When I was a young girl, she taught me about the ancient civilizations of Atlantis, Lemuria, Egypt & Assyria. . . .
>
> When I was seven and eight, I was taken to U.F.O. conventions in the California desert where many people openly thought that my mother and I were from the planet Venus. . . . I saw many U.F.O.s and great fireballs of Light during my childhood; this also was an accepted fact. In my young innocence, I simply assumed that this was a common occurrence for everyone. Fairies, also, were openly discussed and communicated with. [13]

Messages from Aliens

New Age writer Brad Steiger (a.k.a. Eugene Olson, originally from Decorah, Iowa), author of more than 110 books, many dealing with UFOs, says the UFOs do lead into the new age. UFO contactee groups (people who claim to be in touch with aliens through a variety of ways to be discussed later) are a good source for learning more about humankind's awakening to leap into the golden era, he writes.

Steiger, quoting the Mark-Age Metacenter, formerly of Miami and now of California, one of the larger and more established of the UFO groups receiving messages from aliens, says that mankind "is in the interim period before the Golden Age of Aquarius."[14]

"In this forthcoming spiritual cycle on Earth, man is to experience the Second Coming," Steiger continues in summarizing the beliefs of Mark-Age; mankind should do everything in its power to move into a new age. Quoting Jesus, Steiger writes: "What I have done, you shall do; even greater things" (see John 14:12). He adds:

> One of these greater things is for a minimum of one hundred and forty-four thousand in Christ consciousness and in their light or etheric bodies to help lift and transmute Earth and all forms upon it, including mankind, from the third dimensional frequency (physical matter) into the fourth dimensional frequency form (spiritual form of light body which Jesus demonstrated after his crucifixion).[15]

Steiger also quotes a beautiful blonde female UFOnaut named Semjase from the constellation Pleiades in his 1989 book *The Fellowship* (which is partly an attempt to write a new bible based on "revelations" from extraterrestrial beings), who also advocates moving the planet into a new era. And she tells contactee Fred Bell of Laguna Beach, California, that a chosen 144,000 people are about to be raised up and whisked away to the stars. "Realize that all human beings . . . aren't going to become enlightened," Semjase said. "144,000 souls will come and these 144,000 souls may end up in the Pleiades or in other parts of the galaxy."[16] (More about Semjase will be discussed later; she has allegedly appeared to other people throughout the world, including the famous Swiss contactee Eduard "Billy" Meier.)

Steiger, who claims to come from a fundamentalist Christian background, says that the aliens have been struggling for some time to get us to join them in a new age. He equates these new messages from outer space, allegedly being received by countless UFO-New Age enthusiasts worldwide, to the same force that started the Christian church and to the same power that blinded Saul of Tarsus on the road to Damascus. Steiger writes:

> After he had recovered his sight by following instructions given to him in a vision, he changed his name to Paul, became a Christian missionary, and in his epistles to the young churches established a large part of Christian dogma.
>
> Just as Saul was diverted from his journey by a bright light and a period of blindness, the [UFO] contactee literature tells us of [others] who were temporarily rendered sightless and disoriented by a strange and powerful light [UFOs], which appeared above them as they traveled along lonely highways.
>
> When these individuals recovered their sight and their memories, they recalled seeing a spacecraft and an occupant, and receiving a message to share with the world. [Some] have come to devote their lives to preaching of peace, love, brotherhood, and the coming time of transition.[17]

A Spiritual Second Coming

Steiger is well aware of the many UFO groups claiming to have an inside track on the 144,000. And he knows that the 144,000 figure may mean something different depending on the group of people referring to it. A possible answer to the meaning of the 144,000, Steiger wrote in his famous Star People series of books (which have sold more than fifteen million copies), is that the 144,000 are reincarnated space brothers, born during this present time to help mankind witness the second coming and to help the transition into the dawning of the new age.

But what kind of new age do Steiger and other UFO vision-aries look forward to? What does the second coming of Christ mean to Steiger? It is a "second coming" at odds with the one declared openly by Christ in the Bible. And their new age dif-fers dramatically from the millennium described in the Bible.

Steiger's concept of the second coming contrasts markedly with the second coming of Christ described in Scripture. First, Steiger, quoting the Mark-Age people in a favorable light, says the second coming will not be the physical, bodily return of Jesus Christ of Nazareth to Planet Earth, which contradicts Revelation 1:7. The second coming "refers to the entire race as it experiences its second opportunity to express Christ or cosmic consciousness on the Earth, as before the fall of man into physical matter," he writes. What he means is that humankind itself will become "Christed"; it will develop a new consciousness that will be part of Christ, as Steiger has written in many of his books. Second, although a spiritual ruler may return to the planet, the person may be in the form of a reincarnation of Sananda, not necessarily or exclusively Jesus of Nazareth, Steiger asserts, again favorably quoting the Mark-Age people.[18]

> Sananda [is] one of the seven directors of the spiritual govern-ment or Hierarchal [sic] Board of our solar system. Some of Sananda's past incarnations on Earth have been as Jesus of Nazareth, Moses, Gautama Buddha, Melchizedek, Elijah, and the head of the groups known in the Old Testament as the Abels and the Noahs.[19]

The Physical Second Coming

All the orthodox Christian creeds over the centuries have affirmed the doctrine of the physical return of Jesus Christ from the sky. These were not the clever inventions of church coun-cils; they were based on the very words of Christ and the apos-tles recorded in the Gospels and throughout Scripture. In fact, the first thing the disciples were told by the two angels who appeared when Christ bodily ascended into heaven following his crucifixion was, "Why do you stand here looking into the sky? This same Jesus, who has been taken from you into heaven, will come back in the same way you have seen him go into heaven" (Acts 1:11).

Even during Christ's trial before the Sanhedrin he affirmed his bodily return. To the high priest's direct question under oath, "Tell us if you are the Christ, the Son of God" (Matt. 26:63), Jesus replied, "Yes it is as you say. . . . But I say to all of you: In the future you will see the Son of Man sitting at the right hand of the Mighty One and coming on the clouds of heaven" (v. 64).

Earlier Jesus had given his disciples the same account of his second coming, and he clearly said he would come back in the midst of a time of turmoil and religious deception. "At that time the sign of the Son of Man will appear in the sky, and all the nations of the earth will mourn. They will see the Son of Man coming on the clouds of the sky, with power and great glory. And he will send his angels with a loud trumpet call, and they will gather his elect from the four winds, from one end of the heavens to the other" (Matt. 24:30, 31).

The Old Testament's references to Christ's coming further shoot down the idea of a reincarnated person claiming to hold the title of Christ coming to guide the earth into a new age, and they strongly imply that Christ will still have the nailprints on his hands as a sign for all when he returns. At the very least, everyone will know it is Jesus Christ who has returned, the same one crucified on a cross outside Jerusalem.

"On that day [an end-time period during which Israel is attacked by many armies from throughout the world] I will set out to destroy all the nations that attack Jerusalem," God declared through the Old Testament prophet Zechariah. "And I will pour out on the house of David and the inhabitants of Jerusalem a spirit of grace and supplication. They will look on me, the one they have pierced, and they will mourn for him as one mourns for an only child, and grieve bitterly for him as one grieves for a firstborn son" (Zech. 12:9, 10).

Further, God talks about how he will then set up his new age and how he will eliminate sin: "A fountain will be opened to the house of David and the inhabitants of Jerusalem, to cleanse them from sin and impurity. On that day, I will banish the names of the idols from the land, and they will be remembered no more" (Zech. 13:1, 2).

The Hebrew prophet Isaiah also told of the time when the Messiah—Christ Jesus—would rule from Jerusalem:

> He will judge between the nations and will settle disputes for many peoples. They will beat their swords into plowshares and their spears into pruning hooks. Nation will not take up sword against nation, nor will they train for war anymore (Isa. 2:4).

Isaiah also says the balance of nature will change in those days to one in which "the wolf will live with the lamb, the leopard will lie down with the goat, the calf and the lion and the yearling together; and a little child will lead them. . . . The infant will play near the hole of the cobra, and the young child put his hand into the viper's nest. They will neither harm nor destroy on all my holy mountain, for the earth will be full of the knowledge of the LORD as the waters cover the sea" (Isa. 11:6, 8, 9). And Isaiah said it will happen after Christ judges the earth and slays the wicked (v. 4).

Irreconcilable Theologies

Contrast that picture of Christ removing the evil before beginning his new age with the picture given to us by UFO contactees Moi-Ra and Ra-Ja Dove of Lytle Creek, California, who consider themselves "star shepherds" sent to give us a new religion and to help humankind enter the new age. According to Steiger's *The Fellowship,* the new age, the Age of Aquarius, will begin soon when the "teachings of the Plumed Serpent merge with the teachings of the Christ, the Dove."[20] What do these contactees mean? That the serpent in the Garden of Eden who caused Eve to sin was really an "extraterrestrial entity" from a "celestial race" who had helped to develop the wisdom faculty of man, and that celestial beings such as Jesus, Buddha, Mohammed, Krishna, and others were "'the doves that have helped humanity develop its love nature." The implication is that the new age will begin when what was traditionally regarded as evil merges with the good. The claim is that "corruption" and "religious deceit" have caused the serpent in the Garden of Eden to be misunderstood.[21]

Of course, this is a key strand of thought in the New Age movement, that all is one, or monism. This means that "all is interrelated, interdependent and interpenetrating,"[22] and that good is evil and evil is good. Author Doug Groothuis cites the 1980s movie *The Dark Crystal* (produced by the late Jim Henson, creator of the Muppets). The final scene, which many UFO believers would approve, is of a world in which the good guys merge with the bad guys.

In the movie *The Mystics* the lovable good guys merge with the Skecsees, the evil, depraved, wretched monsters, because they are really part of one self, one reality, the one.[23]

Contactees Moi-Ra and Ra-Ja Dove have more "truth" for us about the coming new age as reported by Steiger in *The Fellowship*. They claim that Jesus was not the Christ by himself. *YHWH*, Jesus, and other master souls, have never "really ever proclaimed themselves as the ultimate one GOD! . . . No! They have always proclaimed themselves as but aspects of the one GOD, just as you are!" The religion of the New Age is that we are Christ, that we are God. "The individual will know what the religions of the Ancient Age have always tried to demonstrate: to be STILL and KNOW that YOU are GOD!" these people assert (in this perversion of Psalm 46:10). "Indeed this is the great new religion!"[24]

Comparing what these UFO apostles have said with the New Testament account of the coming new age we see Jesus told his disciples in three different places in Matthew 24, that there would be tremendous religious deception on earth just prior to his coming and the setting up of his kingdom. In verse 5 Jesus gave this warning: "Many will come in my name, claiming, 'I am the Christ,' and will deceive many." Furthermore he said, "At that time many will turn away from the faith and will betray and hate each other, and many false prophets will appear and deceive many people" (Matt. 24:10, 11). Finally, Jesus warned them again about religious deception:

At that time if anyone says to you, "Look, here is the Christ!" or, "There he is!" do not believe it. For false Christs and false prophets will appear and perform great signs and miracles to deceive even the elect—if that were possible. See, I have told you ahead of time. So if anyone tells you, "There he is, out in the desert," do not go out; or "Here he is, in the inner rooms," do not believe it (Matt. 24:23–26).

Messengers of Deception

I believe that something very strange indeed is happening throughout the world today. In the late 1940s began what we refer to as the modern UFO era, when people worldwide reported having seen shiny disks whizz across the sky. The 1950s saw people claiming to be contactees for alien civilizations from within our solar system (mostly from Venus). In the 1970s and 1980s increasing numbers of people claimed to have been abducted by aliens from other star systems. And late in the 1980s an increasing number of UFO enthusiasts began joining the New Age movement.

Many of these people join after they claim to have received messages from space that, if acted on, promise to change the world forever. Many UFO contactees claim to receive messages directly from Jesus Christ, or messages about Jesus. Yet as we have already seen, Jesus himself told us that many false Christs—people claiming to be he—would arise in the last days to deceive many.

I believe that the New Age god of the UFOnauts may be part of that deception, which may be one of the cleverest demonic onslaughts ever launched against humanity. As we shall see, the deception by the UFOnauts involves a clever counterfeit retranslation of many of the future events Scripture says will happen in the time of the tribulation or during the one thousand years of peace God has promised will follow his coming.

Triton's Dedication

In fact, evidence exists that the UFOnauts may be involved in a centuries-old plan to deceive mankind into accepting a counterfeit messiah, a coming world leader the Bible refers to as the Antichrist, who will unleash destruction against the earth and lead to the real Armageddon. As we shall see, the UFOnauts's influence has already helped open the door to a renewed interest in occultism, which some argue may lead to the dissolution of Western civilization as we know it in favor of an India-like Hindu-based society.

On the front page of one of the early books that links UFOs, the occult, and a coming new age is an unusual dedication. The book, *The Magic of Space*, was allegedly written by "Triton," an otherworldly entity who utilized telepathy and automatic writing to communicate the book during five weeks in 1962 to a Tibetan Da. It states, long before the term *New Age* became vogue in American culture: "Dedicated to the New Age World Teacher and to all those who have waited patiently."[25]

The Second Coming According to the Space Brothers

It is said to take place almost silently within about thirty seconds. It almost always happens in the middle of the night and is seldom observed.

But zealous researchers of the paranormal say it has been observed and allegedly filmed at least once, recently, in southern England. In the middle of a wheat field one night near Stonehenge, the famous site where the Druids of centuries past worshiped, a phosphorescent-type light descended from the sky and lit up a portion of the field. The light then changed colors, from orange to yellow to greenish. Suddenly in the middle of the glow appeared what looked to be hundreds of little black rods that started jumping around.[1] When the sun came up, amazed onlookers spotted a circle formed of crushed but otherwise undamaged wheat at the site.

Skeptics and those who research UFOs from a strict scientific viewpoint, however, are not so sure. Many in this camp have long held the view that these formations, or "crop circles" as they are called, are the work of pranksters fueled by sensationalistic tabloid reports in England. The Winter 1992 *Skeptical Inquirer* gave compelling reasons why they could be elaborate hoaxes. Either way, these formations have been well known in the British Isles for many years. But in 1976 their frequency began to climb. According to Andrew E. Rothovius, a researcher who cofounded the New England Antiquities Research Association, two to three dozen were found in 1987, seventy-five in 1988, two hundred eighty in 1989, and more than four hundred in 1990.[2] But what has been most astounding to many is that each year in recent memory the circles have become more elaborate, and in 1990 huge patterns began appearing with the circles that resembled figures some people believe were parts of ancient and nearly forgotten alphabets. (However, the phenomenon may have crested in 1990; the formations didn't seem quite as elaborate in 1991 and 1992.)

What's more, similar circles, though not as elaborately formed, have been appearing elsewhere with increasing frequency. They have been found in thirty countries,[3] including the United States, Canada, the former Soviet Union, and Japan.

No one knows for sure what they are or what they mean, if anything, though many people advance theories. A popular American Bible-prophecy teacher, speaking on his international television program, even guessed that the circles could have been placed there by Christ himself as a sign of his second coming. The teacher quoted Christ's words in Luke 21 telling his disciples that there will be "great signs from heaven" (v. 11) just prior to his coming.

But that speculation is somewhat novel. The two most common explanations for them in the secular media (that includes the tabloid press) are the possibility that UFOs have been orchestrating them as signs for mankind, or that they are formed by an earth force as a herald of the coming New Age. Of course, there are other less sensational explanations, such as that the circles are the work of pranksters or part of a series of rare but natural atmospheric vortexes similar to tornadoes or whirlwinds.[4] In fact, in September 1991, two men in their sixties surfaced claiming they were responsible for many of the crop circles. They demonstrated for the British tabloid *Today* how they made various circles using wooden boards, string, and a sighting device attached to a baseball cap. Newspapers worldwide picked up the story.

The idea that UFOs have something to do with the circles has been played up in the worldwide press more than any other. *USA Today* quoted a Canadian farmer as saying he saw "five shiny, saucer-like objects spinning" just off the ground in

1974 that caused the phenomenon.[5] Most who give credence to the UFO theory also subscribe to certain other elements discussed in other theories. And the one thing that almost every New Ager agrees on is that the crop circles are signs for humankind that the new age is about to dawn. Some say they warn us that the planet is to go through a great tribulation or a "cleansing" and that the second coming of Christ is near.

One Contactee's 'Christ' Is Here Now

British New Age author Benjamin Creme says the crop circles are definitely formed by "UFOs manned by the Space Brothers," and their purpose is to alert humankind that the new age is upon us. "This is a time when highly evolved beings are moving into the world, in every nation and country, giving experiences to people, showing them a higher life, a higher wisdom," according to an article in Creme's monthly, *Share International News.*[6]

More significantly, Creme asserts, the circles are also here to help herald the arrival of the Christ, Lord Maitreya, who in 1977 allegedly descended in a "self-created body" and has been living in the Asian-Indian community in the east end of London. According to Creme, a soft-spoken, white-haired man who has frequently spelled out his beliefs about the coming of the Christ in his writings and newspaper advertisements, that figure is the "World Teacher" who transcends all religions. He is the Maitreya, the Buddha, the Messiah, the Immam Mahdi, or the Christ, he asserts.[7]

According to Creme's Tara Center of Los Angeles, a man claiming to be Lord Maitreya presented his credentials as the messiah before two hundred media representatives and world leaders at a conference in London in April 1990. And according to Tara Center spokeswoman Lynne Craft, he astounded conference participants, including some fifty reporters, by "appearing, then disappearing" in front of them.[8]

The Tara Center also asserted that less than two years earlier, Lord Maitreya appeared as a bearded, white-robed man to six thousand people in Nairobi, Kenya. The Center released a fuzzy photograph of the man.[9]

In spite of Creme's track record in producing his Lord Maitreya to the world, many are skeptical of his claims. It is interesting that, though Craft claims so many prominent people and journalists were at the alleged conference, she would not release the names of anyone who attended, nor did journalists worldwide write a single story about it. According to the *Christian Research Journal*:

> Such proclamations are reminiscent of a previous advertisement (April 1982) for which Creme's organization paid $200,000 to place in prominent newspapers worldwide. It boldly announced, "THE CHRIST IS NOW HERE." Creme followed that advertisement with a press conference in which he proclaimed that Maitreya would appear before the end of spring. (Creme's announcement created a sensation and alarm in some quarters of the church, with several authors claiming that the Antichrist of the Bible was about to be revealed.)[10]

But what a few pundits have picked up about Creme—whether or not his information about the coming of a new world teacher is true—is that Creme is a long-time "contactee" who claims he has been receiving messages and direct orders from extraterrestrial beings, whom he calls "the Space People," since 1958. And since he began taking "telepathic dictation" from them, he claims, the aliens made him part of their plan[11] to reveal their messiah and to bring to earth a new world order.

Rick Branch of Watchman Fellowship (an evangelical Christian ministry to cults) quoted Creme's book, *The Reappearance of the Christ and the Masters of Wisdom*, as saying that Creme became interested in flying saucers in 1953 after reading occult theosophical books by authors such as H. P. Blavatsky (the founder of The Theosophical Society), G. I. Gurdjieff, Alice Bailey, and others.[12] That progressed to direct telepathic contact with Lord Maitreya in 1972, then to Creme becoming one of the world's loudest heralders of the new age and a new messiah. Creme wrote:

In mid-1957, I began to work with a society involved with the U.F.O. phenomenon, which claimed contact with the Space Brothers. With this group I did my first public speaking, but more importantly, discovered my ability to transmit the cosmic spiritual energies from the Space People. . . . Toward the end of 1958 I withdrew from this society and entered into the closest contact with, and work for, the Space Brothers.[13]

New Age Occultic Roots

To be sure, the belief in flying saucers descending to earth to help usher in the new age does not necessarily mean that all UFO enthusiasts are eagerly awaiting the appearance of a Lord Maitreya or another world teacher. Apparently most UFO enthusiasts talk excitedly about a second coming or the arrival of such a coming teacher, but such ideas are a little blurred in the minds of many of them.

Perhaps the reason for the uncertainty among New Age UFO enthusiasts is the fact that the New Age movement itself is not unified on every point. And as we shall see later, the modern UFO movement is eclectic, although it is intrinsically tied to the same occultic Theosophical roots of the New Age movement. As *Christian Research Journal* associate editor Ron Rhodes points out, Theosophy, which was founded in 1875 by Blavatsky, broke off into "four prongs" during the twentieth century, and "each 'prong' has made a significant impact on current New Age Christology."[14] What this translates to when talking about the modern UFO movement is that UFO enthusiasts will often borrow ideas from founders of Theosophy, Anthroposophy (founded by Rudolf Steiner in 1912), the Arcane School (founded by Alice Bailey), and the "I AM" movement (which has included as its major figures Baird Spalding, Guy and Edna Ballard, and Mark and Elizabeth Clare Prophet).[15]

Each of these prongs has a slightly different view of the second coming of Christ, and not all of them believe in the appearance in the near future of a great world leader they call the Christ. Creme was influenced by the Arcane School. But other New Agers involved in receiving messages from extraterrestrial beings do not look at it in the same manner. UFO contactee literature is dotted with alien messages that talk about the second coming as being Christ's incarnation into humanity as a whole, or the quantum leap of humankind into a higher level of understanding or a higher dimension, and not the arrival of any one individual. Steiner, for example, taught that after Christ's crucifixion he became "the planetary spirit of the earth."[16]

The Occult Prerequisite for Contact

What seems to unite the UFO movement as a whole is a widespread belief in matters serious students of Bible prophecy refer to as the last things or eschatology. Most New Age UFO enthusiasts have definite opinions about the end times, and most of them believe the earth is in the last days before a coming new age, even a near-future second coming. Most believe in an Armageddon, tribulation, or "cleansing" time in which the wicked on earth will be punished, a coming UFO "rapture" of sorts (meaning the removal of good spiritual people from the earth during the coming troubles), and afterwards a blissful new age in which UFO believers will see a new Jerusalem or cities of light. And although it is not a major theme with most UFO groups, a few of them even talk about a coming wicked Antichrist that will bring the world to ruin during the cleansing.

Perhaps most surprising about the UFO believers' end-time scenario is that it has parallels to the end-times scenario outlined in the Bible. The contactees claim often to have received the scenario from extraterrestrial messengers themselves and not after hearing an end-times sermon delivered by a dispensational Bible prophecy preacher.

Los Angeles Christian journalist Stuart Goldman has pointed out that there is little interplay or communication between evangelical Christians and those claiming to be UFO contactees or abductees. Goldman, who has appeared on numerous radio and television shows, including *Good Morning, America* and *Hard Copy,* bases his observations on his lengthy investigation of UFO abductee-guru Whitley Strieber, author of the best sellers *Communion* and *Transformation*. In an unpublished manuscript he wrote:

> In looking at the backgrounds of UFO abductees, it quickly becomes clear that almost to a man, they have some background in New Age or occultic beliefs. Interestingly, studies show that there are very few practicing Christians or Jews amongst UFO contactees. What could this mean? Are the aliens racists? Or does this, rather, indicate something about the belief systems of the abductees themselves?[17]

I believe Goldman is correct. The occult often leads to a belief in a glorious new age. And UFOs are often a significant part of that belief system. Furthermore, although the UFOnauts talk about Armageddon, the second coming, the new Jerusalem, and the rapture, what they mean by these terms departs significantly from what the Bible and Christ himself say about these events.

Again, could it be that the similar end-times scenarios being spewed in the form of messages from the space brothers are deliberate attempts to fool humankind about Bible prophecy in the very era of Christ's return? Could the benevolent space brothers that the New Agers talk about actually be some of the "angels of light" deliberately sent by Satan to deceive mankind whom the apostle Paul warned the early Christian church about (2 Cor. 11:14)?

Cleansing of the Old Thinkers

Prolific New Age author Brad Steiger has probably written more books about UFOs than anyone else. He's looked at practically every possible theory about their origin. He has written about the possibility that they are evil, about their alleged link to Atlantis, about their being physical "nuts-and-bolts" visitors from other star systems, and about the possibility that they are interdimensional or multidimensional messengers.

These days, though, Steiger often talks about the possibility they are multidimensional. He favors the intellectual approach that, even though we don't know what UFOs are in many cases, most of them are good, and higher developed powers may be using the UFO as a symbol, a guiding light, to usher humanity into the new age to join them. But first, the planet will go through a time of terrors: Armageddon. He has written:

> Although these paraphysical, multidimensional gods have always co-existed with us, in the last thirty years they have been accelerating their interaction with us in preparation for a fast-approaching time of transition and transformation. This period, we have been told, will be a difficult one; and for generations our prophets and revelators have been referring to it as The Great Cleansing, Judgment Day, Armageddon. But we have been promised that, after a season of cataclysmic changes on the Earth plane, a New Age consciousness will suffuse the planet. It is to this end that the gods have been utilizing the UFO as a transformative symbol.[18]

Marianne Francis started studying the occult and flying saucers at age sixteen. Since then she has become an important figure for the space brothers and the New Age. She changed her name to Aleuti Francesca and became founder and director of the Solar Light Retreat of Oregon. She claims to have communicated with space beings since 1954.[19] She claims to channel (allow her body to go into an altered state of consciousness wherein another entity speaks through the individual) messages from space beings named Orlon, Voltra (an advanced space being from Venus),[20] and others. She says they tell her that earthlings should not be afraid of the difficult times coming to the planet, because it means things are changing for the better. "Meet change with joy and a song on your lips," she said during a channeling "transmission" titled "Cleansing Must Come to Planet Earth."

Francesca says there is nothing to fear if people go along with the new program that includes a brand new way of thinking by individuals and mass "changes of consciousness" that will enable humankind to embrace a new "Age of Light unto the New dimension and the New consciousness which is the Christ consciousness."[21] But for those caught holding on to the old thought patterns, there is something to be terrified of: removal and destruction.

"Prepare yourselves," the extraterrestrial messengers told her, "for the day now closely approaches and those who are not so prepared must vanish from the face of this your Earth. . . . Those who align themselves with the things of the Old must surely be destroyed with that age of decay and darkness."[22]

But while most other New Age writers talk about a coming time of troubles, some of those receiving messages from the space brothers say it's possible for Armageddon to be averted if humankind wises up, ends all wars, and raises its collective consciousness.

Influential New Age leader-author David Spangler, who headed the education department at the Findhorn Community (New Age) in Scotland in the early 1970s, is one. Spangler says he has been in touch with space beings. In his book, *Links with Space*, Spangler, who has returned to the United States and founded another influential New Age organization while continuing his New Age writing career, highlights conversations he said he's had with "Lord Maitreya," an angel, and an entity named John, who Spangler claims is a "spokesman for a group of intelligences on the inner places of Being."[23] John told him that, although mankind is teetering on the brink of destruction, those who embrace "attunement" to a new higher consciousness will be spared the coming suffering in the same way Noah built an ark and was saved from destruction. "That is what is happening now," John said. "You are building the ark [by developing a new mass consciousness associated with the new age]. . . . All who attune to and live this consciousness are absolutely protected, no matter what happens in the outer world."[24]

The Extraterrestrial Concept of Christ

During an eleven-day cold and snowy period from December 27, 1978, to January 6, 1979, New Age writer Ken Carey received an astounding set of revelations from extraterrestrial messengers.

They first communicated with him nonverbally "on waves, or pulsations . . . neurobiologically . . . and my nervous system seemed to become available to them as a channel for communication,"[25] he wrote. They told him of the purpose of life on earth, of coming future events, and that Christ's second coming would be soon.

"I can certainly attest to the truth of what is stated in these transmissions," Carey wrote in the introduction of his popular book summarizing the messages titled *The Starseed Transmissions*. "One's life does indeed begin to change when one decides to work with the approaching forces!"[26]

Despite Carey's endorsement of the book's startling messages to Planet Earth, he admits that he was never sure who was communicating with him during the eleven days. "In the course of my work with these creatures," Carey wrote, "[at] times I considered these extraterrestrial, at other times, angelic. . . . Toward the end of the transmissions, other, more mythical perspectives emerged."[27]

Indeed, near the end of the book, Jesus Christ even transmitted a message to him that set Carey straight on the purpose of Christ's life on earth.

Something about the little book struck a nerve within the New Age movement. In just four years after its first printing in 1983, it sold almost 100,000 copies. Perhaps one of the reasons it has been well received is its encouraging messages about the future new age and its account from extraterrestrial sources that the world is about to experience the second coming of Christ, the coming of a fantastic one-thousand-year new age of peace, and of mankind someday reaching out to the stars in massive floating spaceships of light.

The book also tries to set the record straight on Christ's second coming, for the entities forcefully told Carey that the Christian church has misunderstood the second coming for the past two thousand years. The second coming is "the event that primitive civilizations have looked forward to as 'the return of the gods,'" they said. "The Mayans went so far as to pinpoint its actual occurrence in what you would call the year 2011 A.D."[28]

They also equated the second coming of Christ to the Hindu concept of "the in-breathing and out-breathing of Brahma, the process through which God breathes out all of Creation, and then breathes it all back in again."[29]

> At this point in linear time, we are very close to the middle of the cycle, soon to reach the exact mid-point between the out-breath and the in-breath of God. . . . [and this] will coincide with what has come to be called the Second Coming of Christ.[30]

In other words, the entities behind these starseed transmissions reject the concept of Jesus Christ of Nazareth, who was crucified on a Roman cross and later resurrected from the dead, as being the one who is coming to earth at his second coming. They believe in a concept of Christ linked to Theosophical occult movements discussed earlier. They told Carey that Christ's second coming will be in the form of a collective consciousness coming to the people on earth. "Christ is the single unified being whose consciousness all share," the aliens told Carey.[31]

> [He] is the being who sacrificed, for a time, his unified sense of identity, and cloaked himself in the matter of a planet that a species might share his life. He went to sleep to dream an evolutionary process that would leave him, upon awakening, clothed in a physical body comprised of many human cells.[32]

The Return of a Spiritual Leader

The Mark-Age Metacenter of California, which claims to receive messages from a variety of space people on a regular basis, holds a similar theosophical view of the soon-to-be second coming. But Mark-Age throws in the Alice Bailey-Benjamin Creme view that a spiritual ruler is coming back to earth who has been called by different names (including Jesus and Buddha) in previous lives. Extraterrestrial beings told Mark-Age the earth is in the "latter days, the cleansing period, the purification time."[33]

In this forthcoming spiritual cycle on Earth, man is to experience the Second Coming. This refers both to the entire race as it experiences its second opportunity to express Christ or cosmic consciousness on the Earth, as before the fall of man into physical matter . . . and also the Second Coming of the spiritual ruler of this planet.[34]

UFO Landing Pads

Mother Teresa's trip to St. Paul in north-central Alberta in 1982 was quite a hit with the residents. The townspeople, mindful that the year was designated the International Year of the Child by the United Nations, decided to aid Mother Teresa's mission in Calcutta. When she visited, she addressed a throng of people from atop a large structure: St. Paul's publicly built UFO landing pad, which is the first one ever constructed. A sign at the pad, built in 1967, states in part: "All visitors from Earth or otherwise are welcome to this territory and to the town of St. Paul."[35]

The small town of Lake City, Pennsylvania, near Erie, also built a landing site, billed as the "1st UFO Landing Port in the World." But author Douglas Curran points out that it is not the first; it was built in 1976, nine years after the one in Canada.[36]

"Welcome Space Brothers!" says a large sign at the most famous UFO landing site, near San Diego, California. It is located on a sixty-seven-acre hilly area about twenty miles east of the city[37] and owned by the El Cajon, California-based Unarius Academy of Science, one of the most eccentric UFO cults of all (so far out that they often are not accepted by the rest of the New Age-UFO community). This cult is headed by elderly Ruth Norman, who claims the space brothers instructed her to prepare the landing site for the arrival of thirty-two spaceships that will help bring in the new age. In the early 1970s she often informed the media, usually around Christmas or Easter, that the landing was imminent. Large numbers of reporters bustled about the site waiting for aliens. In 1975, after an all-night vigil attended by numerous reporters, a television station aired a critical broadcast of the event, and Norman, angered by the broadcast, stopped having the landing extravaganzas.[38] But at last report she said the spaceships will land at the site in 2001.[39]

Although no extraterrestrial vehicles have landed at these three sites, the fact that people have considered that possibility strongly enough to build them underscores how thoroughly one of the major tenets of UFOlogy has seeped into modern culture: that humankind someday, and probably soon, will be visited by creatures from another planet. Although there is little doubt the media played a major role in promoting this belief, the media has not yet played a significant role in promoting another stream of thought of many UFO believers: that the space brothers are coming to earth during a time of tribulation and will evacuate a major portion of the population who are spiritually superior.

UFO Evacuation Theory

One popular movie that did display a partial belief in a UFO rapture was *Cocoon,* directed by Ron Howard in the late 1980s, which showed a number of elderly people volunteering to go to the benevolent aliens' planet. Another film in the 1980s that showed it more clearly was *UFOria.* Although the film did poorly at the box office, it showed a young woman (played by Cindy Williams of *Laverne and Shirley* fame) living in the southwestern part of the United States becoming increasingly obsessed with UFOs. No one believed her when she said UFO-nauts were coming to whisk away some of the local population, until it happened in the final scene.

The concept that a portion of "believers" will be rescued from a future time of terrors is that it largely did not originate in UFO groups. It came from Bible scholars studying the deep sayings of Scripture dealing with the end times and the second coming of Christ. The UFO removal theory parallels a popular belief held by many evangelicals that either before, in the middle of, or at the end of the tribulation to come on the earth (depending upon one's viewpoint) Christ will whisk all of his true believers away. Theologians, who have debated the doctrine almost since the beginning of Christianity, have called the event the rapture. As I wrote in my last book, *Soothsayers of the Second Advent*: "Scripture nowhere uses the word *rapture*, but it describes Christians as being caught up at the return of the Lord (1 Thess. 4:16,17; 2 Thess 2:1)."[40]

Many UFO believers who think they soon will be removed from the earth during a cleansing period, describe their views of this future event in their writings. Gabriel Green of Yucca Valley, California, founder of one of the largest UFO groups in America, the Amalgamated Flying Saucer Club, was quoted by *United Press International* as saying:

> The aliens' mission is to raise the consciousness of earthlings so they can "recognize our own individual Godhood" and adopt creative, rather than destructive, attitudes and behaviors to move into the "Aquarian Age" of peace and Harmony. . . .
>
> If Armageddon comes, so will the aliens, swooping down in spaceships to evacuate one-tenth of the population in what Christians call "the rapture". . . . "Only one-tenth of the population will be spiritually qualified to live in an environment of harmony, and there are some limitations on their ability to provide for us, to house us and so forth."[41]

Green also added that the UFO rapture will fulfill the biblical prophecy of the second coming. In fact, "It will fulfill the purposes of all religions simultaneously."[42]

Green has been a colorful figure in UFOlogy. He said that a year after forming his organization a four-foot alien from the star system Alpha Centauri told him to run for president in 1960. Since then, he says, he has been in touch with other extraterrestrial beings through "telepathic" means.[43]

A Warning by Aliens

UFO abductee Lydia Stalnaker said that in 1974 she was abducted by aliens from the planet Orjane (wherever that is) and given a three-hour examination aboard a silvery spaceship. Inside, short, bug-eyed aliens told her that Earth was to be eventually invaded "and all its good people carried away." According to an interview in an Atlanta area newspaper, the aliens told her to "live the Ten Commandments" and "store up food."[44] Lest one wonders why all these alien messages appear to be spoken in the English language, the answer is that they aren't. Contactees often say they are communicated with telepathically. There is also record of aliens communicating messages to people in other languages.

A New Planet for Earth People

The late Hope Troxell of June Lake, California, also claimed to be in touch with aliens. In the fall of 1973 they told her to prepare "24 Books of the Kingdom" that she was to seal up "in a secret place on a mountain, to be preserved for posterity in a similar manner to the Dead Sea Scrolls."[45] She allegedly completed the task a year later. But as a result of more talks with the extraterrestrial beings, she claims they told her that "many people of the Earth" will be transferred to a new planet called "Dominion" in the future when it arrives in the solar system. "But still others shall tour the Galaxy in the Great University Craft—learning in the Father's House of Many Mansions!"[46] Troxell died in 1979, but a small group of people continues her work under the name The New Essenes of Inyo.

Ashtar Command's Great Exodus

The most prominent group in UFO literature with a detailed view of a coming rapture of sorts is the Guardian Action International organization of Durango, Colorado, formerly of Salt Lake City, that channels messages and entire books by the "Ashtar Command." Ashtar, an information source popular with New Age-UFO enthusiasts, is supposedly the supreme commander of a fleet of spaceships circling the earth that are here to help guide humankind into a new age (more on Ashtar in a later chapter). One of the Ashtar Command's most popular books, *Project: World Evacuation*, has on its cover a colorful picture of spaceships hovering over a city and lifting dozens of people into the ships via beam rays. In this 1982 book, the Ashtar Command warns readers that a "great separation" is soon to take place. "Danger is upon you. Drop everything and prepare yourselves. It is time to run toward the shelter of Divine Love and Guidance and to take with you only that which you can carry within the inner citadel of being. The early times of this decade will see the fulfillment of all the prophecies that have been released to the world."[47]

The book, which also claims to have a foreword written by Jesus Christ, talks about hard times coming to the planet, "the cleansing action," and three removals of people from earth that Ashtar calls "The Great Exodus I, II, and III."

A Golden City of Light

Following the cleansing action and the rapture, many space brothers say, will come a golden age after which one (or sometimes more) crystal cities, golden cities, or "cities of light" shall descend to earth. Here again the extraterrestrial messengers have found a firm link with the end times discussed in the Bible.

In the section preceding one of the most poetic parts of the Bible's Book of Revelation, the apostle John records that after God's one-thousand-year new age he will administer a "white throne" judgment for the dead (see Rev. 20). And then the New Jerusalem will appear as the elect's new dwelling place:

> Then I saw a new heaven and a new earth, for the first heaven and the first earth had passed away, and there was no longer any sea. I saw the Holy City, the new Jerusalem, coming down out of heaven from God, prepared as a bride beautifully dressed for her husband. . . . It shone with the glory of God, and its brilliance was like that of a very precious jewel, like a jasper, clear as crystal (Rev. 21:1–2, 11).

Is it a coincidence that Whitley Strieber in his best-selling book *Transformation* wrote that the aliens claimed they "recycled souls" and that they showed him a beautiful golden city? "I have longed for the golden city, have waited and hoped to see it again," Strieber wrote, "but I have never returned. I have thought that perhaps a thing of such beauty is not meant for living eyes."[48]

Is it a coincidence that the *Starseed Transmissions* say that during the new age there will be "great floating cities of light, massive fleets of inter-galactic star ships"?[49]

Is it by chance that when Brad Steiger has talked to many contactees they independently tell him that they remember coming from a "beautiful crystal city" in space?[50] And what about the beautiful, blonde alien from the Pleiades named Semjase who summoned Sherry Hansen of Phoenix (who later became Steiger's wife) to a crystal where she claims she was snatched up and taken on a tour through the universe escorted "by a being of light"? She said she was shown a beautiful city. "Maybe it was the New Jerusalem—where the beauty was far above anything I've ever dreamed possible," she said. "It was like a crystal/diamond planet, reflecting and refracting the purest, most brilliant colors."[51]

The Kingdom Without the King

I don't think any of these matters are coincidences. I have no doubt that many, even most, of the UFOnauts give their contactees messages about the end times that parallel those given thousands of years ago in the Judeo-Christian Scriptures. But after reading literally thousands of messages from the space brothers during the past several years and carefully analyzing their views of the second coming, the coming millennium, new age, Armageddon, the rapture, and the new Jerusalem, I am convinced that these entities are trying to sell humanity one of the biggest deceptions of all time.

I find it extremely interesting that Sherry Hansen's escort through the universe was a "being of light," in view of the apostle Paul's warning that "Satan himself masquerades as an angel of light" (2 Cor. 11:14).

But the real giveaway to me that the extraterrestrial beings are giving contactees messages that could lead the world into delusion is that in each of their biblical parallels concerning the end times, they have carefully excised Jesus Christ from the picture and have substituted a New Age Christ, or none at all. How can the space brothers say that the prophecies in Scripture about the end times are about to be fulfilled when they cut the divine person out of the scenario of whom all Scripture speaks?

Remember, the Bible says that "there is no other name under heaven given to men by which we must be saved" (Acts 4:12). And that name is Jesus of Nazareth, the one who was nailed on the cross two thousand years ago, giving his life, as he put it, "as a ransom for many" (Matt. 20:28; Mark 10:45; see also 1 Tim. 2:6). There is no other "Christ" than Jesus, who said in John 14:6: "I am the way and the truth and the life. No one comes to the Father except through me."

Take the space brothers' end-time scenarios, for example. Jesus Christ will not be in the New Jerusalem, in their view. He is strangely absent, despite the fact that the Book of Revelation states that Christ the Lamb and God the Father will be the lamp and light of the city (Rev. 21:23).

The rapture will not have anything to do with Christ, according to the extraterrestrial messengers. Yet the Scriptures say believers of Christ will be caught up to meet him in the air (1 Thess. 4:17), not whisked off into spaceships.

Likewise, in the aliens' messages about the second coming and Armageddon Christ is also absent, despite the fact that Scripture clearly states that the same Jesus will come back in the height of the battle on a white horse and save Israel and all of mankind from destruction (Rev. 19:11).

After Armageddon, Scripture states Jesus will rebuild the world and rule it directly and physically from Jerusalem in his millennial kingdom. But the UFOnauts' view of the new age is one in which the Prince of Peace, Jesus Christ, is not present. They have eliminated the King from his kingdom.

I believe the UFOnauts' view of future events and their concept of the second coming strikes at the very core of Christianity itself. Virtually every extraterrestrial message I know today denies what the church has always called "the blessed hope": Jesus' personal, physical return to earth that the Bible refers to more than five hundred times. As James J. Brookes put it in

1878, "Among the early Christians there was, perhaps, no doctrine that was more the object of firm belief, and the ground of more delightful contemplation, than that their ascended Master would return."[52]

Set Up for a Fall

Anyone who has read my last book, *Soothsayers of the Second Advent*, knows that I am no fan of reckless speculations and guessing games over specific end-time events and personalities. The book documents grave errors many Bible prophecy teachers have made in fact and judgment by engaging in speculation about the future.

But after reading parallel end-time "prophecies" from the space brothers, and realizing that their teachings about a second coming and the dawning of a new age form the central plank in most of their theologies, I have to wonder if there is a deliberate other-dimensional, otherworldly plan to deceive mankind in what could very well be the era when Jesus Christ returns to Planet Earth.

Consider New Agers' possible mindsets if a great tribulation befalls the earth. What will they think if a world leader does emerge and promises to bring peace to the earth (as the Bible seems to say a coming wicked leader called the Antichrist will do)? Will they mistake that leader (whom the Bible describes as a frightening dictator who will enslave the world, claim to be God and demand worship, kill Christians and Jews, and lead the world to ruin) as the "Christ" or coming world teacher?

What will New Agers think if Christians really do disappear? Will they think the wicked have been removed as some of their "prophecies" have implied, or will they think they will be the next ones on the program to be beamed aboard a spaceship?

And when the world is falling apart, will they look for a spaceship to save them instead of the God who formed the universe?

When most people embrace a new one-world religion, will they think they have achieved "Christ consciousness" and experienced the second coming?

Delusion

The Bible predicts earthlings will be deluded on a massive scale by the Antichrist. Indeed, it is difficult to imagine that in our modern world masses of people actually believe in science-fiction mythology. But the apostle Paul, writing to Timothy, predicted this very thing:

> For the time will come when men will not put up with sound doctrine. Instead, to suit their own desires, they will gather around them a great number of teachers to say what their itching ears want to hear. They will turn their ears away from the truth and turn aside to myths (2 Tim. 4:3, 4).

3 The Second Coming According to Jesus

Imagine a history professor at a major university teaching that Adolf Hitler was a great man, that Hitler did not want the Jews exterminated, that he did not actually attack Poland in 1939 and set off World War II, and that he did not later send his blitzkrieg against France, England, and the Soviet Union.

Imagine the professor citing for "proof" new documents he uncovered that were buried in the ground and that various mediums and channelers had confirmed his findings.

Most likely the professor immediately would be censured and dismissed, and it would probably become a national story, a scandal, and rightly so. The horror of World War II is still etched in the world's memory. The extermination of six million Jews is fact. We can go to the remains of some of the gas chambers today, and we can visit Yad Vashem, the Holocaust museum in Jerusalem, for plenty of evidence.

The professor would be guilty of not only grossly misrepresenting history but of misrepresenting Hitler and his legacy of hate by trying to portray him as a man he was not.

Today proponents of the New Age constantly talk about another historical figure and they have likewise, though perhaps unknowingly, misrepresented him. They have produced documents that are the exact opposite of the historical record of his sayings. They have rewritten history to say something different from what he said his purpose was, and they have misinterpreted the motives and actions of millions of his followers through the centuries.

Although certain occultists have written down their own ideas about him for many centuries, not until late in the nineteenth century did some of the more influential ones go to work. Better communications and other factors helped these occultists pave the way for the twentieth-century occult and spiritistic traditions that blossomed into the New Age movement. And today the trend to dispense new information about him through a variety of ways, including trance channeling, automatic writing, and other means, has increased. On top of that, various mediums and channelers have "confirmed" many of these new writings. And increasingly, voices that claim to come from other planets, other galaxies, other dimensions, are coming through the UFO and New Age communities either confirming these writings about him or giving new revelations about him.

The he I refer to is Jesus Christ.

Most of the otherworldly messages seem to say that Jesus Christ of Nazareth is not who Christians claim he is—not God in human flesh, the second person of the Holy Trinity, as the Christian church has taught for twenty centuries—but simply a way shower, an avatar, a spiritual leader, in the same league as other prophets from the Old Testament or other religious figures. Most of those messages claim that the world has been living a twenty-century-long error concerning Jesus, because the church through deliberate falsehoods, greed, and ignorance covered up what Jesus actually taught. They say, among other things, that Jesus did not die as an atonement for sin, that he taught reincarnation not resurrection, and that humans can become gods, or at least attain "Christ consciousness," just as Jesus did. Perhaps the Bible verse the extraterrestrial messengers most often quote is Jesus saying that anyone who has faith in him "will do what I have been doing. He will do even greater things than these" (John 14:12).

And to back up these New Age revelations, many contactees supposedly receive confirming messages from sources in outer space who claim to be Jesus himself.

Moreover, all of these voices, including those claiming to come from Christ, contradict what Christ's apostles said about him. They also, in one way or another, contradict what many Jewish Scriptures (what Christians refer to as the Old Testament) teach about the Christ and his coming to earth. More seriously, these modern messages about Jesus contradict what Jesus himself said about his life, mission, and second coming. For Jesus talked extensively about his return, as recorded in all four Gospels, and it is Jesus who gave, and spoke directly in many parts, the entire Book of Revelation to the apostle John.

But most troublesome about the new messages is that they cannot be verified or put to the test. They have usually come through occult means—channeling, automatic writing, authors' opinions—that cannot be supported with empirical evidence. Worse yet, in an age where channeling is popular, the messages demonstrate the fact that many of the world's leading channelers are not always on target when they dispense information (more on this later).

The Bible: A Historical, Reliable Document

In contrast, the biblical record of Christ, and what he said and did, is about a proven historical figure and was written down by eyewitnesses. The apostle John wrote:

> That which was from the beginning, which we have heard, which we have seen with our eyes, which we have looked at and our hands have touched—this we proclaim concerning the Word of life. The life [Jesus] appeared; we have seen it and testify to it, and we proclaim to you the eternal life, which was with the Father and has appeared to us (1 John 1:1, 2).

The apostle Paul also appealed to the historical record, and even stated that Christ appeared to more than five hundred people, following his resurrection from the dead:

> He was buried, that he was raised on the third day according to the Scriptures, and that he appeared to Peter, and then to the Twelve. After that, he appeared to more than five hundred of

the brothers at the same time, most of whom are still living,
though some have fallen asleep. Then he appeared to James,
then to all the apostles, and last of all he appeared to me also
(1 Cor. 15:4–7).

But just because early Christian church leaders wrote about
Christ, can we really trust what they said? Yes.

If you were injured in an accident, whom would you want to
testify on your behalf on the witness stand, an eyewitness who
saw the accident happen or a self-proclaimed psychic claiming to have had impressions of the accident from a hundred
miles away? Whom would the jury find more credible?

Many scholars throughout history have verified the authenticity of Scripture, for it has withstood rigorous testing. As R. C.
Sproul puts it, "You should trust the Bible because the Bible
has been proven trustworthy."[1]

Christ's resurrection from the dead is a proven historical fact.
D. J. Kennedy in his book *Why I Believe* wrote:

> The evidence for the resurrection of Jesus Christ has been exam-
> ined more carefully than the evidence for any other fact of his-
> tory! It has been weighed and considered by the greatest of
> scholars. . . . I have met many people who do not believe in the
> resurrection of Christ, but I have never met one person who has
> read even a single book on the evidence for the resurrection
> who did not believe it.[2]

Skeptics' explanations for the supernatural event of the resurrection of Christ are harder to believe than the mere fact that
he was raised from the dead. The explanations range from "the
swoon theory" (Jesus was not actually dead, but revived in the
tomb after his crucifixion and a two-ton stone was pushed away
from the tomb's entrance) to the first-century lie that the apostles stole his body (and almost all gave their blood in martyr's
deaths to defend a lie). All such attempts to explain away the
eyewitness accounts of the events are as ludicrous as to say
that little green men took the body away in a flying saucer.

In light of the documented historical evidence, we ought to take seriously what Jesus himself had to say about his second coming and compare it very rigorously with what the UFO-nauts say about it.

Christian View of Prophecy

I would be remiss if I didn't mention the fact that all Christians do not interpret Bible prophecy and the events leading to the second coming of Christ the same way. Christians differ on various aspects of terms that I have used thus far, such as the great tribulation, the rapture, the Antichrist, and others. And I certainly do not want to leave the impression that the great tribulation and the Antichrist are definitely just around the corner because the world looks dark. Yes, humankind appears to be rushing toward judgment, and yes, it looks like all of the signs that Jesus said would herald his coming have either been fulfilled or are in the process of fulfillment. But it is also true that the timing of all future events is in God's hands, and that Christ may not come back for a long time.

But one thing all Bible-believing Christians agree on is the imminent personal, physical return of Jesus Christ and the establishment of his kingdom on earth. The Bible cannot be construed to say that someone other than Jesus of Nazareth will return at the second coming. It is heresy for a Christian to profess the second coming to be a nebulous leap of humankind's consciousness to a higher level.

The back cover of the book *The Meaning of the Millennium: Four Views*, by Robert G. Clouse, states: "Christ is coming again. With this Christians have agreed since the first century. But since the first century there have also been many disagreements. How will Christ return? When will he return? What sort of kingdom will he establish? What is the meaning of the millennium? These questions persist today."[3]

Who Is the Real Christ?

New Age and flying-saucer literature is packed full of references to the Christ, Christ consciousness, the Christ self, becoming Christed, and other terms that sound religious. But those familiar with the Bible know that the use of all these derivatives of the term *Christ* differs greatly from the Hebrew Scriptures, which are the origin of the concept of Christ.

Straightforwardly, *the Christ* is the term that can only fit one person for all time—Jesus of Nazareth. It means God's promised Jewish Messiah. *The New International Dictionary of the Bible* states:

> *Christ*, meaning "anointed one," is the Greek equivalent of the Hebrew word *Messiah*. Its function as a title is emphasized by the fact that often it occurs with the definite article, which gives it the force of "the promised Christ," the one who fulfills the concept of Messiah as set forth in the OT [Old Testament] Scriptures. . . . Of special interest is the development that led to the use of "Christ" as a personal name. It must have taken place early in the life of the church, for we find it reflected, for example, in the opening verse of Mark's Gospel—"The beginning of the gospel of Jesus Christ, the Son of God."[4]

If we go by this alone, that narrows the field down as to who the Christ could be, "the one who fulfills the concept of Messiah as set forth in the OT Scriptures." First and foremost, he had to be a Jew and a direct descendant of King David (1 Chron. 17:12–14; Isa. 11:1). This alone disqualifies Benjamin Creme's Lord Maitreya who, he claims, lives in London and was a Tibetan.[5] And it certainly eliminates the possibility of anything nonliving, not flesh and blood, or of a collective enlightenment.

Scripture is even more specific about who Christ would be. In *Soothsayers of the Second Advent* I pointed out some of these specifics: he would be born in Bethlehem (Mic. 5:2); he would be born of a virgin (Isa. 7:14); a messenger (John the Baptist) would precede him (Mal. 3:1; Isa. 40:3); he would open the eyes of the blind and heal the deaf, dumb, and lame (Isa. 35:5,6); he would come into Jerusalem on a donkey (Zech. 9:9); he would be betrayed for thirty pieces of silver (Ps. 41:9; Zech. 11:12); he would be beaten and killed (Isa. 53; Ps. 22); he would be pierced (Zech. 12:10); some would gamble for his clothing (Ps. 22:18); and he would be resurrected (Pss. 16:9, 10; 21:4).[6]

But a good percentage of the Old Testament verses about the Christ have to do with his future role as the literal king of Israel and the ruler of the world (Ps. 2; Zech. 6:12, 13). And that separates Judaism from Christianity. Most Jews today are still looking for their Messiah and reject Jesus, because he did not establish his kingdom in Jerusalem at that time. In other words they tend to look at only the Old Testament verses that talk about a conquering Messiah. They have failed to discern the verses that show us the full picture of the Messiah, the ones that discuss his crucifixion, resurrection, and return to earth in glory at his second coming (Zech. 9:9, 10; Isa. 42:1–4; 53; 61:1, 2).

Finally, the Messiah would be uniquely God in human flesh according to Isaiah:

> For to us a child is born, to us a son is given, and the government will be on his shoulders. And he will be called Wonderful Counselor, Mighty God, Everlasting Father, Prince of Peace (Isa. 9:6).

The apostle John verified that Jesus of Nazareth is uniquely God clothed in human flesh: "In the beginning was the Word, and the Word was with God, and the Word was God. . . . The Word became flesh and made his dwelling among us" (John 1:1, 14).

All extraterrestrial definitions of Christ fall short of the biblical one. The Bible's Christ is one of a kind; the New Age Christ is one of many gods or is a mere level of spirituality that anyone can attain.

The Physical Return of Christ

Who Christ is and who he is not is a crucial concept for understanding what the Bible has to say about his second coming and the coming new age. As we will see, the Hebrew Scriptures' account of his coming is at great odds with the event recorded in the gospel according to extraterrestrial beings.

The Old Testament prophets consistently referred to the "Day of the Lord" as part of the end-times scenario leading to the physical coming of the Messiah to earth, not the birth of a new messiah or the coming of a new consciousness or feeling to humankind. Daniel referred to it as one coming "like a son of man" (Dan. 7:13). The Book of Joel, likely written about 400 B.C., describes the event as happening when the "multitudes" are in the "valley of decision" (Valley of Armageddon) and "the LORD will roar from Zion and thunder from Jerusalem; the earth and the sky will tremble. . . . Then you will know that *I*, the LORD your God, *dwell in Zion*, my holy hill" (Joel 3:14, 16, 17, emphasis added). The fourth chapter of the Book of Micah, written about 750 B.C., is another passage that talks about the Messiah living in Jerusalem and presiding over the new age. Although there are a number of passages like this one in the Old Testament, it says that during that time people from many nations will go to Jerusalem where "he will teach us his ways, so that we may walk in his paths" (Mic. 4:2).[7]

Furthermore was the fact that the apostles believed strongly in the physical return of their Messiah. The Christian church, following the lead of the apostles through the ages, has maintained that belief. In the Nicene Creed of 325 A.D. and the Apostle's Creed of the seventh century, which are recited in unison in churches of many denominations to this day, are almost identical statements that the same Jesus who was crucified and resurrected shall come again to judge the living and the dead.

The apostle John urged his readers to continue living in a manner pleasing to Christ "so that when he appears we may be confident and unashamed before him at his coming" (1 John 2:28).[8] He also adds that everyone who has the hope of the return of Christ "purifies himself" (1 John 3:3).

Paul repeatedly stressed the physical return of Christ. In 2 Thessalonians 2:8 Paul talked about Christ coming back to overthrow "the lawless one" (the Antichrist) with "the splendor of his coming." In saying this about the event, Paul verified Jesus' own testimony that he would return to judge the world during a time of rebellion, war, and religious deception.

I've already discussed Jesus' words about his physical return from the sky, but to go a step further, Jesus revealed to the apostle John that his coming would be so physical that "every eye" would see him: "Look, he is coming with the clouds, and every eye will see him, even those who pierced him; and all the peoples of the earth will mourn because of him" (Rev. 1:7).

The Coming of the Lawless One

The Bible's picture of the events leading to Christ's second coming are very detailed. It talks about the time being one of incredible rebellion, and one in which a false leader who will proclaim himself to be God will hold sway over the world. Answering rumors that abounded in the first century (and that still crop up from time to time) that the "day of the Lord" has already come, Paul gave the Thessalonian church a detailed description of why it wasn't so and of what they should look for:

> Don't let anyone deceive you in any way, for that day will not come until the rebellion occurs and the man of lawlessness is revealed, the man doomed to destruction. He will oppose and will exalt himself over everything that is called God or is worshiped, so that he sets himself up in God's temple, proclaiming himself to be God (2 Thess. 2:3, 4).

Five verses later Paul explains this:

> The coming of the lawless one will be in accordance with the work of Satan displayed in all kinds of counterfeit miracles, signs and wonders, and in every sort of evil that deceives those who are perishing. They perish because they refused to love the truth and so be saved. For this reason God sends them a powerful delusion so that they will believe the lie (2 Thess. 2:9–11).

Overall, it is a frightening picture. The Bible clearly prophesies that a world leader will arrive on the scene calling himself God. Daniel said he will rule deceitfully (Dan. 11:23) and adds, along with the apostle John, that he will deny and oppose

God (Dan. 11:36, 37 and 1 John 2:22). The Book of Revelation states that he will force everyone to worship him, and all peoples will be forced to receive his mark on their foreheads or hands to be allowed to buy or sell. And those who refuse will be beheaded (Rev. 20:4).

Christ repeatedly warned his followers that in the days prior to his return many would come claiming to be Christ, and they would come with great signs and wonders. He said they were not to believe it (Matt. 24:26). To further reinforce this, Paul said it didn't matter who the source was. If anyone, "even an angel," claimed to have come down from heaven preaching a different gospel, "let him be eternally condemned" (Gal. 1:8). Paul also warned against those who proclaimed "another Jesus, whom we have not preached" (2 Cor. 11:4 KJV).

Nevertheless, Scripture plainly states that the world will follow after false christs and false prophets, and that in the end time one will claim to be God in human flesh, the promised Christ. He will be a false christ, an Antichrist, because he will fail to fulfill hundreds of biblical prophecies designated for the true Christ. Some scholars, citing Scripture, seem to indicate that the Antichrist will come from Europe (although in my judgment there is nothing very clear about his origin), not from Bethlehem as the Scriptures declared Christ would. And there is no indication that the Antichrist would be a Jew, a direct descendant of King David. Jesus of Nazareth, on the other hand, had two of his ancestral lineages, for both his mother and earthly father, published in the Gospels of Matthew and Luke. And through both Mary and Joseph he was a direct descendant of David.[9]

Fascinating to this discussion is the fact that if a man claiming to be Christ comes to earth in these last days and presents his credentials as the Jewish Messiah, there will be no way for him to prove he is a direct descendant of David as Jesus did. In A.D. 72 Titus's Roman army sacked Jerusalem, destroyed the Jewish temple, and obliterated the genealogical records of Israel. For that reason most Jews today have no clear idea from which of the twelve tribes of Israel they descended. Was Jesus referring to the Antichrist and other false prophets when he talked about his rejection by the Jews and commented that "if another shall come in his own name, him ye will receive" (John 5:43 KJV)?

A Technological Savior

The late Walter Martin, one of the twentieth century's leading authorities on cults and the occult, while not directly saying that the Antichrist will come walking out of a flying saucer someday, left open that possibility. After all, Martin said, Scripture talks about "signs in the heavens and the wonders that will precede the second coming of Jesus Christ." He argues thus:

> Suppose the sign of antichrist is not to appear in normal fashion, but instead, to be a technological saviour, not a spiritual saviour. A superior technological intellect, a supernatural being with all power, signs and natural wonders. Suppose he could cause the deserts to be irrigated and end famines. Supposing he could impose a benevolent despotism upon the world and stop national fighting and squabbling about boundaries. . . . Supposing he could give us cures for cancer, AIDS, herpes, diabetes, arterial diseases. Suppose this super technology presented us with signs and lying wonders. Do you think the world would build him a temple and worship him? I do. I think they'd go to Jerusalem on their knees and kiss his feet, because the world isn't looking for a spiritual redeemer.[10]

Although Martin explored other options to explain UFOs, he was aware that many of the alleged messages from the UFO-nauts were spiritual in nature, for they talked about the coming new age that they were helping humankind ease into. Today, years after Martin's speech, UFOlogy has been thrust squarely into the mainstream of the New Age movement. People who channel extraterrestrial beings, talk about them, and write about them are major speakers at almost every New Age conference, and an increasing number of key New Age leaders claim to be in contact with extraterrestrial beings. What is unsettling to some New Agers, though it's seldom openly discussed with a few notable exceptions,[11] is the fact that most New Agers do not fully know who the aliens are, and they do know that the space brothers have lied to them in the past and will probably lie to them again.

"It seems to me that the UFO entities may have been fibbing to us about their true identity and their true place of origin since our earliest antiquity," Steiger wrote. But he says not to worry about it; it may be part of some "supercosmic jigsaw puzzle" by the superior UFOnauts to help mankind piece together a "complete picture of the UFO enigma."[12] Steiger, addressing concerns about the lying messages, asserts this:

> If one can find certain shiny grains of truth in this murky swirl of metaphysical sand and silt, then he will charge himself not to dismiss lightly the steadily unraveling scrolls of the Space Brothers' apocalyptic apocrypha.[13]

The Channeling Housewife

Los Angeles housewife-turned-trance-channeler Penny Torres was a rising star in New Age circles. In 1986, she claims, an entity named Mafu came to her and said he wanted to use her body to spread his message to the world. "Mafu claims to be a member of the 'brotherhood of light' in the 'seventh dimension,' last incarnated as a leper in first-century Pompeii."[14]

NBC's old television show *West 57th Street* did a segment on channeling featuring Torres and came up with an unflattering picture of her abilities. She claimed Mafu had healed someone of AIDS and that he had taken the pressure off the earth's tectonic plates in California to prevent another earthquake. The show also had Mafu speaking through Torres, wowing a crowd when she picked a random man in the audience and told him that Mafu knew about the future pyramid-building project he was working on. "I didn't know you knew about that," the startled man said to Mafu.

But when *West 57th Street* checked Torres's story about these matters, it found that the man supposedly healed had never had AIDS, and pressure was still threatening California with an earthquake. They also caught on camera Torres's friends telling her prior to the channeling session that the "random" man (whom Torres already knew by name) was soon going away to begin the building project.

What was Torres's response when confronted with these facts? "It's not my truth that it's not true," she said. "All I can tell you is that the information that was given to me was quite different than the information that you're now giving to me. I allow both of those things. I allow both of those fantasies."

"But they're not fantasies," objected reporter Meredith Vieira.

"I consider everything a fantasy, because I've gained a lot of wisdom, . . . " Torres replied. "It doesn't matter to me 'cause I'm not here to prove anything to you. If you are attempting to prove that this is all fraudulent and that's the opinion you gained, I allow you that."

Vieira objected to that, too, and commented that the audience seemed dazzled by the "all-knowing Mafu."

"If that's what they need to their fantasy to follow an entity, then he is going to provide this circumstance," Torres responded.

"That's a convenient out," snapped Vieira.

"Is it? It's my truth," Torres said.[15]

Create Your Own Reality

Although the show pointed out that certain other New Age channelers considered Torres a fraud, her you-create-your-own-reality approach ("It's my truth") forms a central part of the messages coming through the channeling movement, according to *Christian Research Journal* editor Elliot Miller. The other parts of the message are that you are God and that all is one, Miller asserts.[16] These three points also seem to serve as the central theme in extraterrestial messages. While it's true that the messages coming from the UFO movement are a bit more apocalyptic than the standard New Age message, essentially we may be dealing with the same thing.

Penny Torres is just one of many examples I could cite as a bridge between the two. Whom does she say she is channeling? An extraterrestrial being or an alleged deceased human? Both.

God Tells the Truth

In contrast, messages humans have received from God are dramatically different. Reality is clearly defined by God. Things are true and things are false. God is light, the serpent is darkness. Adam and Eve were banished from eternal life and the Garden of Eden for their very first lie. And later, when Moses led the wandering Jews out of Egypt to the Promised Land, God engraved his Ten Commandments into stone for his people to remember. You may not lie ("give false testimony against your neighbor") (Exod. 20:16) was one.

God did not change in the New Testament, as Paul pointed out in declaring that "God . . . does not lie" (Titus 1:2). Since Jesus was God in human flesh, he also never lied or broke any of God the Father's commandments. Peter, quoting an Old Testament prophecy about Christ, wrote: "He committed no sin, and no deceit was found in his mouth" (1 Peter 2:22; see also Isa. 53:9).

Thus the gospel of Jesus Christ is quite a bit different from the gospel according to extraterrestrial beings and New Age channelers.

The Modern Myth Becomes a New Religion

While piloting his private plane near Mount Rainier, Washington, on June 25, 1947, Seattle businessman Kenneth Arnold said he spotted nine large disk-shaped objects "skipping" above him in the sky at fantastic rates of speed. The incident marked the beginning of the modern UFO era, for it captured the public's imagination. By the end of the year the term *flying saucers* was in use and more than 800 sightings had been reported.[1]

Since that time millions of people, including many of prominence (like former President Jimmy Carter), claim to have seen unidentified flying objects, dozens of organizations have sprung up everywhere to study the UFO phenomenon, and thousands of books have been published about the mysterious sightings.

But the truth of the matter is that we are no closer to the solution to the UFO mystery today than Kenneth Arnold was decades ago. Despite all the organizations springing up to research UFOs and all the books being written about them, there is little agreement among UFOlogists over almost anything regarding them. Few agree on the point of origin, the purpose, or the technology that empowers UFOs into impossible (by earthly standards) maneuvers that sometimes include changing shape and vanishing like Cheshire cats. In fact, the debate still rages today—just as it did in the 1950s—as to whether or not UFOs pose a threat to humankind.

That debate, however, has abated while many leading voices in the New Age movement have linked UFOs and otherwordly visitors to the dawning of a new golden era. More and more the idea of the UFO as a symbol of transformation is taking hold.

But not all voices are convinced that this new belief is good for society. UFOlogist Jacques Vallee notes that society, whether we like it or not, is being transformed by the saucers:

> Belief in the reality of UFOs is spreading rapidly at all levels of society throughout the world. Books and periodicals on the subject appear at an ever-increasing rate. Documentaries and major films are being made now by young people of the UFO generation (young men and women who were born just after World War II and who grew up with flying-saucer stories) who have moved into influential positions in the media. . . . Many of the themes of yesterday's counter-culture can be traced back to the "messages from space" coming from UFO contactees of the forties and fifties.[2]

Although Vallee's remarks were published in 1979, I believe they are still valid. The belief in UFOs as a force for good has quietly entered the psyche of the modern culture. I did not realize how pervasive this was until I began the research for this book. Then one day I observed my two young daughters mesmerized by *Sesame Street*, the popular television show featuring the Muppets created by Jim Henson. Friendly aliens landing is a popular theme on the children's show, and to be honest, I'm not sure if it is harmful; I personally laugh when I see the Muppet aliens equipped with antennas on their heads going "Yip, Yip, Yip, Yip, Yip." Recently, when I took my family out to a local fast-food restaurant and bought one of my daughters a kid's meal containing a prize, I was surprised to see a plastic flying saucer, equipped with a floor hatch and fold-down descending stairs, as the gift inside.

Then there is the closest thing humankind has to a world festival, the Olympics. Those who watched the extravaganza on the final night of the Los Angeles games, transmitted around the globe, saw the clever illusion that a flying saucer was descending on the Coliseum during a gyrating Lionel Ritchie tune.

Most Americans Believe in UFOs

According to 1978 and 1981 Gallup polls, most North Americans believe that flying saucers exist and that they are controlled by beings from another world.[3] According to an August 6, 1990 Gallup Poll, 14 percent of Americans claim to have seen a UFO. That's up from 9 percent in 1978 and 11 percent in 1973. One writer states that some twelve million Americans claim to have seen a UFO.[4]

That's a far cry from not so long ago when no one took UFOs very seriously. According to a 1947 Gallup poll, "virtually no one considered the objects to be from outer space," and most thought they were illusions, hoaxes, secret weapons, or phenomena that could be explained.[5]

According to Douglas Curran a number of myths or folk tales have sprung up over the years in the UFO community, and some of them are with us to this day. Rumors of massive government conspiracies, crashed disks, mysterious men in black who try to silence witnesses who have seen UFOs, and many others permeate the UFO movement. Although Curran did not comment on whether any of these myths were valid, he did document how most of the folk tales had a definite starting point and then became established in the collective mindset of UFO enthusiasts and investigators.

Much of the following section on the modern history of UFOlogy is borrowed from Curran's book.

1947

The Arnold sighting marked the beginning of a UFO "wave." As researcher Jacques Vallee has documented, UFOs historically have usually come in great numbers that have then died down, only to reappear later at irregular intervals. But the 1947 wave was especially ferocious. In those days many observers somehow connected it to the end of World War II and the advent of nuclear weapons. Vallee wrote:

When the 1947 wave started, a total of five atomic bomb explosions—Alamogordo (July 16, 1945), Hiroshima (August 6, 1945), Nagasaki, Crossroads A and Crossroads B—had already taken place. . . .

Hence the suggestion . . . that other galactic communities may have kept a long-term routine watch on earth and may have been alarmed by the sight of our A-bombs as evidence that we are warlike and on the threshold of space exploration.[6]

That year also marked one of the most controversial events in UFO history: the alleged recovery of a crashed disk near Roswell, New Mexico, on July 8. What confused the public was that original newspaper reports, transmitted everywhere, indicated that the government had recovered a crashed disk, but by the next day military officials had concluded the device was "evidentally nothing other than a weather or radar instrument of some sort." Widely distributed pictures of the wreckage showed military officers holding up what appear to be pieces of tinfoil and wood that were scattered on the floor of a military office.[7]

Almost immediately some people suspected a coverup, and rumors began surfacing that the government had recovered as many as four alien bodies near the site. Fantastic stories of what the government "really" discovered near Roswell remain to this day, and books continue to be written that highlight testimony from new "witnesses" who claim to have had access to secrets from the Roswell site.[8]

In 1947 for security reasons, the United States government also began to look into the flying-saucer reports. "The public position of the Air Force on flying saucers was that they were misidentifications," notes Curran, "but privately its greatest concern was that they were actually Russian secret weapons."[9]

1948

In January 1948, after Captain Thomas Mantell, an Air National Guard pilot, died while chasing a metallic and "tremendous in size" UFO (according to his last radio transmission), the public was even more suspicious of a government coverup. According to reports of the incident, Mantell did not have oxygen equipment and lost consciousness at 20,000 feet before his plane crashed. The Air Force said Mantell had died "while in pursuit of the planet Venus, having mistaken it for a UFO," and the public and press were incredulous over the explanation.

Less than six months later, in another highly publicized incident, two commercial pilots reported seeing a large UFO that streaked past them "at an estimated 700 miles per hour, made a sharp angular turn, climbed into a clear sky," and abruptly disappeared.

1949

By 1949 the Air Force stepped up its investigation, reorganized its UFO investigations team, and codified procedures for dealing with UFOs under the code name Project Grudge.

The mass media also had a lot to do with feeding the insatiable appetite the public was beginning to have for UFOs. In a two-part *Saturday Evening Post* article in early 1949, material supplied by the Air Force said that most of the UFO sightings could be explained by tricks, hoaxes, and easily explained sightings. But the public was skeptical over this, too, because part two of the article blasted the Air Force's conclusions. The Air Force responded with a press release sticking by its position, and another rash of UFO sightings took place.

1950

Donald Keyhoe, a retired Marine Corps major, was another important figure in UFOlogy in its early days. His January 1950 article in the magazine *True* and his later book, *Flying Saucers Are Real* set off a sensation. Keyhoe claimed that aliens from another planet had been observing Earth for the last 175 years.

The captured-alien scenario first surfaced in 1950 with publication of the best-selling book *Behind the Flying Saucers,* by Frank Scully. The book alleged that the Air Force had asked a doctor to conduct a secret autopsy on sixteen dead aliens (said to be about four feet tall) recovered from three crashed disks. And although the story turned out to be a hoax, the spectre of the government having alien bodies has remained to this day.

In 1951 UFO sightings dropped off, but just when the Air Force began to dismantle Project Grudge, several daytime sightings occurred involving military radar and pilots that resulted in a new investigation called Project Blue Book. The project ended in 1969, with the Air Force admitting that 29 percent of the UFO cases it studied could not be explained.

UFOs Buzz the White House

The next year, just after *Life* published the popular article "Have We Visitors from Outer Space?" UFOs buzzed the White House. It started at 11:40 P.M. on July 19 when seven objects appeared on the radar screen at Washington's National Airport. At the same time two other radar centers picked up the objects on their scopes, one reported as traveling at seven thousand miles per hour. Airline pilots in the area noticed, too. Some radioed messages that they were being followed by unknown aircraft.[10]

But it didn't end there. A week later radar again picked up strange objects. F-94 interceptor jets were scrambled to the scene only to discover that the objects had vanished. But as soon as the jets returned to their base, the UFOs came back, and the Langley Air Force Base in Virginia received calls of strange lights in the sky. An F-94 was scrambled again, but as soon as the pilot made visual contact with one of the lights it disappeared. Minutes later, after more UFO blips appeared on the radar screen, two more jets were scrambled, but as soon as the planes closed in on them, even making visual contact, the lights disappeared. Three days later, during a long Air Force press conference, General John A. Samford, director of intelligence, admitted he had no good explanation for the sightings. He added that about 20 percent of all UFO sightings could not be explained and that they came from "credible observers."[11]

The Sinister Men in Black

During the same time period another strange myth entered the picture. Like the belief that the government is secretly housing alien bodies, this myth has endured in a slow stream of newly published books that keeps flowing and gives the world the latest about "the UFO silencers" or "the men in black." This phrase can be traced back to Gray Barker's terrifying 1953 book *They Knew Too Much about Flying Saucers*. The premise of the book is that mysterious "men in black" suits were at work in the world trying to thwart UFO investigators. According to most "silencers" scenarios, these strange beings make threats against people involved in UFO research. Steiger writes:

> Ever since organized flying saucer research began in the early 1950s, a disturbing number of serious UFO investigators have suffered personal harassment, unusual accidents, and even mysterious deaths. In some cases, sinister voices have whispered threats over the telephone and warned certain researchers to terminate specific investigations. Ufologists have been visited by ominous strangers who have made it physically and painfully clear that their orders to discontinue all UFO investigation would be violently enforced.[12]

The myth was reinforced when one of Barker's friends, Albert Bender, founder of an international flying saucer group, suddenly got out of the business and refused to talk about it. Years later, however, Barker and others convinced Bender to tell why in a book titled *Flying Saucers and Three Men*. In the book Bender stated that he became the victim of "strange paranormal experiences that had left him drained and frightened." His house became haunted, as he was the victim of rappings on the walls and strange footsteps in the night. Later three men in black visited him and gave him the "truth" about flying saucers. They told him that "in short, they were responsible for just about every strange or unexplained thing happening on this planet of ours." They also informed him there was no life after death, no God in heaven, and that Jesus was not God and was not resurrected from the dead.[13]

Contactees and Abductees

UFOlogy continued to grow throughout the 1950s, but some of the wind started to be taken out of its sails by the number of highly publicized "contactees" who began to surface claiming they were whisked away to other planets by UFOnauts. The public was rightly incredulous and later irritated by many of these stories that were so fantastic that only a lunatic could believe them. Some of the main "contactees" like George Adamski were quickly exposed as frauds. And by the end of the 1950s, UFOlogy was demoted to the rank of supermarket tabloid material.

But that all changed in the 1960s because of a new myth: the abductees. Although there are earlier accounts of people claiming to have been abducted by aliens in UFOs, the names Betty and Barney Hill became household words in the 1960s. In the book *The Interrupted Journey*, by John G. Fuller, which later became a major motion picture starring James Earl Jones and Estelle Parsons, the Hills claimed they were abducted by a UFO on September 19, 1961, while driving enroute to their New Hampshire home after a short vacation in Canada. The Hills didn't remember the abduction, but they were troubled by strange dreams and a missing two-hour period.

Later they underwent hypnosis, which revealed what allegedly happened that night (and their stories agreed with each other's in most respects). They were taken aboard a flying saucer, underwent various physical examinations, and were given a hypnotic suggestion that they would forget about everything that happened. In 1964, under hypnosis, Betty Hill drew what she claimed was a star map she had seen aboard the craft. At first, astronomers couldn't find the star formation, but in 1969 two stars called Zeta 1 and Zeta 2 Reticuli were discovered[14] by astronomers in a formation that closely resembled Betty Hill's map. That was the apparent start of another UFO myth that continues, that a race of aliens often called "the greys" visit Earth on a regular basis and conduct unknown—some say sinister—experiments with humans for unknown purposes.

The Debunkers

The 1960s also saw the rise of UFO debunkers. Astronomer Allen Hynek, the Air Force's investigator on Project Blue Book, did not set out to be a debunker when in March 1966 he suggested that some UFO reports might be due to "swamp gas."[15] Philip J. Klass, a senior editor with *Aviation Week and Space Technology,* was one who came to prominence and has become one of the most voracious UFO skeptics. In 1966 he stated that hundreds of UFOs are in reality identified. "In most cases they are plasmas of ionized air, sometimes containing charged dust particles," he wrote. "A few may be vortices of tiny charged ice particles."[16] Klass has also added a further challenge to the UFO community: the offer of a large cash reward to anyone who can prove beyond the shadow of a doubt the existence of UFOs.[17]

The biggest debunking of all came in 1969 with the release of the Condon UFO study, spearheaded by a University of Colorado research team (at the encouragement of the United States government), that pooh-poohed most UFO sightings. But the study backfired. It became the easy target of efforts by the UFO community to debunk the debunkers, as many UFO believers saw it as yet more evidence of a government coverup. There were so many holes in the study that even Klass, though he was supportive of the study's conclusions, had to admit, "I cannot endorse the Colorado investigation as having been well managed."[18]

Despite the debunkers, however, UFOs continued to fascinate and confuse the public. Even NASA had no firm answers for what they could be—though not necessarily flying "saucers"—UFOs were spotted by American astronauts during the Apollo 11, Apollo 12, Gemini 7, Gemini 11, and Skylab 3 missions, according to renowned science writer and NASA consultant James Oberg.[19] NASA, however, has not indicated these unidentified flying objects were manned by aliens, or that they were saucers, or that they were indeed manned. Many explanations for them surfaced, with some centering on the possibility they were caused by natural forces, or that some could have been "space junk" caused by previous launches.

The 1970s

The 1970s was an interesting time for UFOlogy as the spectre of abductions became more ingrained in the public's mind. Part of the reason was the intense publicity generated when two Mississippi men claimed they were taken aboard a UFO while fishing from an old pier in the Pascagoula River in 1973. They passed lie detector tests.

The 1970s were also curious for the famous "Bo and Peep" UFO cult. In the mid-1970s two Texans heavily involved in the occult, Marshall H. Applewhite and Bonnie L. Trusdale, became convinced they were the two witnesses of the Book of Revelation. They left everything (including their families) and began touring the country looking for followers who, they promised, would be carried away by UFOs. They called their organization Human Individual Metamorphosis and dubbed themselves "Him and Her" (while the news media labeled them "Bo and Peep"). But their notoriety was short lived; many became disenchanted by the movement, particularly after newspapers delved into the backgrounds of the two and noted that many families were divided by the sect.[20] The movement quickly went underground and faded into obscurity. Trusdale died in 1985, but the sect still had a small following in 1988.[21]

It was also a noteworthy time in the sense that the UFO movement began to turn increasingly religious and respectable. Hynek, who made the infamous "swamp gas" statement in the 1960s, found himself leading the charge in the 1970s to label UFOlogy a science. He also initially supported the extraterrestrial-beings hypothesis that UFOs are real and are manned by beings from other planets.

Nuts and Bolts versus Other-Dimensional Reality

But by 1970 even the extraterrestrial-beings hypothesis began to be challenged. It snowballed with the publication of John Keel's 1970 book *UFOs: Operation Trojan Horse,* which showed a strong link to the occult of many of those involved in UFO research. Keel also explored the possibility that UFOs could be from another dimension and perhaps demonic in nature. Conservative Christians like John Weldon, Zola Levitt, and Clifford Wilson expanded on the theme in their books. The respected Spiritual Counterfeits Project of Berkeley, California, was another evangelical group asserting the theory. In August 1977, SCP put together a strong thirty-two-page journal that contained a drawing of how UFOs could perhaps be demonic entities from another dimension. But not all professing Christians agreed. Presbyterian minister Barry Downing's 1968 book *The Bible and Flying Saucers* asserted that UFOs were probably angelic in nature.

But the late 1970s and early 1980s saw two significant heavyweights also assert the interdimensional theory. In his 1979 book *Messengers of Deception* Vallee strongly supported the interdimensional theory and expressed his fears that mankind was being manipulated by the UFOnauts to change society for its own purposes. Vallee, who is without a doubt one of the most influential UFOlogists in the world (he served as a model for the character Lacombe, a UFO investigator, in Steven Spielberg's 1977 film blockbuster, *Close Encounters of the Third Kind*) still upholds the interdimensional theory. He also said the UFOnauts may be very dangerous, and they may be responsible for a series of worldwide animal mutilations—and even deaths.

Hynek also began to switch sides in 1982, as noted by Curran:

> Hynek submitted that perhaps UFOs were part of a parallel reality, slipping in and out of sequence with our own. This was a hypothesis that obviously pained him as an empirical scientist. Yet after thirty years of interviewing witnesses and investigating sighting reports, radar contacts, and physical traces of saucer landings no other hypothesis seemed to make sense to him.[22]

But despite such heavyweights jumping to the interdimensional-theory side, the prominent position of most American

believers is what is often called the nuts-and-bolts hypothesis—that UFOs are metallic machines from distant planets or
stars. Vallee, mystified by this tendency, calls it "specifically
American" and adds that almost all UFOlogy around the globe
has embraced the interdimensional hypothesis.

> What American ufology wants to talk about is the message that
> UFOs are here, they are extraterrestrial, they are alien, inter-
> planetary visitors that use nuts and bolts spacecraft. . . . they
> laughed down any suggestion, for example, that there might have
> been descriptions of UFOs in folklore, going back to the ninth
> century, and so on. The suggestion that there might be psychic
> phenomena; that there might be phenomena that went beyond
> the normal extraterrestrial interpretation was something that just
> couldn't be tolerated. I'm sorry, but we have to be guided by the
> data [that they might be psychic or interdimensional].[23]

Thanks to the work of Vallee, Keel, Hynek and others, the
interdimensional school has gotten much larger in America.
And as we will see later, the rise of the New Age movement in
the 1980s also may have helped it grow.

Government Conspiracy?

What also got more pronounced in the 1980s was the continuing theme that the government is hiding something. For
example, the United States Supreme Court in 1982 refused to
order the National Security Agency to disclose what it knows
about unidentified flying objects. A group calling itself Citizens Against UFO Secrecy sued the government, seeking all
the executive branch agency's documents relating to UFOs; the
agency had withheld some files after the UFO group filed a
Freedom of Information Act request.

The biggest explosion UFOlogists cite to prove a government
coverup is the release in 1988 of the so-called Majestic 12 document to author Timothy Good. In his book *Above Top Secret*,
he reveals an alleged briefing document to President-elect
Dwight D. Eisenhower from a former CIA director that details
the recovery of a crashed UFO near Roswell, New Mexico, in

1947. Good also talks about the formation of a secret government group called MJ-12 allegedly assigned to retrieve crashed saucers and keep their existence secret until the right political climate is reached. Many have attacked Good's documents as phony, but even if they are clever forgeries, as I believe they are, large numbers of rumors of a government coverup will remain and circulate.

For example, in "her unpublished biography *The Great One* Beverly McKittrick, former wife of Jack [*sic*] Gleason, claims the comedian visited Homestead Air Force Base in Florida in 1973 in the company of his friend President Richard Nixon and that—under extremely tight security—he was shown the bodies of four aliens, which were allegedly embalmed and displayed on operating tables. It reportedly made Gleason ill for days."[24]

In 1990 Howard Blum, a former *New York Times* writer, added another twist to the government conspiracy scenario in his book, *Out There*. He claims the government has formed a "UFO Working Group" called "Project Aquarius" that is trying to determine through the use of psychics and "people with alleged extrasensory powers" whether there is life in outer space. But he adds that the government is also involved in a dirty "disinformation campaign."

> What they have been doing in certain cases is taking UFO believers . . . onto air bases in New Mexico, for example, and showing them documents that tell of fantastic stories, stories that there are wars between gray and white aliens, that Jesus was an alien, that Moses was an alien, spying on these people. . . . Now why is the government doing this? It's just not sheer maliciousness. It seems these UFO groups have been making a nuisance of themselves. They've been going to the periphery of airbases in the southwest with their video cameras and they've been filming nighttime maneuvers of top secret military craft because they believe these are captured UFOs.[25]

Blum, whose book ironically has been trashed by large portions of the UFO enthusiasts community, added that the government wants to discredit the UFO believers so "nobody will take them seriously."[26]

UFOlogy Worldwide

Another interesting aspect of the 1980s and early 1990s is the incredible spread of UFOlogy throughout the world both in sightings and in symbolism. "In Yokohama, Japan, a large white saucer dominates a peace park hillside, and in the barrios of Rio de Janeiro crudely painted UFOs decorate tin shacks."[27] In the former Soviet Union a thriving interest in UFOs accompanies a growing occult revival. For the first time ever, *Tass*, the official news agency, released a vivid report of a UFO landing in central Russia in 1989,[28] and it appears as if *glasnost* unleashed "a vigorous UFO culture" in the former Soviet Union that included the government sharing information on UFOs with Western New Agers.[29] In Belgium during 1990 there were more than 2,600 sightings of a triangular UFO.[30]

Truly something does seem to be happening out there. And it seems to be increasing in frequency as humankind presses toward the year A.D. 2000. But in my opinion these increasing physical manifestations of UFOs have not nearly matched the growing religious movement people have attached to UFOs as a symbol of transformation related to New Age occultism. People are looking to the stars for enlightenment and salvation in these perilous times. And the message from the UFOnauts is one many people want to hear: a nonjudgmental universalism.

"We believe everyone is a natural medium, and that all roads to God are good," said a banker from Brazil quoted in a 1985 article. The man had become one of 70,000 followers of a strange cult that mixes flying saucers, Christianity, Hinduism, and many occultic ideas.[31]

A New Religion

UFOlogy has, to some people, become "in fact part of a religion," according to Tom Wolfe, the famed chronicler of American culture.

"And that religion is, at bottom, not terribly different from most other new religions of the past two millennia," Wolfe noted. "Most of them, the successful ones as well as those that have vanished, have been based on the belief that there exists Another Order, invisible to the great mass of humanity."[32]

New Age
Channelers Owe
a Lot to UFOs

J. Z. Knight, one of today's most popular New Age channelers, was a teenager at a slumber party when it happened. She remembers that a Bobby Darin hit was playing on the record player when "an eerie red glow" lit up the room.

Running to the window she looked up. "Several hundred feet above the rooftop" was "a huge orange ball twice the size of the house."

"It didn't make a sound," she wrote in her autobiography. "It just hung there, suspended in midair. I thought it looked like a planet of some sort, for it seemed to have craters all over it. Then, all of a sudden, blinding flashes started coming off of it. I panicked and ran from the window to the bed. I started praying. The thought came to me that the world had ended."[1]

Knight, an attractive blonde-haired woman from the Seattle area, today channels Ramtha, a 35,000-year-old warrior from Atlantis. In her book she did not clearly explain what seeing the UFO had to do with her development into one of America's best-known New Age leaders, but she was sure that the event was a significant step. The more she gravitated toward New Age occult channeling, the more she placed significance on the UFO sighting, she wrote.

Knight is not the only New Age leader having had an early experience with UFOs. The fact is that many people involved in the New Age movement have had experiences with strange otherworldly entities early in life. They range from Brad Steiger writing about seeing a fairy peering through the window of his home when he was a child, to his ex-wife Francie (who assisted him with some of his UFO books) seeing an "angel" when she was young, to Uri Geller, the famed metal-bending, mind-power psychic who claims he was "only three or four years old when he was visited by a flying saucer."[2]

Actually, the New Age Movement, and specifically the New Age channeling that is popular today, owes a lot to UFOlogy. In *The Flying Saucer Contactee Movement: 1950–1990*, J. Gordon Melton and George Eberhart note that New Agers have borrowed the term *channeling* from the early flying-saucer movement of the 1950s[3] when a number of people started going into trances and letting the so-called space brothers talk through them. This common link, and its affinity with the message of the New Age, may be one of the reasons that UFO channeling is being thrust from the fringe into the mainstream of the New Age movement in the 1990s.

The Channelers of the 1950s

There's little wonder that until recently UFOlogy had been considered the domain of crackpots, frauds, and publicity hounds. Most UFO contacts, during the 1950s in particular, fit this category. UFOlogy was so ridiculous that many to this day do not like to talk about flying saucers because of the stigma associated with it, and the saucer movement was further scorned when in the early sixties a woman who had channeled space brothers from Jupiter since 1953 died as the result of a fast ordered by an extraterrestrial message.

George Adamski

Most experts agree that the "modern era of the Extraterrestrial Contact Movement began on November 20, 1952, with George Adamski's alleged encounter in the California desert with a long-haired man from Venus named Orthon."[4] Melton and Eberhart write:

Whether prophet or faker, possibly both, Adamski inspired a
number of others who also claimed contact with extraterrestrials.
Characteristic of the contactees of the 1950s were encounters
facilitated by some means of psychic phenomenon, usually the
reception of telepathic messages over a period of time (what is
today called channeling) and a subsequent call for a religious
response to the content of the channeled messages. Most of the
contacts also resulted in the formation of a spiritual group which
resembled either a spiritualist or theosophical organization.[5]

A common characteristic of the early contactees was their
claims, in almost every case, to be in contact with aliens within
our own solar system. Aliens from Venus were the most common, but Mars, Saturn, the moon, the moons of Jupiter, and
other nearby planets were also said to be the origins of other
extraterrestrial messengers.

Perhaps Adamski had something that America wanted to
hear. Many channelers were warning the world through the
space brothers to clean up our act or be destroyed in a self-
inflicted nuclear war. And in the post-World War II and atomic
bomb era, the fear that humankind could annihilate itself was
universal.

Whatever the reasons, Adamski's books sold like hot cakes,
making him an instant celebrity as he jetted throughout the
world telling about his experiences. His first two books, *Flying Saucers Have Landed* (1953) and *Inside the Space Ships*
(1955), were his most famous. By the time *Flying Saucer
Farewell* was published in 1961 (later reprinted as *Behind the
Flying Saucer Mystery*) Adamski had become the focus of
intense criticism. (Adamski also wrote many smaller booklets
dealing with his alleged flying saucer experiences and his
resulting religious philosophy.)

Not only did Adamski claim to have been aboard magnetic-
powered saucers, he claimed he traveled the solar system with
the space brothers and eventually was taken to a "galactic council" meeting on Saturn as Earth's intergalactic representative.
Adamski also claimed to have photographed the saucers, which
he called scout ships, and cigar-shaped mother ships on sev-

eral occasions, and he reproduced some of those photographs in his publications.

But by 1954 he was under fire from the scientific world. That year author Arthur C. Clarke in the *Journal of the British Interplanetary Society* labeled his pictures phony. "The uncanny resemblance (of the 'scout ships') to electric light fittings with table tennis balls fixed underneath them has already been pointed out," he said.[6] *Yankee* further illustrated the point by publishing two pictures side by side in its May 1954 issue. One was of Adamski's "scout ship" and the other of a model made from a Chrysler hubcap, a coffee can, and three Ping-Pong balls. The two pictures were nearly identical.

In 1957 James Moseley, editor of *Saucer News,* further attacked Adamski's credibility. His staff documented misquotations in Adamski's first book, exposed his phony educational degrees, produced evidence that one of his desert meetings with a Venusian was an orchestrated fake, and showed how he allegedly faked other matters. Later he was exposed for substituting the words *Space Brothers* and *Cosmic Brotherhood* where *Royal Order of Tibet* had appeared in an earlier (1936) book from another author.[7]

By the early 1960s Adamski was facing open discord and defection from his own camp based in Palomar, California, and in 1965 he died a largely discredited man. But the controversy didn't end; there are still those who strongly endorse his work,[8] and his George Adamski Foundation, based in Vista, California, lives on.[9]

George Van Tassel

An early follower of the UFO scene compared George Van Tassel to John the Baptist.[10] Van Tassel lived in the wilderness of the Mojave Desert. The task an alien named Solganda gave him was to build a machine that would eliminate old age.

Van Tassel never finished the job. He died in 1978, and to this day on his estate in Yucca Valley sets a strange, dome-topped building he called the Integratron—his fountain of youth machine—that was built without nails, bolts, or metal.

Following his 1952 book *I Rode in a Flying Saucer* his annual spacecraft conventions held at the site became a rallying point for the UFO community. Van Tassel claimed to have made his first contact with Ashtar in 1951, whom he said was commander of an orbiting space station. Later he communicated with space brothers Zoltan and Desca and began public channeling sessions with them in a grotto under a huge rock on his property. He published the communications from space in his "Proceedings" newsletter.

Despite the broken promise that he would have his Integratron finished back in 1961, it was never operational.[11]

Other Contactees

Other early UFO contactees include Daniel Fry, who claims he was picked up by a saucer in 1954 and zoomed over the earth (he, too, has produced contrived photographs); Reinhold Schmidt, who claims a spaceship from Saturn picked him up near the Platte River in Nebraska; Howard Menger, who also claimed to have been visited by Saturnians; and Buck Nelson, who wrote a 1956 magazine article titled, "I Visited Mars, Venus, and the Moon!"

George King's Aetherius Society

Two significant UFO contactee "churches" or organizations were founded during the 1950s and are still operating: the previously mentioned Unarius Foundation run by Ruth Norman, and George King's colorful Los Angeles-based Aetherius Society. King actually founded the sect in his native London in 1955 after "a great master of yoga from India" walked through a locked door and into his flat. That contact enabled him to make telepathic connections with a being from Venus,[12] and in 1958 he received his first message from Jesus, who, he claims, resides on Venus.

Since those days the Aetherius Society has spread around the globe, and King has wowed a number of UFO conventions with his on-stage channeling of beings from Mars, delivered as he wears dark goggles.

The Contactee Movement Begins to Slacken

Weird contacts continued into the 1960s, but as the American space program began to advance in its task to map the planets, the number of contactees claiming to talk to aliens within our solar system decreased. New ones began to surface claiming contact with aliens from other solar systems. One exception, however, was Van Nuys, California, contactee Frank Stranges, who maintains, just as he did in the early 1960s, that he is being visited on a regular basis by a Venusian named Val Thor. But Stranges has changed his tune slightly. He says his Venusian lives underground on that planet, away from the 900 degree temperature scientists say permeates its surface.[13]

The Death of Gloria Lee

There was also a decrease in the number of space-brother channelers in the 1960s, and some of it may have had to do with bad publicity generated by the December 2, 1962, death of Gloria Lee at the behest of a space brother she called J. W. According to various published reports Lee hooked up with the Mark-Age group of Miami and in 1962 went to Washington to try to warn the government to change its warlike ways. J. W., whom she identified as an etheric being from Jupiter,[14] allegedly ordered her on a fast to purify herself for the task. She fasted sixty-six days, fell into a coma, and died.

The public also had a much more critical attitude toward contactees after Lee's death. Melton and Eberhart noted that two of the best-known contactees of this period, Eduard "Billy" Meier of Switzerland and Uri Geller, "both suffered from heavy criticism as hoaxers."[15] Geller, an Israeli, claims he channels Spectra, a computer aboard a spaceship from a distant galaxy under the control of an entity named Hoova.[16]

What Is Channeling?

Not all agree that channeling is mediumship, writes New Age author Jon Klimo. Quoting California parapsychologist D. Scott Rogo, Klimo reports:

Mediumship is the art of bringing through spirits of the dead specifically to communicate with their relatives. Channeling I define as bringing through some sort of intelligence, the nature undefined, whose purpose is to promote spiritual teaching and philosophical discussion.[17]

Klimo further defines channeling thus:

The communication of information to or through a physically embodied human being from a source that is said to exist on some other level or dimension of reality than the physical as we know it, and that is not from the normal mind (or self) of the channel.[18]

Klimo thinks channeling can be used for good, but he warns of the drawbacks. It takes people away from reality; the "sources" of channeled messages often do not help; and all channels are vague.[19] He also notes that trance channeling, popular in New Age and UFO circles, is more narrowly defined by William Kautz of the Center for Applied Intuition in San Francisco as: "a mental process in which an individual (the channel) partially or totally sets aside waking consciousness, to allow knowledge that lies beyond conscious awareness to flow into the mind."[20]

Although messages from alleged aliens come through trance channeling, there are at least seven ways to receive alien or other channeled messages, wrote Steiger in his famous Star People series of books. First is trance or sleep mediumship in which one's body is taken over by "past incarnations" or "astral beings." The late Edgar Cayce, known as the sleeping prophet, often received revelations in this manner in the middle of the night. Second, is automatic writing, drawing, or music; third, "clairaudience (clear hearing), clairvoyance (clear seeing), clairsentience (clear sensing of feeling)" which Steiger defines as spontaneous "voices, visions, information channeled . . . without our conscious control or desire"; fourth, mental telepathy or thought transference; fifth, space beams ("Extraterrestrial spacecraft can use electromagnetic beams to transmit

thoughts and words to, or physical control over, those on Earth.
. . . Space beams are usually felt physically"); sixth, inspiration, intuition, or hunches; and last, through the I-am consciousness, the "direct knowing and experiencing from the God
Self within." [21]

Are any of these methods valid? *Christian Research Journal*
editor Elliot Miller provides a critique of channeling and mediumship in his book *A Crash Course on the New Age Movement.*
He says that channeling fits the definition of spiritism, which is
the "direct antithesis of inspired prophecy and Scripture."[22]
He points out that it is not scriptural; Deuteronomy 18:9–12, 15
and Isaiah 8:19, 20 specifically condemn the use of mediums,
spiritists, or the practice of calling up the dead.

He further points out that although the Bible affirms the
existence of good spirits, "efforts to contact them are never
encouraged but rather prohibited." He adds that the prophet
Saul lost his kingdom when he asked a medium to call up
Samuel, who had died, rather than consult with the Lord
(1 Chron. 10:13, 14).[23]

I agree with Miller's analysis, but there are also additional
logical arguments against channeling, or receiving messages
from alleged space brothers or entities, to consider. First, channelers of aliens can never be sure of who or what they are really
channeling. As we have seen previously, these otherworldly
entities readily accepted as space brothers often lie and are
usually vague about their points of origin. This can be dramatically illustrated in the case of Whitley Strieber. Throughout
his book *Communion* Strieber is not sure what the visitors are
or where they come from. And at the end of his sequel, *Transformation,* with two more years of abductions under his belt, he
still is not sure of their point of origin or what they are, yet he
wants us to trust them.

Second, the Scriptures teach that evil spirits can sometimes
tell us factual things (Acts 16:16–19) but always with falsity
mixed in, and just one false statement from an otherworldly
entity disqualifies the entire message. Why? Messages and
prophecies from God are always true and always come to pass.
Titus 1:2 states that God does not lie; 2 Corinthians 5:21 and

Hebrews 6:18 tell us that God's Son, Jesus Christ, was totally sinless and did not lie. And in the Old Testament, when a prophet spoke for the Lord, everything he stated had to come to pass or he could be subject to death (Deut. 18:20–22).

Walk-ins

Another indication of the increasing religious nature of the UFO movement in the 1980s and 1990s is the proliferation of people claiming that aliens have literally taken over their bodies and are here to help usher in the New Age.

They call themselves walk-ins, a term popularized in 1976 by Ruth Montgomery's book *Strangers among Us: Enlightened Beings from a World to Come.* She further explained the concept in her 1985 book *Aliens among Us*:

> Some of our "unearthly" visitors . . . have emerged from spaceships to test our environment, take samples of our flora and fauna to reseed in other galaxies, and conduct harmless experiments with human beings, manifesting themselves and their spacecraft here by reassembling the pattern of the atoms. But a significantly larger group of spacelings, the Guides insist, volunteered to be born into earthly bodies, or to become Walk-ins through the utilization of unwanted human forms.[24]

Although Steiger rarely uses the term *walk-ins* he has also promoted the same concept through his Star People series of books. According to Steiger, many people are living on Earth whose real home is in other solar systems. He calls them star people and says that they have voluntarily come to help Earth usher in a new era.

How can Montgomery speak so authoritatively about walk-ins? Because she is possessed by so-called guides who have made her a "pathfinder" for the world, and these guides possess her daily as she churns out books on occult topics via automatic writing. "My Guides are souls like ourselves who have had many previous lifetimes but are currently in the spirit plane, as we will be when we pass through the mysterious door called death," she writes,[25] adding that "the Guides write through my typing fingers, we have jointly produced eight books on subjects of their own choosing that run the gamut from life after death to reincarnation, and from a prehistoric view of the world to Walk-ins who rejuvenate dying or unwanted bodies in order to help humankind."[26]

Lest one think that Montgomery is some crackpot, fringe New Age writer, consider her credentials. She was at the top of the journalism profession as a syndicated columnist, a *Meet the Press* television panelist, and top Washington reporter. She worked for the *New York Daily News* and the International News service covering the White House, Congress, and the state department, and wrote a book about Lady Bird Johnson. In her office where her guides work through her typing fingers are autographed inscriptions from the six presidents she covered, from Franklin D. Roosevelt to Lyndon B. Johnson.[27]

Despite her spectacular career in a field that claims to use facts as its basis for reporting, Montgomery's life story also further illustrates a subtheme of this book: that occult dabbling often leads to encounters with UFOs and extraterrestrial beings, and almost always leads deeper into the occult.

Wimbish wrote this about Montgomery:

> The occult world is an exciting and expanding place. There's always room for a new experience or two, a new type of being or two. Disembodied spirits have always lived there, of course, along with assorted other ghosts and goblins. But in the 1980s, space beings moved in.
>
> According to Montgomery, they have come here in ever-increasing numbers. Some are quite content to zip through our atmosphere in their spaceships, even though they are of such a spiritually advanced nature that they don't need mechanical devices for traveling through space. Others have entered human bodies—some in a benign form of possession and others through birth.[28]

Montgomery's first encounter with the occult occurred when a relative invited her to a seance where she allegedly communicated with her dead father and other deceased relatives. Later she met Arthur Ford, a well-known medium, who encouraged her into "automatic writing."[29] She also met psychic-astrologer Jeanne Dixon and helped her co-write the book, *A Gift of Prophecy,* which made Dixon an international celebrity.[30]

As she began her attempts at automatic writing, a spirit guide by the name of Lily came to her (who claims to have been a writer of "great note"), and later a group of twelve spirit guides came to assist her. And how does she write messages? According to a *New Age Journal* article she "says she sits at her typewriter, meditates, goes into the 'alpha state' and waits for the keys to fly."[31]

How accurate are the spirit guides? About as accurate as Jeanne Dixon's predictions, which is not very high. According to *Aliens among Us,* the guides told her that President Reagan would not be able to serve out his second term. She also noted that years ago the guides told her a big-spending Democrat would succeed Jimmy Carter as president. Did they flub? Probably, but not necessarily, says Montgomery, since "Reagan had been a New Deal Democrat most of his adult life."[32]

What does Montgomery say the future holds for America? Americans will knowingly elect a walk-in as president during the 1990s. "He will become a world leader who will harness the energies of the people and guide them aright," she wrote.[33] She also claims that the earth will shift on its axis "in the year 2000," and that although the event will be chaotic, a new golden era will follow and a Christ spirit will come to earth. Contradicting the biblical record concerning Christ's second coming, Montgomery writes: "The Christ spirit will enter a perfected person within some twenty to thirty years after the earth has restabilized."[34]

Other Walk-ins

Bill Cox, the globetrotting occult researcher, claims he has been gathering evidence documenting the existence of other walk-ins around the globe. At the National New Age & "Truth about UFOs" Conference in San Diego in March 1991, Cox showed the dazzled gathering strange photographs from South America of individuals who seemed to be able to dematerialize if they wanted to. He calls them blends or walk-ins because "they were born of earthly parents, but at some point they were merged with highly intelligent life forms in order to get human-kind through the troubled times we find ourselves in."[35] Cox showed another photo of a woman he claims is a walk-in who was born with the picture of the galaxy she came from on her back.

Another famous walk-in is Penny Harper, publisher of a UFO newsletter called "New Age Dawning." She claims she first came to this planet around 2,500 years ago.[36] But perhaps the most extreme example of the phenomenon is an entire group living in Sedona, Arizona, called Extraterrestrial Earth Mission. Accord-ing to UFO mythical literature seen at conferences, a doorway to outer space and other dimensions allegedly exists near Sedona. "We are extraterrestrial masters," states a flyer for the group. "We have 'walked in' to the bodies of beings who wished to leave and continue their spiritual unfoldment elsewhere. There are many extraterrestrial beings on this planet. It is time for us to make our presence known to you."[37] What makes this Arizona group bizarre is that its members claim that different alien enti-ties possess their bodies every couple of years. The aliens, in effect, play musical chairs with the host bodies.

It's hard to keep up with who's who in this group, because when the aliens enter their bodies the people go by their new extraterrestrial names. Thus the same person is pictured in the group's 1991 newsletter as going by the name Avinash from March 1986 to May 1987; Aktivar from May 1987 to March 1988; then to Savizar and, at this writing, ZaviRah.

A Biblical Analysis of Walk-ins

The Bible teaches that it is possible for entities from other realms to exist in people. But there is no evidence to indicate that "good beings"—entities associated with God—ever pos-sessed Old Testament prophets in the same manner of the walk-in of the modern UFO movement. Likewise, the outpouring of the Holy Spirit to the church in the New Testament does not resemble the walk-in phenomenon in which the spirit actually takes over a body and begins speaking out of believers. Rather,

the Christian's experience with the Holy Spirit is that of a relationship that complements the individual's life.

The Holy Spirit, according to orthodox Christian theology,
is the third distinct person of the Holy Trinity but does not
override the individual. Jesus called the Holy Spirit the Counselor, not the possessor (John 14:26), who will guide us into
all truth (John 16:13). Paul warns the believer not to grieve the
Holy Spirit by failing to follow his guidance (Eph. 4:30). Furthermore, the Holy Spirit is a helper who gives Christians spiritual gifts that fit together with gifts he gives to others in the
task of proclaiming the gospel. The result of the Holy Spirit in
Christians' lives is sanctification, a process in which all believers become more Christ-like (2 Thess. 2:13). Spirit-filled believers will demonstrate that the "fruit of the Spirit is love, joy,
peace, patience, kindness, goodness, faithfulness, gentleness
and self-control" (Gal. 5:22, 23).

But the Bible does talk of another type of possession very
similar—and I maintain identical—to the walk-in phenomenon. God's Word calls it demon possession.

The popular media have done a great disservice to truth
when they constantly portray demonology in an *Exorcist*-movie
kind of light with the demon growling through its victim, spit-
ting, and flipping his or her head into circles while talking in
strange voices. Although Scripture does talk about this type of
possession, it also tells about another type in which individuals had occult spirits and were apparently able to make a living
off the powers these spirits gave them. In Acts 16:16–19, Paul
cast out of a slave girl a spirit that predicted the future.

I believe there are in the Sedona, Arizona, group parallels of
walk-ins to a biblical story. Mark 5 gives an account of a possessed man who lived in the tombs who was so powerful that
he could not be bound by chains. But when Jesus saw him, he
cast out the demon, who called himself "Legion, for we are
many" (Mark 5:9). Jesus cast the spirits into a herd of pigs who
threw themselves off a cliff into the Sea of Galilee. Where
would the multiple spirits afflicting the Sedona group flee to
if they were cast out? Into their spaceships?

Whitley Strieber, I believe, has also reached the level of possession. In *Transformation* he concludes that he is learning to call the visitors into his life on a continual basis "and make use of what they have to offer. . . . The most effective technique seems to be simply to open oneself, asking for what one needs the most without placing any conditions at all on what that might be."[38]

But to anyone with logic, such a move of turning one's life over to someone he doesn't know or understand is foolhardy. Strieber, who also advocates out-of-body experiences as a benefit he learned from his abduction experiences, never determined the identity of his visitors. And just a few pages earlier in his story, Strieber tells us that he was still struggling with fears that the visitors were evil:

> They were predators and they were going to eat our souls; they were demons and they were going to drag me off to hell; they were vicious aliens and they were going to steal us all for some kind of experiment.[39]

Would you turn your life over to entities you don't know or understand? Of course not. Yet New Age UFO enthusiasts do it all the time.

Barbara Schutte was one contactee who turned her life over to extraterrestrial beings, and for a spell an alien named Quastas was communicating through her by automatic writing, although other alleged alien entities also came to her. Schutte was also an abductee; part of her story is recounted in Steiger's 1988 book *The UFO Abductors*.[40] But her obsession with contacts with aliens almost destroyed her life, she said in an interview, and after falling under conviction that there was really something evil about her extraterrestrial contacts, she accepted Christ as her Savior in 1984, and her contacts with all entities ceased.

Now she believes her contacts with the extraterrestrial beings were part of a demonic latter-days' deception that trapped her for a while. "I could see where people would very easily jump on board a UFO if they thought that was going to be their way out," she said, "especially if they didn't have to admit to sin or anything."[41]

Communion, MacLaine, and Occult Myths

Whitley Strieber's *Communion* and *Transformation*

Horror writer Whitley Strieber describes what happened to him at his cabin in New York State on December 26, 1985. Small beings entered his room, woke him up, kidnapped him, and performed medical experiments on him. He was terrified. "What was left was a body in a state of raw fear so great," he wrote, "that it swept about me like a thick, suffocating curtain, turning paralysis into a condition that seemed close to death."

> Tiny people were now moving around me at great speed. Their quickness was disturbing, and in a curious way ugly. I had the thought that I was being taken away, and remembered my family. An acute, gnawing feeling of being in a trap overcame me. It was a truly awful sensation, accompanied as it was by the sense that I was absolutely helpless in the hands of these strange creatures.[1]

The above account is from the early pages of Strieber's *Communion*, one of the most successful books in publishing history and the best-selling UFO book ever. Published in January 1987, the book, with a strange picture of an almond-eyed alien on the cover, quickly rose to the number-one position on *The New York Times* best-seller list and stayed there for almost the entire year.[2] Later the book was made into a major motion picture starring Christopher Walken as Whitley Strieber. It flopped

100

at the box office, but it is still making its rounds via cable and video rentals.

(However, in May 1992 CBS ran *Intruders,* a two-part miniseries on prime time that was similar in many ways to *Communion.* It reached millions of homes and ranked number-one on the Nielsen ratings for the week.)

Communion is about Strieber's abduction experiences, which he did not remember until he recalled them in vivid detail under hypnosis. It turns out that "the visitors," as he calls them, had been watching him all of his life and had been abducting him periodically for unknown purposes. Under hypnosis he remembered the small beings (of different shapes and varieties) implanting something into his brain with a needle through the nostril and jamming another object into his rectum.[3] In one of the more memorable lines of the book, the female visitor, pictured on the cover of the book, asked him during the brain operation, "What can we do to help you stop screaming?"

> My reply was unexpected. I heard myself say, "You could let me smell you." I was embarrassed; that is not a normal request, and it bothered me. But it made a great deal of sense, as I have afterward realized.[4]

Strieber's book, and its best-selling sequel, *Transformation,* are filled with religious imagery. Although the visitors terrified him, he discovered that he really loved them and that the female aroused him sexually. Their purpose, asserts Strieber, although he was never sure about it, was to seek communion with humankind for the betterment of the planet. In *Transformation* Strieber claims he was abducted many more times by the visitors, and he continued to draw conclusions about their real purpose.

Strieber's books are not the stuff of typical flying saucer lore. They are quite different, for Strieber has taken "a much more Shirley MacLainesque approach" to the problem of extraterrestrial visitors[5] and has been the force perhaps most responsible for bringing the UFO phenomenon into the mainstream of the New Age movement.

Why? First, Strieber's message fits well into the parameters of the New Age movement. He says that the visitors "are not extraterrestrial at all, but rather interdimensional beings who have come here to take man on a journey through his own consciousness" for the betterment of the planet and in preparation for the new age. But at the same time he links these creatures to UFO reports; just prior to his abductions there were reports of flying saucers in the vicinity of his home. He claims that the sightings and abductions may be part of a new emerging religion[6] and that "perhaps the visitors are the gods. Maybe they created us."[7]

Whatever they are, Strieber writes, they told him he was their "chosen one"[8] and they placed triangles on his left forearm,[9] symbols, perhaps, of a new trinitylike relationship they were forming with humankind.

The visitors, Strieber says, are trying to open us to their presence, and "everything depends upon our understanding that." Coming together with them means the creation of a third and great form which will supplant us in a new age, he wrote,[10] adding that he likens it to being conquered by the visitors in the same manner Cortez conquered Native Americans to bring forth something new, a marriage.[11]

In *Transformation* Strieber takes his ideas about the visitors further, because they continued to abduct him at will as they taught him more profound things. Strieber links them more firmly to the spiritual world; he says they told him that their role is to "recycle souls,"[12] and they became more of an integral part of him. He says the visitors were still vague as to their point of origin; they told him they were from "everywhere" and that Earth is a "school."[13] After he learned that, his relationship with the visitors deepened.

> After this the voice changed dramatically. No longer was it a distinct sound, heard as if it were coming from a small speaker just to the right of my head. It became much more thoughtlike. I suspect that it was very much like what some people hear when they channel.[14]

Strieber always admitted that there was a dark side to the visitors. They repeatedly scared him, pushing him to the edge of sanity. They greeted him in the night with strange rappings on the side of his cabin in Upper New York State (a phenomenon often linked to seances and poltergeist activity). They punished him on occasion, because he wasn't living the kind of lifestyle they wanted. They falsely told him he was going to be killed in an accident. He called them "soul eaters" and "predators" and said the idea of having a relationship with them was disturbing. "Mostly they terrified me," he wrote. "One does not want to develop a relationship with a hungry panther."[15] Yet despite this, Strieber steadfastly refused to believe the visitors could be demonic.

> So far the word *demon* had never been spoken among the scientists and doctors who were working with me. And why should it have been? We were beyond such things. We were a group of atheists and agnostics, far too sophisticated to be concerned with such archaic ideas as demons and angels.[16]

Near the end of *Transformation* the visitors helped him develop further metaphysically into levitation and out-of-body experiences. Finally, he said, he began to stumble onto the truth: They were probably behind all of the world's religions and responsible for many of the world's paranormal events.

> Whatever the visitors are, I suspect that they have been responsible for much paranormal phenomena, ranging from the appearance of gods, angels, fairies, ghosts, and miraculous beings to the landing of UFOs in the backyards of America. It may be that what happened to Mohammed in his cave and to Christ in Egypt, to Buddha in his youth and to all of our great prophets and seers, was an exalted version of the same humble experience that causes a flying saucer to traverse the sky or a visitor to appear in a bedroom or light to fill a circle of friends.[17]

And finally, Strieber began to see a link between the visitors and the ancient pagan religions. He attended a Wiccan (witchcraft) ceremony in Wisconsin; he experienced an odd manifestation and noted that one of the participants had seen a "lighted disk sailing along beneath the cloud cover."[18]

Strieber concludes the book by implying that the visitors hold the key to solving all the problems of Planet Earth:

> We will walk a narrow way between dangers. To our left there will be a sick planet and all the social discord and economic misery that must accompany its suffering. To our right there will be the rigorous, demanding, and wise unknown that is the visitors. . . . At last, we will see.[19]

Reaction to Strieber's message has been mixed. The traditional nuts-and-bolts UFOlogists have been hostile to Strieber because of his religious approach. Some members of the Mutual UFO Network (MUFON), a scholarly UFO-research group, aware of Strieber's one-million-dollar cash advance for *Communion*, have said that Strieber is simply writing about UFOs for the money. He has also given debunker Phil Klass a lot to write about, as Klass has attacked major portions of the story. He, too, is disturbed over Strieber's new, religious approach. In *UFO Abductions: A Dangerous Game* Klass writes: "Strieber's remarks suggest that he now sees himself as a modern-day messiah who has been chosen to warn the people of this planet, bringing them not the Word of God, but of the omniscient UFOnauts."[20]

Los Angeles Christian journalist Stuart Goldman, who claims he infiltrated one of Strieber's *Communion* support groups, is also concerned over the religious aspect of the Strieber phenomenon. Goldman has been on television's *Good Morning, America* and *Hard Copy* warning the public about Strieber's religious movement. Goldman, who also investigated Strieber's background, believes that Strieber's experiences are directly related to his dabbling in the occult, and outside the pages of his UFO books he has admitted it, Goldman writes. Although Strieber wrote that he was surprised by the abduction experiences, Goldman notes:

Rather, it's quite clear that Strieber's experiences were the direct result of his forays into mysticism and the occult. At a San Francisco conference entitled "Angels, Aliens and Archetypes," Strieber said exactly this. "I made choices a long time ago that brought me into this experience," he told the audience.[21]

Goldman has said that Strieber was a fifteen-year follower of occult mystic G. I. Gurdjieff and that his belief system is shrouded with occultism including Zen, alchemy, tarot, witchcraft, shamanism, hermeticism, and "mystical" Christianity. Moreover, says Goldman, "in an interview with author Douglas Winter in *Faces of Fear*, a book profiling horror writers, Strieber says, 'I am a student of the great thirteenth-century mystic, Meister Eckart. I have been a witch. I have experimented with worshipping the earth as a goddess/mother.'"[22]

Up to the publication of *Communion*, Strieber was a moderately successful horror writer. He wrote *The Wolfen,* which was made into a Hollywood movie, *Black Magic, The Hunger,* and other books. He was also co-author of two environmental concerns books titled *Warday* and *Nature's End.* And perhaps, noted Ed Conroy in *Report on Communion*, it was Strieber's stature as a writer and a good storyteller that contributed to the success of *Communion*.[23] I believe Conroy was right in this assessment. In reading *Communion* and *Transformation* I became aware of the fact that Strieber is an excellent writer and extraordinary storyteller. He was also perceived as an outsider to the UFO community, and his emergence onto the scene undoubtedly helped draw attention away from UFOlogy's fringe elements.

Is Whitley Strieber a fraud, as some allege? While critiques of Strieber indicate he is advocating a new, non-Christian religion, the jury is still out on him in the UFO community. And in late 1990, after three straight UFO-related books, he began steering away from UFO-related topics and is back writing horror novels. But even if the UFO community thoroughly rejects him, (as it looks like it will) his books have made a profound impact on UFOlogy, and he is more responsible than anyone else for thrusting UFOlogy into the mainstream of the New Age movement. Strieber became a gurulike figure overnight; he became a media gadfly, touring the country with enormous energy making dozens of radio and television appearances. It's no coincidence that just after the publication of *Communion* the demand for UFO writers and speakers increased at New Age conferences everywhere.

The reason it looks like the UFO community is in the process of rejecting Strieber is that Strieber has rejected them. In July 1991 he announced he was ceasing publication of his *Communion Letter* (his quarterly newsletter) and claimed that "UFOlogists are probably the cruelest, nastiest and craziest people I have ever encountered. Their interpretation of the visitor experience is rubbish from beginning to end. The 'abduction reports' they generate are not real. They are artifacts of hypnosis and cultural conditioning."[24] More recently Strieber has begun claiming that his alien abduction experiences were not real. He was "the *victim of a hypnotist* who implanted the alien experiences deep in his mind as well as in the minds of other 'abductees' under his care."[25]

Shirley MacLaine: Out on a Flying Saucer

Although she has not written much on the topic, actress-author and New Age enthusiast Shirley MacLaine is arguably the second most important person to have thrust UFOlogy into the mainstream of the New Age movement.

Although MacLaine's best-selling book *Out on a Limb* was published in 1983, not until the mid-eighties did some of her occultic ideas really take hold. And in 1987—the same year *Communion* was released—ABC ran a highly publicized TV miniseries, *Out on a Limb,* starring MacLaine, that showed the actress' evolution into occultism in vivid detail. And, just as Strieber claims he was chosen to spread the word of the UFO-nauts in *Communion*, MacLaine near the end of the series boasted that she had been chosen by aliens to spread the word of the coming New Age.

To be sure, MacLaine's idea of a New Age has appeared to many to be faddish, and comedy writers had a field day making up Shirley MacLaine jokes. She was even a humorous topic in the cartoon strip *Doonesbury*. But despite it all, she became a rallying point for the growing New Age; many Americans grew fascinated with the occult world she unveiled. She subsequently wrote two sequels to *Out on a Limb*, *It's All in the Playing* and *Dancing in the Light*, which became best sellers and expounded on her themes of reincarnation, contact with the spirit world through channeling, out-of-body experiences, crystals, and contact with aliens.

Klimo wrote:

> Critics and fans alike concur that MacLaine has done more than any other single person in recent times to soften the ground for people to believe and participate in things they once avoided for fear of being thought "flaky."[26]

MacLaine's belief that UFOnauts are at work attempting to guide the destiny of the world forms a central theme in her work. In *Out on a Limb* MacLaine is pictured at first as having an affair with a married British politician but unable to understand her obsession with him. As she continues her search for the meaning of life, she goes to "trance channeler" Kevin Ryerson (who appeared as himself in the telemovie), who relays information from a spiritual entity named John that she was once married to the British politician in a previous life on Atlantis, the lost continent. What's more, she learns that she had at least two past lives in Atlantis—one as a man and the other as a princess, and that in other past lives she had been a Buddhist monk, a court jester during the reign of Louis XV, a voodoo worshiper in Brazil, a ballet dancer in Russia, an elephant-riding child in India, and an Inca boy in Peru.

MacLaine never claimed nor intended to be a New Age guru or spiritual leader. Rather, she says, the revival of occult mysticism developed because of the inner need people have for spirituality. Near the end of *Out on a Limb* she writes that the more she began talking about her experiences, the more people began opening up to them.

Studio executives, bank presidents, journalists, actors and actresses, musicians, writers, househusbands and housewives attended the spiritual channelings that I had been introduced to. No one questioned the validity of the process anymore. They only wrestled with the information they received—past-life information, psychological information, dietary information, medical and scientific information: information about Atlantis, Lemuria [the mythical lost continent in the Pacific], the creation of the cosmos, extraterrestrials . . . everything one could think of to ask. The spiritual entities (not in the body) became their friends and confidants.[27]

MacLaine's affair with the British politician collapsed in the book and movie for the same reason it collapsed 300,000 years ago on Atlantis, she alleges. He was too busy with his political job to pay much attention to his relationships and spiritual development. In his previous life in Atlantis his political job had been to arrange cultural exchanges with visitors from other planets.

Later in the book MacLaine was influenced by David (her occultic guide), who introduced her to metaphysical ideas. Almost right away he began talking to her about extraterrestrial contacts. David ought to know, according to the book; he claimed to have had contacts with an attractive female explorer named Mayan from the Pleiades. Later David took her to Peru on sort of a New Age pilgrimage, and there, while she meditated in an "alpha state," a huge UFO passed over her head and "I began to have flashing feelings coming toward me in another language."[28]

What can we make of MacLaine's "revelations?" The first thing we can note is that her ideas about aliens are directly related to her dabbling in the occult. Reporter Antonio Huneeus, who is sympathetic to her, wrote:

An important part of Shirley MacLaine's message has to do with her conviction that we are not alone, and that extraterrestrial civilizations have visited Earth in the past, and continue to do so at an increasing pace. This realization came to her during a gradual process of becoming acquainted—and accepting—other non-mainstream ideas like reincarnation, spiritualism and channeling, eastern meditation, etc., which led to her experience of a divine cosmic energy, or God-force, which she says exists within all of us.[29]

Another thing apparent from MacLaine's occult dabbling is that it has led her into a continued quest for contact with extraterrestrial beings, the idea of lost continents, and a fascination with the possibility that it was ancient astronauts from space, not God, who planted humans on earth. MacLaine has also been linked with Billy Meier in Switzerland, who claims to have been visited by a woman from the Pleiades, and she is fascinated by the theories of ancient-astronaut scholar-author Zecharia Sitchin, who put together the famous Earth Chronicles series. More on Sitchin later, but he is arguably the most famous ancient-astronaut teacher in the world today. Sitchin claims to be able to read ancient Sumerian texts and says they reveal that the Nephilim of Genesis 6 in the Bible were aliens from "the 12th planet" in our solar system. They created humans through genetic engineering with animals, he asserts, and they portrayed themselves as gods (including the God of Israel and the Greek gods) in the ancient world.

Huneeus, who had dinner with Sitchin and MacLaine at the actress' Upper East Side apartment in New York, wrote that during the meeting MacLaine said she had heard rumors that there are "33 extraterrestrial civilizations currently visiting or operating on Earth" and that the "Russians have had encounters with aliens in space, and were allowed to keep their cosmonauts and space station in orbit so long as they abstained from military operations."[30]

Huneeus's story about MacLaine's beliefs in extraterrestrial beings, which appeared in *UFO Universe*, delves into other relationships MacLaine has had with UFO contactees. In *It's All in the Playing* MacLaine cites the story of a Peruvian who claims to be in contact with tall, highly evolved humanoids from the star Apus (which is in a faint constellation in the southern skies). Their message is similar to MacLaine's, she notes in the book, so therefore it does not matter whether the

Peruvian's claims of contact with them is contrived. "Whether they were 'real' or not seemed irrelevant to me," wrote Shirley, "the message was clear, a spiritual shift in consciousness would benefit humankind."[31]

Of course, Shirley MacLaine did not invent these ideas herself; she is not the founder of modern-day occultism. Rather, a quick reading of her books indicates that she is only a student of occult traditions, which in some cases is centuries old. The reason she has so influenced popular culture is her high visibility in an age when society is particularly idolatrous over famous people and movie stars in particular.

The New Age movement is not even new, although it has certainly been repackaged and popularized for contemporary culture. In 1985, when the evangelical church was just beginning to grapple with the growing movement, Dr. Gordon Lewis of Denver Theological Seminary sponsored a conference designed to help evangelicals develop a posture for the movement. On the final night of the conference Walter Martin delivered a speech that many of us will always remember. He said the movement was simply a revival of the very first lie Satan told Eve in the Garden of Eden—that you shall become like God (Gen. 3:5).

So when MacLaine, in one of the most famous scenes in her miniseries, stood on the beach screaming, "I am God, I am God," she was simply affirming her belief in the soul destroyer's original lie.

Occultism has come a long way since the Garden of Eden; there are adherents of occultic mysticism throughout the world in every religious tradition. Christian apologists who study occultism are quick to point out how readily occultists accept myths without a single shred of evidence to substantiate them, and when they do have "evidence" it is in the realm of the subjective, which no one can see or prove.

MacLaine, then, in believing these myths has become a willing participant in the revelations of some of the best-known figures of occultism. And while we cannot discuss the origins of all her occultic ideas, we will trace some that have certainly influenced her relationship with extraterrestrial beings.

H. P. Blavatsky

As previously mentioned, one of the most significant occult leaders of the nineteenth century was the founder of the Theosophical Society, Helena Petrovna Blavatsky, who was born into a noble Russian family in 1831 and traveled to Egypt and Western Europe early in life. She founded the society, whose beliefs are known as Theosophy, in New York in the 1870s and developed a large following, despite the fact that she "was thoroughly debunked in her day" as a hoax.[32] L. Sprague de Camp provides some background on her colorful life before she started Theosophy.

> [She] was the estranged wife of a Russian general, and had been successively the mistress of a Slovenian singer, an English businessman, a Russian baron, and a merchant from the Caucasus living in Philadelphia, and had made her living as a circus bareback rider, a professional pianist, a businesswoman, a sweatshop-worker, and a Spiritualist medium.[33]

Despite her past, Blavatsky made "extravagant claims about her early life," writes Paul Zweig. They included claims she had visited the interior of Tibet, was a virgin and had never married, and had been wounded fighting with Garibaldi in Italy. "These myths became cornerstones of Theosophical faith . . . [but] reality was sadder, although adventurous enough." Actually, she married at age seventeen and left her husband three months later. She was addicted to hashish, and she had a "defective illegitimate son named Yuri whose death so devastated her that she invented the story of his having been mutilated in battle."[34] She also never visited Tibet, the very place she claimed she received contact with disembodied spiritual beings she called mahatmas or "the masters."

Her two chief works, *Isis Unveiled* and *The Secret Doctrine* (which reportedly plagiarized at least two other books without credit),[35] are still widely used by Theosophists today.

Blavatsky also received numerous messages from spirit beings—aliens—as early as the 1880s. Steiger wrote that

Blavatsky's beings "were part of a governing hierarchy between man and the solar rulers of the universe."

> It is said that the mighty beings who would later become Earth's adepts came from Venus six and one-half million years ago. Venus is said to be the original home of the Lord of this World, the Head of the Hierarchy of Masters, and the Three Lords of the Flame.[36]

Klimo adds that both Blavatsky and Alice Bailey channeled messages from other "highly evolved spiritual beings" including "the 'masters' 'Hilarion' and 'Saint Germain'; 'K. H.' ('Koot Hoomi') and 'D. K.' ('Djwal Kul')."[37] L. Sprague de Camp's excellent book *Lost Continents* gives us a compelling account of other writers, some of whom were offshoots of Blavatsky's, developing more complete histories of humankind that also indicated links with beings from Venus.

In Blavatsky's view the universe is constructed through multiple planes of existence as planets follow each other "like the horses on a carousel." But perhaps her most influential contribution to occultism is her theory, allegedly channeled to her by the mahatmas, that humankind evolves through seven cycles—root races, she called them. We are now in the fifth root race, nearing the sixth, she wrote. The last two root races were the egg-laying Lemurians and the Atlanteans, earlier forms of humans that once lived on now-sunken lost continents.[38] Other occultists took her ideas about the lost continents further. Rudolf Steiner of the schismatic Anthroposophy Society, for example, wrote extensively about the psychology of the peoples of both lost continents.

Today in Western occult literature, which includes that of the New Age-UFO movements, Atlantis and Lemuria are central fixtures. New Agers and UFO enthusiasts don't always agree on the locations of Atlantis or Lemuria. Blavatsky placed Lemuria just off the east coast of modern Africa. But most others place it in the South Pacific ocean.

Many channeled alien messages today talk about these mythical places as fact, and all kinds of fantastic stories about them are imparted to enthralled listeners. Many go further than Blavatsky did. They talk about Lemuria and Atlantis as being realms where highly developed human societies once existed. Many, just as Shirley MacLaine affirmed, say these mythical continents were centers of technological achievement in direct contact with fantastic alien societies. Brad Steiger has even asserted that as the New Age begins to burst upon the world within this decade, Atlantis will arise from the watery depths of the ocean by the year 2000.

Another writer to popularize Lemuria was James Churchward, who wrote a handful of books about a land he called Mu. But Churchward's revelations about the lost continent came through a means every bit as suspect as Blavatsky's. He claimed his knowledge about Mu came from clay tablets, which like the mythical golden plates of Mormonism were never recovered. And to supplement his voluminous books about Mu, Churchward recalled that he had visited Mu in previous lifetimes while in a trance.[39]

Did Lemuria Ever Exist?

But first things first. Was there once a lost continent named Lemuria? Perhaps there was such a land mass, says de Camp, but he notes that science does not confirm the existence of any of the lost continents of occultism. In 1887 a German biologist hypothesized that an Indo Madagascan land bridge might explain the distribution of lemurs (nocturnal creatures that look like a cross between a monkey and a squirrel) in both Madagascar and India. He speculated that the land sank. Others suggested that Lemuria was part of a larger continent. But de Camp said that even if they did exist at one time during the formation of the earth to its present form, they were there and gone long before the appearance of man. "Nevertheless they have been exploited by occultists and Atlantomaniacs for their own purposes," he wrote.[40]

De Camp also bemoaned the fact that occultists apply a double standard to science to "prove" the existence of Atlantis and Lemuria. They hold up questionable and quack "scientists" to prove their existence, but when pressed by reputable scientists who say that they never existed, occultists denounce science and cite "Akashic Records," clairvoyant visions, or occult-divine revelation as proof.[41] He writes sarcastically:

> If you insist upon evidence, there are plenty of records of lost continents, but these are concealed in the Fourth Dimension, or in secret underground libraries in Tibet open to qualified occultists only. . . . So if we really want to get to the bottom of the lost-continent problem, we must leave the occultists to their dream-worlds—very pretty, but not for us.[42]

Atlantis According to the Sleeping Prophet

In the twentieth century, Atlantis became an increasingly popular theme and subject of speculation by Hollywood and the popular press. Contributing to the rise of interest in the topic was the work of Edgar Cayce (1877–1945), the so-called sleeping prophet, who founded the Association of Research and Enlightenment of Virginia Beach.

It is not surprising that Cayce claimed to have seen "little people" or "play folk," who appeared to him as a child,[43] along with other apparitions.

Cayce, who claimed to be able to read the universal mind,[44] would put himself into a sleep trance during which he propounded metaphysical "truths" that included a new, unbiblical view of Jesus, reincarnation, gnosticism, astrology, monism, and Atlantis. These "truths" were not always true. For example, he predicted that New York City would sink into the ocean in the 1970s. Nevertheless, over 14,000 of Cayce's trance sessions have been transcribed, catalogued, and placed in a fireproof vault at his organization's offices now run by his son, Hugh L. Cayce.

Cayce had an interest in UFOs and linked them to work that supposedly must be done on earth. He described strange metal ships that flew about Atlantis[45] and claimed that Atlantis would rise from the ocean floor in the twentieth century.

Although de Camp expressed doubts about Atlantis, there is less evidence that it ever existed than there is for Lemuria's existence.

In their article "The 'Evidence' for Atlantis: Addressing New Age Apologetics" that appeared in the Summer 1989 *Christian Research Journal*, Irv and Karla Hexham noted that the father of the Atlantis myth, Greek philosopher Plato (428–348 B.C.), referred to Atlantis as only a mythical lost island, and that "Plato expected his readers to understand that it was a literary device used to make a philosophical point." The Hexhams further noted that when Plato described the city of Atlantis, there was nothing remarkable about it. It was not seen as the wonder of the ancient world in technological advancement as many UFO enthusiasts and New Agers believe it was. They also wrote that all Greek or Roman writers who discussed Plato's Atlantis took for granted that it was a fictional story.[46]

With the work of Ignatius T. T. Donnelly (1831–1901) a revival of interest in Atlantis was born, the Hexhams note. And although Donnelly's reasoning is easily debunked, it made a good story and captured the public's imagination. In addition, the occultists ate it up with glee. De Camp noted that Blavatsky was accused of plagiarizing Donnelly's book *Atlantis* (and other books in her *The Secret Doctrine*) "without credit and used in a blundering manner that showed but skin-deep acquaintance with the subjects under discussion." In fact, he noted, Blavatsky's entire lost-continent theory seems to have been based on Donnelly's and a few others' ideas.[47]

Lost Civilizations Justify Other New Age Beliefs

If these lost continents never really existed, then why do New Agers and UFO enthusiasts treat them as fact? The Hexhams say that since so many New Agers' experiences are subjective in nature (such as Akashic Records, channeled messages) and beyond falsification or verification, they need to cite certain facts to make a point:

The New Age usage of the Atlantis theme—as well as related occult works about Lemuria, Mu, and a host of other lost civilizations—serve a very different function. In contemporary occultism, legends of lost civilizations are linked with the ruins of various historic civilizations to make an apologetic point. Specific extraordinary claims are made about the technology, religion, and general social order of certain known civilizations of antiquity. These claims are then seen in terms of "mysteries" which are solved by reference to earlier civilizations which eventually lead back to places like Atlantis and Lemuria. Therefore, rather than being statements of faith, New Age claims about lost civilizations are presented as verifiable facts which justify other New Age beliefs.[48]

In addition, I believe that strange stories of lost continents, UFOs, and supercivilizations are attempts to cut away at the credibility of the Bible, God's Word. Scripture never mentions former high-technology civilizations. In fact, it teaches the opposite: people's slow progress since the time God sent them out of the Garden of Eden dressed in animal skins. Archaeological discoveries also confirm the slow progress of man up to the time of the Industrial Revolution. In many cases the lost continent stories are littered with accounts that their inhabitants were seeded by aliens from the stars and not deliberately placed on Earth by God.

The Seth Material

It's obvious that Blavatsky and Cayce, though perhaps indirectly, have influenced MacLaine in her staunch support of lost-continent theories. There is also evidence that she was influenced by Jane Roberts of Elmira, New York, who channeled spirit entities from the 1960s until her death in 1984. Klimo credits Roberts, who channeled an entity known as Seth and gathered about her a small following, as the starting point of the modern era of channeling.[49]

Roberts, in the 1970s, wrote several books outlining Seth's pontifications, and after that other books containing Seth material came from some of her followers. Roberts, in a manner similar to Cayce's, would receive her messages while in a trance, and her husband would write them down in shorthand.

And did Seth talk about the identity of flying saucers? He surely did, though not often. He spoke of them as "visitors from another reality" at times.[50]

Does Truth Count?

One of the major problems surrounding the merging of the UFO movement into the New Age is that both movements, as I have shown, are founded partly on myths, not facts. And while Shirley MacLaine may not think it's important whether certain of her associates are telling the truth about their alleged UFO encounters, and while Whitley Strieber doesn't think it signif- icant that his "visitors" have lied to him and are evasive as to their point of origin and purpose, any rational human being would think it is important.

Likewise, New Age leader David Spangler, writing about con- tacts with the "space brothers and other Beings on higher dimensions," said there is nothing wrong with their lying to us or giving us false information, if it helps humankind avert destruction by embracing the New Age. Spangler's definition of a prophet, unlike the criteria of 100 percent accuracy God gives the prophets of the Bible, has nothing to do with their telling the truth all the time:

> The best prophet, in other words, is a false prophet, for he seeks to help people to transmute negativity and avert the conse- quences of fear and destruction; he does not seek to enhance his own ego and reputation by amassing a record of successful prognostications.
>
> In many cases the space brothers and other Beings on higher dimensions, working with sensitive and dedicated groups and individuals on the physical earth dimension, have fulfilled this role of Prophet.[51]

And what one believes, including reliance on Jesus Christ alone for salvation, is apparently not important to the UFO- nauts. As the channeled entity Triton asserted: "If you are on

God's side then you are one of us, and it does not matter at all whether you call yourself a Hindu, a Buddhist, a Christian, or a Mohammedan."[52]

But history is important, and it is important what a person believes. Christianity is a historical religion, a faith based on fact. Almost every detail in the Bible can be historically verified, from the foundation of Abraham's chosen nation to Christ's crucifixion to the letters written to the church in the first century.

The central fact of Christianity is that Christ claimed to be the only way of salvation for the world. "I am the way and the truth and the life. No one comes to the Father except through me," he said (John 14:6). The apostles also affirmed this, and throughout the centuries those who denied this truth were said to have denied the faith. One simply could not practice any other religion such as Hinduism and Islam and be considered a Christian. As Peter testified before the Jewish Sanhedrin just after Jesus' resurrection: "Salvation is found in no one else [but Jesus], for there is no other name under heaven given to men by which we must be saved" (Acts 4:12).

The Bible clearly warns us not to be intrigued with secret knowledge, which includes strange tales of lost continents and lost civilizations. While it's true that the Bible does not answer all of our questions regarding history, it gives us all we need to know about the one thing God deems most important: salvation in Jesus Christ.

There is something fascinating about lost continents, UFOs, mystical power, clairvoyance, and such things. But the intrigue and mystery are traps that the evil one has set for us, for the world of the occult is so big and unknowable we could spend our entire lives trying to figure it out. This is another reason for believers not to study UFOs too much: It focuses our eyes away from Christ, God's Son, and onto the stars, God's creation. We need to be busy fulfilling the Great Commission in these last days instead of pursuing never-ending, tail-chasing quests for secret knowledge. Paul warned Timothy about "what is falsely called knowledge, which some have professed and in so doing have wandered from the faith" (1 Tim. 6:20, 21).

I have seen people obsessed by the New Age movement, the occult, and flying saucers. Some people are so absorbed by these topics they can never fully understand that they waste a good portion of their lives on intrigue. This is another danger Paul warned Timothy about: "devote themselves to myths and endless genealogies. These promote controversies rather than God's work—which is by faith" (1 Tim. 1:4).

Is Hollywood Setting Us Up for the Next Generation?

Francie Steiger was only five years old when she was visited by a fair-haired robed angel.

Although she was young, she remembers the incident vividly, because he sang-talked to her. "He began to speak," she said, "but his voice kept rising very high, then falling in tone, as one would sing and talk at the same time."

She didn't comprehend much of what the angel was trying to tell her, but one phrase he sang to her stands out: "Like unto another Christ child you will be." She says she has come to understand that her visitation had to do with her job as a star person (meaning that she believes her origin is another planet), which is to "help bring as many souls as possible to a higher state of awareness."[1]

Francie, a brunette former model who has gone on to become a yoga teacher, psychic, and an internationally known mystic, is still popular in New Age circles today, despite her divorce from New Age writer Brad Steiger. She continues to receive messages from the angel in a kind of spirit-guide relationship. She calls him Kihief, and he told her that he is "from Lealand," which is a place "like unto Venus," she wrote. He talks to her "continuously. . . . When I call on him, I usually get an answer."[2]

But in the 1950s, Kihief, whom she says is "multidimensional," gave her some astounding information: Aliens in flying saucers were planning to make mass landings on Planet Earth to begin a relationship with humankind. Furthermore, they began a program of positive conditioning to prepare people for the event and for the coming New Age.[3]

"I have been told that we are definitely in the change time, the cleansing time, before the New Age comes," she wrote.[4]

How are they conditioning humankind? Through the media and entertainment industry, which is "the most thorough way of affecting the culture," she said Kihief told her. They are subtly controlling television and Hollywood filmmakers such as Stephen Spielberg and others so that we will begin to see the prospect of partnership with aliens as beneficial, she said. First they affected children's programming; the children grew up and became important enough to influence society into accepting the aliens as benevolent, she said.

Why the need to change society to accept them? Partly because of the horrible images of aliens seen in the media in the first decade of the modern era of UFOlogy, she said, adding that 1950s movies like *The Blob* and *The Thing* did not help the image of the benevolent space brothers.[5]

Just because Francie Steiger says UFOnauts are directing Hollywood to prepare for a mass landing does not mean that it's so. Occultists are good at exaggerating their claims and bragging about accomplishments that never happen. We have to be careful not to necessarily believe everything they tell us, because it can lead to paranoia and fear.

For example, in the early 1980s an author frightened Christians everywhere by drawing on the work of New Ager Benjamin Creme, the occultist who had taken out newspaper ads worldwide declaring that "The Christ Is Now Here." Spelled out in speaking engagements and in a book, the scenario advanced by this author convinced many that the Antichrist of the Book of Revelation could be revealed as early as 1982. While leading cult researchers dismissed the conspiracy theory findings, Spiritual Counterfeits Project cofounder Brooks Alexander faulted the author for believing occultists' and New Agers' inflated claims about themselves. In other words, just because occultists *say* a world leader has arrived doesn't make it so. Alexander, a veteran occult researcher, proved to be right.

Hollywood's Shift in Perception

But there has been an undeniable shift in the way the mass media perceives what used to be an alien threat. In the early part of the century aliens were almost always portrayed as invaders bent on destroying and taking over Earth. This, of course, was the theme of the infamous 1938 radio program, "Invasion from Mars" that sounded so real it sent many people fleeing from their homes in fear of reptile-like Martians who possessed fantastic weapons.

Scary alien movies eventually followed, including the *Invasion of the Body Snatchers*, *The Crawling Eye*, *Invasion of the Flying Saucers*, and others. In the 1953 classic *Invaders from Mars* the Martians were ugly large-eyed, weapon-toting thugs who tunneled underground and captured earthlings by making them fall through sand pits. Sinister aliens of many shapes was also a prominent theme in the two old television series *The Twilight Zone* and *The Outer Limits*. In one memorable *Twilight Zone* episode aliens came to the United Nations offering to help humans solve their problems, bringing a book with them called *To Serve Man*. It turned out to be a cookbook on how to eat humans. Similarly, an *Outer Limits* episode that scared me to death as a child featured the Zantes, small insect aliens swarming over a house and attacking humans.

About the only exception to the aliens-are-coming-to-take-over movies was the 1951 classic *The Day the Earth Stood Still*, in which a flying saucer landed on the White House lawn in a futile attempt of its occupants to dissuade humankind from continuing its warlike ways.

But the tide began to turn in the 1960s and has increased to the present, though it was slow at first. Although the mid-sixties television series *The Invaders* portrayed aliens as looking like humans but seeking domination over the planet, films began hinting that perhaps aliens are benevolent beings seeking to help humankind in its progress.

The leading film that portrayed aliens in a good light was Spielberg's 1977 hit *Close Encounters of the Third Kind*, which to many resembled a religious film. Mark Albrecht, formerly of the Spiritual Counterfeits Project, suggested this about the movie:

> The huge "mother ship" [that descends to the Devil's Towers in Wyoming at the end of the film] looks less like a space vehicle than a vast city of light descending from the heavens. Whether the parallel is deliberate or not, Spielberg's offer of this ersatz New Jerusalem (cf. Revelation 21) as the answer to Mankind's spiritual longings is a slick con-job indeed. Roy Neary's "conversion" under a beam of bright light while on the road to Chrystal Lake is said to have been consciously modeled after St. Paul's conversion on the road to Damascus.[6]

Spielberg's 1982 box office smash *ET* was also packed with religious imagery as it portrayed the alien as a reptile-like friendly creature who was resurrected from the dead through love energy. Advertisements for the film were distinctly religious as well. In a scene almost identical to God touching the finger of Adam as portrayed in Michelangelo's painting on the ceiling of the Sistine Chapel, ET's bony finger touches the finger of a child.

In *Star Man*, released in the mid-eighties, the alien who comes to Earth to experience life in the body of a woman's deceased husband is also a good player. He fills the void in the grieving widow's life with a sexual interlude and resulting pregnancy, and the woman loves him so much that she cries when she finds out he must return to the stars without her. In *Batteries Not Included* the aliens are also good. They help ward off developers taking over an apartment building doomed to destruction.

In *Enemy Mine* the alien reptile race with whom humans had been warring turned out to be misunderstood. A human and an alien crashed on a planet and eventually became the best of friends despite their vast differences.

The portrayal of aliens by Hollywood grew more mystical from the late seventies to the present. In George Lucas's *Star Wars* trilogy, none of the characters were earthlings, because the film was set a long time ago in "a galaxy far, far away." But the principal characters were humanoids, and some of the aliens were good while others were bad. But the series promoted an Eastern worldview where an impersonal force aided both the good and the bad characters as they vied for power. The good won in the end, but the hero, Luke Skywalker, found that the "dark side" was also a part of him. Darth Vader, the epitome of evil in the series, was really his father.

Dune was also a religious film, although it was a box office flop. It was set on an oppressed desert planet that turned green again when ancient prophecies were fulfilled by the return of a conquering messianic figure.

Cocoon, directed by former child star Ron Howard, and its sequel were very mystical, portraying aliens as benevolent, advanced spiritual beings that could reverse the aging process and take senior citizens to their utopian planet. The film showed the aliens communing with dolphins, a theme often proposed at various New Age conferences where dolphins are sometimes channeled.

The Serpent People

Just suppose Francie Steiger's extraterrestrial angel was right—that aliens have been influencing movie directors and entertainers such as Shirley MacLaine and others to prepare for a coming New Age in which we will grow in partnership with the space brothers. If that's for real, then perhaps we should look at some of the other things Kihief told her.

It turns out they are astounding, since Kihief gave her an alternate history of the world and explained a way of salvation—a different gospel—from the one outlined in the Bible and believed by Christians for twenty centuries. In world history according to Kihief, the serpent people, who, he says, were represented by the serpent described in the biblical Garden of Eden, helped create humankind. Following is the Genesis story according to the angel Kihief. Francie Steiger says we should believe him, because "he speaks only of God and of goodness."[7]

The star gods stumbled upon earth about 12,000 years ago as some of them were trying to escape their planet in another solar system that was about to be wiped out by their sun going into supernova stage. They found that an extraterrestrial reptilian species had arrived on Earth first, which had through genetic engineering created a fast-evolving civilization and had tampered with "the natural evolutionary pace of humankind" by producing beings "without soul knowledge."

The star gods, angry at the reptilians for failing to instill spiritual teachings in people, decided to provide humankind with spiritual seeding. This anger over the reptilians' genetic experiments is where the biblical story of God becoming angry at the serpent in the Garden of Eden came from, according to Kihief. They were also angry at the reptilians for violating the galactic laws of noninterference with the evolution of beings from other planets, he added.

So the star gods began to supervise humankind's progress. They instructed humans in Atlantis, Sumer, and Egypt, often materializing into and dematerializing from being humans at will. Kihief said that was no problem for them; since their own star and planetary system was rising in frequency "in a return to pure energy," it was a simple matter for them to manifest themselves as supernatural beings. Later, when Atlantis sank, the star gods guided the survivors to new areas where they could keep civilization going. They also placed in certain members of humanity the "Star Gods' spiritual seed" to be passed on through the generations to let them know they are really from the stars and what their mission is.

What did the star gods teach humans? The same thing that Shirley MacLaine wants us to know—that God is within each individual. They also taught the human race the power of crystals, which were used to power Noah's ark and provided the energy the Hebrews needed to communicate with aliens through the ark of the covenant.[8]

Francie says that the reason many star people are being awakened today is that it's time to head into a new era, and she refers to the Bible to back her up. "According to Revelation," she says, "there will be a gathering together of God's children, so to speak. I've seen many indications of such a gathering of a New Age flock."[9]

She also refers to the Bible to rebut potential claims that her angel, Kihief, could be a lying demon:

> I would refer them to the parts in the Bible wherein the disciples spoke to Christ about wanting to cast someone out of the city who was teaching of God, but was not of their group. Jesus would not permit this. He said that if they spoke of God, they were from God even if they were not from their group. I must say the same thing of Kihief.[10]

But a look into the Bible shows that Francie Steiger has just misquoted and used it out of context twice to prove her point. In Mark 9:38 the apostle John told Jesus that they saw a man driving out demons in Christ's name and they told him to stop it "for he was not one of us." Jesus replied: "Do not stop him. No one who does a miracle in my name can in the next moment say anything bad about me, for whoever is not against us is for us. I tell you the truth, anyone who gives you a cup of water in my name because you belong to Christ will certainly not lose his reward" (Mark 9:39–41).

The obvious flaw in Francie's argument is that her Kihief is not acting in the name of Jesus. He is proclaiming the divinity of man, the idea that all are Christ, a blasphemous idea that Jesus himself warned the apostles about (see Matt. 24, Mark 13, Luke 21).

In the second instance the Book of Revelation does talk about the gathering together of God's people. But they are gathered together to live with God in the New Jerusalem (Rev. 21) after all people have been brought before God, "before the throne," (Rev. 20:12) in judgment. God will separate his people from the unbelievers and, Revelation 20:15 states, "if anyone's name was not found written in the book of life, he was thrown into the lake of fire."

Lest there be any misunderstanding over who will live on with God throughout eternity in the New Jerusalem, Christ reinforces the principles of who would be saved during his earthly ministry.

I am the Alpha and Omega, the Beginning and the End. To him who is thirsty I will give to drink without cost from the spring of the water of life. He who overcomes will inherit all this, and I will be his God and he will be my son. But the cowardly, the unbelieving, the vile, the murderers, the sexually immoral, those who practice magic arts, the idolaters and all liars—their place will be in the fiery lake of burning sulfur. This is the second death (Rev. 21: 6–8).

As seen above, the Bible condemns those who practice magic arts which includes consulting with mediums, spiritists, or calling up the dead. God, in Deuteronomy 18:9–12, calls it detestable. It is later condemned in Isaiah 8:19–20. It would also appear that Kihief, an alleged angel, is not qualified to live in the New Jerusalem, based on Christ's "belief" criteria. He does not proclaim that Christ died on Earth to save sinners. He says we all are Christ.

The Metamorphosis of *Star Trek*

If it is true that Hollywood is setting up humankind for a New Age in which we will commune with aliens, there is no better example than the long-running transformation of the popular twentieth-century folk tale *Star Trek*.

I realize that what I say might be misinterpreted by Christians who seem addicted to the popular television and movie series that was resurrected as "The Next Generation" (featuring a new crew) a few years ago. But don't be defensive, truth is truth, and I have a secret: I am an unabashed "Trekkie." Although I have never donned Vulcan ears or shown up at *Star Trek* conventions dressed as Captain Kirk, I can confidently say I have seen most episodes in the original series a number of times, I've seen every movie in the series, and I'm hard pressed to miss a show in the new series (which I maintain is superior to the original series because of better character development and electronic wizardry).

There has been a noticeable slide from a humanistic worldview in the original series of the sixties to a decidedly New Age, mystical worldview in the nineties.

In the sixties series in an episode called *Children of the Sun,* the crew of the *Enterprise* reached a planet in which a small persecuted religious group was facing a society not unlike the Roman society of the first century. The small group had a strange belief—the worship of the sun—so the *Enterprise* crew thought. But as the story reached its climax, the truth was told. They were not worshiping the sun, they were worshiping the Son of God (and the implication to some was that it was Jesus Christ who had just arrived to save that planet from its sins). The look of wonderment on Lieutenant Uhura's face in the final scene was memorable. However, although this episode was popular with some Christians, most episodes reflected the humanistic philosophy of its creator, the late Gene Roddenberry.

The tone began to change decidedly when the sixties series became a movie series. In *Star Trek V*, which was panned by the critics, some of whom called it "Star Trek Finds God," the crew of the *Enterprise* meets up with a fanatical, mystical religious leader who hijacks the starship and takes it to a hidden mythical location thought to house God. The "god" they find is mean spirited and irrational and threatens to destroy all who don't believe in him. After they make their getaway at the end, Captain Kirk (played by William Shatner) proclaims a central tenet of New Age thinking: Maybe God isn't out there somewhere; maybe he's within our hearts.

In *Star Trek: The Next Generation*, set more than seventy years into the future from Captain Kirk's crew, a mystic is on board (Marina Sirtis who plays Counselor Troi) who can read human emotions. But other than that, some of the episodes could have come right off the pages of Shirley MacLaine, Marilyn Ferguson, or standard UFO literature, although a strong humanistic philosophy is still intact.

In the 1990–91 season episode called "Transfigurations" written by Rene Echevarria, the *Enterprise* picks up a survivor from a crashed ship. After the severely injured humanoid male recovers he has an unusual and good effect on the crew. He cures certain members of their shyness and other problems and is able to heal people. He is seen as having wonderful, good spiritual qualities. At one point he brings Lieutenant Worf, the

Klingon, back from the dead. But despite the power he is also plagued by periodic pains, as though his cell structure begins to mutate. Eventually the *Enterprise* crew finds out that "John Doe" is from a nearby planet, and they want to take him back. He says he doesn't want to go, because he came to space to "escape." It turns out that beings from his planet were hunting him down because of religious bigotry in perhaps the same manner as the Roman Catholic Church's inquisition in thirteenth- to fifteenth-century Europe. They fear John's spiritual powers, and declare him "a disruptive influence." But at the end of the episode, John's pains continue until he turns into a bright multidimensional creature of light that is symbolic of the way Francie Steiger's star gods claimed they changed their vibrational qualities to move up into the next dimension. It turns out that John was the first of his species to make the next quantum leap, as he explains, in "wondrous evolutionary change, a transmutation beyond our physical being."

Captain Jean-Luc Picard (played by Patrick Stewart) welcomes the New Age being. "It is our mission to seek out life in all forms," he says. "We are privileged to have been present at the emergence of a new species."[11]

Two episodes right out of UFO literature were one in which the Federation of Planets (to which the *Enterprise* belongs) is engaged as "watchers" of an evolving society, and another in which Captain Picard contacts a government official in a rapidly advancing society on another world to let them know that the Federation (an alien society to them) exists and is ready to begin a beneficial relationship with them. It turns out that a religious bigot from that planet blocks progress by not approving of a new relationship with the superior aliens. He would prefer that his planet stick to the old ways. The *Enterprise* winds up leaving, because the people are not quite ready to advance.

The creator of *Star Trek* is the late Gene Roddenberry; even a cursory examination of his philosophy could give clues as to where he might take *Star Trek*. For example, in an interview conducted by Brad Steiger and Andrija Puharich, an occultist and former partner of Uri Geller, Roddenberry declared another tenet of the New Age: "I think all religións come together, because if the Gods are indeed all-powerful, they could have gone 'Zap!' and all men would have been good." He also declared in the same interview that he associated himself with UFO contactee Geller and that he believed in another tenet of the New Age movement: the possibility that we can create our own reality with mind power.[12]

Have Science Fiction Writers Also Helped Set Us Up?

Long before Hollywood began churning out positive movies about friendly aliens, literary giants were at work setting the stage. In a 1977 issue of *Spiritual Counterfeits Journal* chronicling the rise of the UFO movement on the worldwide scene, writers Woodrow Nichols and Brooks Alexander tried to trace a link between science fiction and the new Eastern consciousness.

They noted that the father of the modern science fiction story, Edgar Allan Poe, shortly before his death wrote the poem called "Eureka," which outlines "his solution to the mystery of the universe." His conclusion "could have been lifted verbatim from the scriptures of Eastern mysticism," they wrote.[13] Poe wrote that the universe of stars is God's "present expansive existence," that someday man will recognize his existence as that of Jehovah, and that in order "that God may be all in all, each must become God."

But one of the most important modern science fiction stories that helped set the stage for contemporary New Age-UFO thought was Arthur C. Clarke's first full-length book, published in 1953, *Childhood's End*. In it Clarke portrays a last generation of humankind seeing "its offspring transformed into something totally nonhuman, but superior to humanity."[14]

"It is probably not too much to say that Clarke's novel became a cornerstone for the developing world view of a whole generation," wrote Nichols and Alexander. They added:

> In the book itself, UFOs arrive on earth at a critical stage in the international arms/space race to save us from a nuclear holocaust. The ships are crewed by "the Overlords," a race with mas-

sive intellects, but a curious reluctance to show themselves to the earthlings whom they proceed to rule with a dictatorship that is orderly as well as truly benevolent. After a long duration, they reveal themselves, and lo! they look like devils. But no . . . they are actually high-minded guardians, watching over mankind on behalf of the mysterious "Overmind," as it prepares to guide us through enormous and inconceivable evolutionary transformations.[15]

In the book "Clarke has pulled off an ideological coup by his deft reversal of values in giving the demonically countenanced Overlords a benign role as protector and guide," the SCP researchers noted. The largest opposition to their coming rule comes from "a potentially dangerous group of misguided religious fanatics."[16]

Arthur Clarke has gone on to be a giant in modern science fiction and in the study of the occult. Besides being the author of two books, later made into major motion pictures, that infused Eastern mysticism into futuristic space tales (*2001: A Space Odyssey* and *2010*), he was the guiding force behind the television series syndicated worldwide called *Arthur Clarke's Mysterious World* that explored (and often debunked) occult topics such as ghosts and poltergeists, ESP, and many other metaphysical topics.

In *2001*, the movie directed by Stanley Kubrick, an ancient alien artifact found on the moon stimulated the brains of prehistoric apes, propelling them forward in evolution into humankind and then back to its place of origin.

Why Are Evil Aliens Not Emphasized?

Many Hollywood actors and actresses besides Shirley MacLaine push a New Age agenda connected with extraterrestrial beings. Telly "Kojak" Savalas recently became the narrating star of the home video *UFOs and Channeling* (Genesis III Publishing), which explores the stories of several people who claim to have seen UFOs and who have become "gifted channels of information and art," according to a flyer advertising the tape.

But no matter how hard the UFO community and Hollywood try to portray aliens in a positive light, they can never shake the possibility that extraterrestrial beings could be evil. Troubling is the fact that they seldom talk about so-called evil deeds of aliens, yet they want us to put our faith in the so-called good aliens. They seem unwilling to entertain the idea that the good ones could somehow be wolves in sheep's clothing. Take Fred Bell, for example. He claims to be in contact with Semjase, a beautiful blonde-haired female from the Pleiades. He admitted at a recent New Age conference that he believes the "greys," a mythical reptile race of aliens allegedly from Zeta Reticuli, are succeeding in the process of poisoning the earth's water supply. Yet, what was more important to him was his occasional solo contact with the good alien.[17]

Similarly, at a national New Age-UFO conference in San Diego five months later, speaker after speaker began by saying they did not want to talk about the bad extraterrestrial beings. Only speaker William Cooper focused on the likelihood of an alien threat.

Jacques Vallee is also mystified over why there is not more scientific research into the alleged misdeeds of aliens. He devoted a large section of *Messengers of Deception* (1979) to the evidence that aliens might be involved in a series of bizarre cattle mutilations. And in *Confrontations: A Scientist's Search for Alien Contact* (1990), he took issue with Whitley Strieber's view of alien contact as beneficial. Their "'scientific' experiments [on people they abduct] are crude to the point of being grotesque. The 'medical examination' to which abductees are said to be subjected, often accompanied by sadistic sexual manipulation, is reminiscent of the medieval tales of encounters with demons," he wrote.[18]

According to Vallee, there's a lot more evidence that aliens could be evil rather than good. *Confrontations* investigated one hundred UFO events from around the globe. "Many of them involve secondary physical and medical effects, including twelve cases of fatal injuries in which the victim typically survived less than twenty-four hours."[19]

But to Hollywood's credit they have not totally ignored an alleged alien threat. The movie *Alien* in the late seventies set a high standard for fear when an evil predatory extraterrestrial being got aboard a ship and grew, eating everyone alive except for Sigourney Weaver, who managed a harrowing escape at the end. *Aliens* in the late eighties and *Aliens III* released in 1992 continued the theme of grotesque killers. And few movies could outdo *Predator* of the late eighties starring Arnold Schwarzenegger, which illustrated an evil man-eating alien menace.

Are We Being Prepped for an Alien Landing?

Many New Agers and UFO enthusiasts boast of a near-future mass landing of flying saucers boarded by benevolent space brothers to usher in a New Age. While I would be reckless in speculating that I think something like that might happen as part of an end-time delusion, I will guide you to the central fact about extraterrestrial beings, the New Age, and alleged contacts with otherworldly beings: Whatever they are, their foremost concern seems to be to change the way we think about God. They are almost equally interested in changing God's Word, the Bible, and inserting in its place a type of universalism that says it really doesn't matter what one believes in matters of religious faith as long as one is sincere. Truth is irrelevant.

We saw it in Francie Steiger's channeled message from the "angel," Kihief, in which he gave her an opposing view of the Bible's Genesis account that made the serpent people (equivalent to the biblical devil) co-creators of the human race. And the star gods (which were equivalent to the monotheistic God of the Bible) were simply aliens from another planet who taught humankind that we are also gods.

A Scripture verse comes to mind. Francie Steiger and many others throughout the centuries who were in touch with entities and angels have not paid it much heed. It was delivered by the apostle Paul to the young church in Galatia in the first century. "But even if we or an angel from heaven should preach a gospel other than the one we preached to you, let him be eternally condemned! As we have already said, so now I say again: If anybody is preaching to you a gospel other than what you accepted, let him be eternally condemned" (Gal. 1:8, 9)!

8

Evil Lurks

Extending just south of the old walled city of Jerusalem is the Valley of Hinnom. It starts near the Jaffa Gate on the city's west side, then turns eastward until it joins the Kidron Valley. From the Mount of Olives, just beneath the site where Christ ascended into heaven, is a picturesque view of Jerusalem, and looking south you can see the texture of the land where the Kidron and Hinnom Valleys join.

The Valley of Hinnom was not a pretty place in 650 B.C. An area of the valley was called Topheth, and had you been looking down at it in those days you would have been horrified. It was a place of hellish torture and deathly screams. It reeked of burning flesh. It was there—practically in the shadow of God's temple in Jerusalem—that human sacrifices were offered to the ancient god Molech.

At that time the reigning king of Judah was Manasseh, who assumed the throne at age twelve. "He did much evil in the eyes of the LORD," 2 Kings 21:6 states, "provoking him to anger." Like King Ahaz had done decades earlier, Manasseh sacrificed his son to Molech and brought back Baal worship to Judah. He ordered idols of other gods placed throughout the land and "bowed down to all the starry hosts and worshiped them." He even built altars to the stars and planets, "practiced sorcery and divination, and consulted mediums and spiritists," the Bible states (2 Kings 21:3–5).

134

According to the *New International Dictionary of the Bible*, Molech was a "heathen god, especially of the Ammonites, who was worshiped with gruesome orgies in which children were sacrificed. At least in some places an image of the god was heated and the bodies of children who had just been slain were placed in its arms."[1]

God, through his prophets, repeatedly denounced the foreign gods and the lewd murderous rituals that took place as part of their worship. He was particularly angered by the practice of some who sacrificed their children then walked to the temple to worship him (see Ezek. 23:37–39 and Jer. 7:9–11).

Speaking through the prophet Jeremiah he said:

> For they have forsaken me and made this a place of foreign gods; they have burned sacrifices in it to gods that neither they nor their fathers nor the kings of Judah ever knew, and they have filled this place with the blood of the innocent. They have built the high places of Baal to burn their sons in the fire as offerings to Baal—something I did not command or mention, nor did it enter my mind. So beware, the days are coming, declares the LORD, when people will no longer call this place Topheth or the Valley of Ben Hinnom, but the Valley of Slaughter (Jer. 19:4–6).

Who Was Baal?

Although God had used mighty Elijah to reveal Baal for what he was by putting to death the 450 "holy" prostitute priests whom Elijah had challenged to a duel to see which was the true God, Baal and pagan deity worship continued on and off in Israel. Almost as soon as a good king arrived on the scene to stamp it out, three evil kings emerged to promote it; some kings employed hundreds of prophets of foreign gods, while others brought pagan deity statues into God's temple so the people could worship them.

Why bring this up? Because after studying the pagan religious system of the day, I have come to the conclusion that the same "gods" that may have led the people into murderous and perverted orgies throughout the ancient Middle East could be the same ones who claim to be the space brothers of today.

To be sure, the ancient pagan "gods" to be discussed in this chapter are not gods. The Bible teaches that there is only one God, Jehovah, and that an idol "is nothing at all" (1 Cor. 8:4). However, the apostle Paul said that the worship of many false gods represented by idols was in reality the worship of demons (1 Cor. 10:19–21). We must also recognize that it is possible that the idols represented real demons; even Jesus recognized—and did not rebut—the assertion by the Pharisees that one of the idols of his day, Beelzebub, was the "prince of demons" (see Matt. 12:24–29; Mark 3:22; and Luke 11:15–19). Let's take a brief look at the ancient Canaanite cult gods.

"Baal became the proper name for the most significant god in the Canaanite pantheon, or company of gods."[2] In other words, Baal (who was known as Hadad, the god of wars and storms, in Syria) was the chief of many gods throughout the region, similar to the way Zeus was considered to be the father and most powerful of all gods in ancient Greece. The term *Baalim,* the plural of *Baal,* referred to other manifestations or aspects of Baal, or of local, less important Baals in charge of certain areas or responsibilities. Baals were thought to own and control the land and were responsible for the increase of crops and livestock.[3]

However, some Baals, such as Baal-Zebub who was worshiped by the people of Ekron (about twenty miles due west of Jerusalem near the Mediterranean), were responsible for other areas. Baal-Zebub was identified with Satan by Christ and other Jewish religious leaders in the New Testament. His name (also spelled *Beelzebub*) signified "lord of the dwelling," and he was considered to be prince of the demons.[4]

Sacrifices of incense and animals were made to Baal, and sometimes even humans were sacrificed to Baal. But primarily he was a fertility god, and worship of him was marked by bizarre sexual orgies presided over by prostitute priests in religious shrines throughout the Middle East. "Baal worship involved the most debasing immorality imaginable," noted Old Testament scholar F. Duane Lindsey.[5]

Chemosh was another god in the Baal family. In the pagan system he may have been in charge of the land of Moab (located in today's southern Jordan east of the Dead Sea), and he apparently had influence well north of that area in the land of Ammon, the region of the modern capital Amman, Jordan (see Num. 21:29 and Judg. 11:24). Chemosh was allegedly brutal; children were sacrificed to him.[6]

Molech was considered to be an "aspect" of Baal according to the *Davis Dictionary of the Bible*.[7] He was mostly linked to the sacrificial killing of children in fiery valleys and altars throughout Israel and Judah.

Baal worship was extremely strong throughout the entire region. In fact, it was the principal reason for the downfall of Solomon, whom the Bible says was the wisest man who ever lived. First Kings 11 states that despite God's order for the Israelites not to intermarry with foreign women, "because they will surely turn your hearts after their gods," Solomon "held fast to them in love" anyway (v. 2). He had seven hundred wives and three hundred concubines (v. 3), and they led him astray. As Solomon got old he followed the Baal gods and even built high places for Chemosh and Molech directly on the Mount of Olives (v. 7).

Ashtoreth and Venus

Solomon also followed Ashtoreth, the goddess of the Sidonians (v. 5), who lived in an area along the seacoast from modern Lebanon in the north to the Gaza strip in southern Israel. But Ashtoreth's influence went even further. According to *The Bible Knowledge Commentary*, in Syria she was known as Athtart and in Babylonia as Ishtar.[8] She was considered to be the goddess of fertility and was the consort of Baal.

But there is much more. Somehow Baal worship was intrinsically fused with the worship of the hosts of heaven such as the sun, stars, and planets. This was especially true of Ashtoreth, "whose worship involved licentious rites and worship of the stars."[9] According to the *New International Dictionary of the Bible*, Gesenius, the biblical scholar, "related the name Ashtoreth to the Persian word 'sitarah' or 'star' and connected it with Venus, goddess of love."[10]

Josiah Cleans House and Finds the Law

Manasseh, who had led the charge to fill Judah with the worship of the Baals, reigned for fifty-five years and was replaced by his son Amon, who was assassinated after two years. Then Josiah, who was only eight years old at the time he was crowned king, ruled for thirty-one years. Scripture calls Josiah one of the best kings Judah ever had, because he reformed the nation and tried to bring the people back to God (see 2 Kings 22:1–23:30).

He ordered repairs on God's temple, recovered God's law, got rid of all the priests of Baal and Ashtoreth, and removed "all the articles for Baal and Asherah and all the starry hosts" (2 Kings 23:4) from the temple. He also got rid of all the child sacrifice altars throughout the land and so totally desecrated the site where Molech was worshiped in the Valley of Hinnom that it was never again used in this manner. Old Testament scholar Thomas Constable writes that Josiah rid the land of aspects of sun worship and star and planet worship:

> He also removed the sacred horses that were used in formal processions honoring the sun. These animals had been dedicated by the kings of Judah (probably Ahaz, Manasseh, and Amon) and were stabled in the temple courtyard. Josiah also burned up the ceremonial chariots used in these idolatrous processions.[11]

Molech's Planetary Link

Molech, too, was linked directly to space. According to *Boyd's Bible Handbook*, the heathen nations linked astrology with fortune telling, divination, mediums, consulting with familiar spirits, witchcraft, and other practices, and star worship was a part of idol worship. It notes that the prophet Amos (5:26) likened human sacrifices to Molech to sacrifices to Chiun, or Saturn and adds that when Stephen was about to be martyred in the first century, he named one of Israel's sins as idolatry, "mentioning 'Rephan,' which is Saturn or Chiun (Acts 7:41–43)."[12] Donald R. Sunikjiarn's exposition of Amos backs up Boyd's. He states that the words for shrine and

pedestal in connection with sacrifices to Molech in Amos
5:25–26 "could be translated as 'Sakkuth' and 'Kaiwan,' foreign deities associated with the starry heavens, especially with
the Planet Saturn."[13]

Who Is Ashtoreth?

One of the commonly cited space brothers today is an entity
named Ashtar. It was Ashtar who came to George Van Tassel
in 1952 near Joshua Tree, California, claimed to belong to the
"Council of the Seven Lights," and pledged assistance "to save
mankind from himself. . . . We are concerned with their [earthly
governments] deliberate determination to EXTINGUISH
HUMANITY AND TURN THIS PLANET INTO A CINDER. . . .
Our missions are peaceful, but this condition occurred before in
this solar system and the planet Lucifer was torn to bits. We
are determined that it shall not happen again."[14]

But UFOlogists such as Dr. Clifford Wilson and John Keel
associate the modern UFOnaut Ashtar with Ashtoreth, the
Canaanite deity. Wilson also associates Ashtar and other UFO
phenomena to occultic vampires, spiritism, demon possession,
and demonic activity.[15] Keel writes:

> Thousands of mediums, psychics and UFO contactees have been
> receiving mountains of messages from "Ashtar" in recent years.
> . . . Ashtar is not a new arrival. Variations of this name, such as
> Astaroth, Ashar, Asharoth, etc., appear in demonological liter-
> ature throughout history, both in the Orient and the Occident.
> Mr. Ashtar had been around a very long time, posing as assorted
> gods and demons and now, in the modern phase, as another
> glorious spaceman.[16]

Of course, Wilson and Keel could have been wrong in linking
UFOs to the ancient demon "gods," but it is interesting to note
that the names Astaroth, Beelzebub, Chemosh, Ishtar, and Molech are all listed as "infernal names" of Lucifer in the Invocation to Satan in *The Satanic Bible* by Church of Satan founder
Anton LaVey.[17] Further, Ishtar, Astarte, or Ashtoreth are among
the many names recognized by witches for their goddess. "She

is the goddess of ten thousand names," notes Johanna Michaelsen, who carefully documented how Astarte was called Tanit in the ancient city of Carthage. Michaelsen states that when the Romans arrived in Carthage in 146 B.C. they were appalled to find a vast cemetery that had been in use for six hundred years. "Their battle cry, 'Carthage must be destroyed!' was fanned by their determination to put a stop to the practice of burning children alive."[18] Michaelsen further notes: "Little ones, anywhere from birth to around four years of age, were given by their parents as burnt offerings to the Great Goddess in fulfillment of a vow or in exchange for her favor."[19]

Ashtar, or Astoreth, was declared by God to be a danger to Israel even before Moses led the tribes of Judah into the Promised Land. As God was fashioning the Ten Commandments onto stone tablets atop Mount Sinai he said that upon entering the land the Israelites must "Break down their altars, smash their sacred stones and cut down their Asherah poles" (Exod. 23:24; see also Deut. 12:3; 16:21.) But it wasn't long after Moses' successor Joshua's reign ended that Israel "served Baal and the Ashtoreths" (Judg. 2:13) and incurred God's wrath.[20] Thereafter are numerous accounts in the Old Testament of the Jews being under condemnation for their participation in Ashtoreth worship. Scripture frequently refers to Asherah poles, which were generally elongated images of Ashtoreth that were sometimes carved in stone or wood and placed on poles for worship.[21]

His relationship with Ashtar proved to be costly for Van Tassel, also. After meeting up with Ashtar and eventually other space brothers and sisters, Ashtar and friends sent him on a lifelong wild-goose chase of recording their words, organizing massive UFO conferences to spread the message of the benevolent space brothers, and building the Integratron building, which was supposed to reverse the aging process by revealing the "rest of this secret of the cross [of Jesus]."[22]

Curran noted that Van Tassel repeatedly promised his age reverser machine would be ready soon, and he sometimes tried to get the wealthy to contribute to his Integratron project with the promise they would have their youth restored. "Think about it, some of you tired-out millionaire playboys!" Curran quoted Van Tassel as saying.[23]

But Van Tassel died suddenly in 1978, and his never-completed Integratron building stands today as a monument to the "wisdom" of Ashtar and friends. It turns out that Van Tassel should have known he was being duped. The space brothers were pathological liars. Ashtar and friends gave him biblical insights, including the "fact" that Jesus was actually a UFO-naut[24]; that a future chapter of the Bible would be written about Van Tassel; that the Great Pyramid in Egypt in 1967 gave truthful information about future events and prophesied the soon destruction of modern Israel;[25] that the beginning of the "third woe" of the Book of Revelation would begin August 20, 1967, which signified that a nuclear attack by the Soviet Union would soon take place and wipe out much of the southeastern United States.[26]

Thelma Terrell, of the previously mentioned Guardian Action Publications organization of Durango, Colorado, also channels Ashtar. Using her "spiritual name" Tuella, she compiled Ashtar's rapture scenario in a book titled *Project: World Evacuation*. Ashtar lied to her, too. In the 1982 edition of the book, the Ashtar Command tells Tuella that "the early times of *this decade* will see the fulfillment of all the prophecies that have been released to the world" (emphasis mine).[27] In other words, the UFO rapture and mass destruction unleashed upon the world were to have taken place in the early 1980s.

More serious is the fact that Ashtar lied concerning the nature of God and the nature of Christ. Ashtar defines the Trinity not as Father, Son, and Holy Spirit, but as a coalition headed by Commander Ashtar, Lord Sananda (Jesus), and Lady Athena (who was the Greek goddess of wisdom and arts and was identified with the Roman goddess Minerva).[28] And according to other Ashtar Command literature, Ashtar is considered to have more authority than Jesus; Jesus works for Ashtar.

Jesus Is Not Who He Says He Is, Ashtar Claims

That view of Jesus working as Ashtar's underling is quite all right with the Universarium Foundation of Portland, Oregon, a nonprofit organization that also claims to be in touch with Ashtar. In fact, Ashtar is really a "High Being" from the Milky Way directing a fleet of one million UFOs stationed in the atmosphere waiting to beam worthy earthlings on board. The commander of the fleet is Jesus, and they claim Jesus' function is not necessarily that of saving souls as "the orthodox religionist" believes. His job is also to beam New Age messages to earth through his channels:[29]

> Now, if you think for one moment that the sole function of Jesus of Nazareth in the Spiritual Realm is to save souls from Hell and damnation and that He will greet you and hug you when you have finished your Earth incarnation, and welcome you to His Celestial City paved with gold, you are in for a great surprise.[30]

Ashtar Possessed His Body

Ashtar really turned out to be a liar when he possessed the vocal chords of T. James, author of the 1956 book *Spacemen: Friends and Foes*. According to James's account, after George Van Tassel taught him telepathy, a force empowered him to do automatic writing. Later a force seized control of his speech, and he found himself saying: "I am Ashtar. I greet you from Schare. Your interest in our cause is well known and we would like you to help us. Would you wish to do so?"[31]

Thereafter Ashtar agreed to a question-and-answer session with James during which he affirmed that the earth is hollow and that a morally degenerate race lives there (a theory popular to occultists); that the hoaxter George Adamski was indeed entertaining aliens; and that people allied with Satan live on the moon. Ashtar also affirmed the Lemurian myth, and claimed one of their cities still existed in Antarctica from which Lemurians keep—and fly—their UFOs.[32]

Billy Meier Also Talks about Ashtar

Famous Swiss contactee Billy Meier also speaks about Ashtar. According to his 1975 transcripts that he says he got directly from the Pleiadeans, Ashtar used to be an evil alien, but he has seen the light and is now working with Jesus, helping to prepare for "the rapture."[33]

Should we believe this new account of Ashtar, that he's really good? I think it would be wise to take the advice of Dave Wimbish: "Although thousands of people believe every word that purports to come from outer space, I personally would have a difficult time buying a used car from Ashtar and his buddies."[34]

New Age Ashtar Messages

Messages from Ashtar are continuing to come to the world in the wake of the rise of the New Age. Timothy ("Mr. UFO") Beckley's Inner Light Publishing Company has just produced a book of messages "channeled by the Ashtar Command." The 1990 book titled *New World Order: Prophecies from Space* boasts that it is based on thirty-five transmissions coming from a several-miles-long mother ship commanded by Ashtar circling the earth near the equator. According to its introduction, the messages began on July 4, 1980, when a "well-established" New York City businessman fell into a trance and his vocal chords were taken over by Ashtar.[35] The book, which contradicts the Bible from brim to brim, quotes Ashtar as saying that "Jesus does not wish to be worshipped"[36] (see John 20:28, 29; Luke 19:37–40; Rom. 14:11; Phil. 2:9–11; Heb. 1:6; Matt. 2:2; John 9:35–38; Matt. 28:17; Rev. 4:9–11) and that Ashtar and a whole cast of characters (Monka from Mars, Aura Raines, a beautiful spacewoman from Clarion [in UFO lore an alleged planet in our own solar system going the same speed as the earth but constantly being hidden by the sun], and others) have arrived to assist humankind into the New Age following coming calamities. "Ashtar says that the Space Brothers are willing to assist with our transformation into a higher plane of consciousness brought about by the heightening of our planet's vibrations as we are about to enter the Aquarian or New Age."[37]

Beckley's New Age organization is also selling another recent book by a mysterious Commander X called *Underground Alien Bases* that talks about the aliens having more than fifty underground bases in the United States alone. In an article by Commander X, he states that a hot site for alien contact and the site of potential meetings with living nine-foot-tall Lemurians and "the knomes, the elves and the fairies" is at Mount Shasta, the New Age mecca in California. Also from that site a woman is able to channel "Ashtar as well as other Space Guardians."[38]

A Further New Age Link

Although some New Agers are skeptical of channeling aliens, they will channel spirit guides who often give them similar messages about coming catastrophes that will lead to the new age.

Asher, the spirit guide of John Randolph Price, a moving force behind the New Agers' "World Instant of Cooperation" (on December 31, 1986, in which thousands of meditators worldwide simultaneously concentrated on world peace hoping to cause a critical mass launching into the New Age) told him that two billion people who didn't go along with the New Age would be wiped off the face of the earth during the coming cleansing.[39]

Isn't it strange how Price's Asher has a message about the future similar to the various space brothers named Ashtar? It's hard to believe anyone would trust any entity named Ashtar at all, considering the track records of such beings with the same names being liars and tricksters with agendas of trying to change the way we think about Jesus Christ and the historic Christian faith. Considering this behavior, it is not surprising that the name Ashtar has been linked to Satan and to Lucifer. It also makes sense that today's UFOnauts who go by the Ashtar calling card may be the very same entity that led Israel and Judah to ruin by seducing Israel into the Baal-Asherah pole star and planet worship of centuries past.

Modern Star Worship?

The striking similarities between ancient Baal worship and the new gospel according to extraterrestrial messengers make one wonder if it will lead the world to delusion and end in destruction in the same manner as it did centuries ago when the nation of Israel provoked God's anger by their sin. Lest you say today's UFOnauts don't teach us to worship the stars, consider Ashtar's instructions in the 1990 book *New World Order:*

> Yes, there are consciousnesses all through the solar system. Mercury is a very high planet. It is the planet of healing, of light rays, of warmth.
>
> Meditate upon Mercury if you wish to feel these warm healing rays. Venus is the planet of love and harmony. Mars is the planet of spirit and higher consciousness and scientific order in the solar system.[40]

"Say to yourself," instructs Ashtar in another place, in a line that sounds suspiciously like the sins of the tyrant king of Babylon (recounted in Isa. 14:12–15) that led God to cast him down to earth: "I am the Light of the Universe. I am powerful. I am glorious. I am a living being. . . . Send out positive thoughts, send out harmony, send out love, and meditate on the wholeness of the solar system in the galaxy."[41]

New Agers and UFO enthusiasts don't seem to be very concerned over the possibility that channeled messages from any source may be part of an evil, satanic plot to destroy men's souls and lead the human race to ruin. It's a stunningly illogical omission, especially in light of the Bible's clear admonition to "test the spirits to see whether they are from God" (1 John 4:1). The apostles frequently warned the first-century church not to believe different spirits or entities and to reject the pagan religions' practice of sacrificing food to idols.

Like George Van Tassel's monument to the lying space brothers in Yucca Valley, California, the UFOnauts' false statements and prophecies have been recorded in books, magazines, and in the wreckage of human lives for all to see, yet many New Agers fail to test them. It's almost as if they are blinded by intrigue and misconception; they don't want to believe Peter's warning that "your enemy the devil prowls around like a roaring lion looking for someone to devour" (1 Peter 5:8).

I believe that many New Agers' involvement with sorcery, mediumship, familiar spirits, and other deep things of the occult instead of the truth has caused God to have given up some of them to follow their intrigues, as he said he will just before Christ returns to judge the world (2 Thess. 2:9–12).

Not only do they refuse to acknowledge the possibility of a satanic conspiracy, but in fact, a good number of UFO enthusiasts and New Agers have either redefined Satan himself (such as Lucifer being a planet) or have publicly declared Lucifer to be good. We have already seen a lot of that in this book, and be assured God's curse is on such people. Isaiah 5:20 says: "Woe to those who call evil good and good evil, who put darkness for light and light for darkness."

Lauding Lucifer

David Spangler, one of the world's most influential New Age leaders, who claims to be in touch with a variety of entities including aliens, states that we must be initiated into Lucifer to enter the New Age:

> Lucifer comes to give to us the final gift of wholeness. If we accept it then he is free and we are free. That is the Luciferic initiation. It is one that many people now, and in the days ahead, will be facing, for it is an initiation into the New Age.[42]

We've already seen instances where contactees like Moi-Ra and Ra-Ja Dove of Lytle Creek, California, and Francie Steiger have stated that Satan or the serpent in the Garden of Eden was not really the monster the Judeo-Christian tradition says he was. But we haven't yet seen what the El Cajon, California-based Unarius Foundation teaches about Satan, Christ, and Christianity for a real lesson in the reversal of values. For instance, Ernest L. Norman, founder of the sect and late husband of its current leader, Ruth, wrote a book that said Judas and Paul conspired in a plot to contaminate Christianity and make it into the "immoral" religion that it is, and that he (Norman, who died in 1971) is the second coming and the reincarnated Jesus.[43] The foundation also produces a book allegedly channeled by John the Baptist featuring his "apology" for his sin of advancing Jesus of Nazareth as the Jewish Messiah.

But more pertinent to our discussion is literature Unarius puts out that proclaims Satan to be a good guy now. The Normans' reasoning? That their emergence into the world in 1900 and 1904 (the years in which Ernest and Ruth were born) resulted in their overcoming "the forces of darkness, evil and destruction":[44]

> The soul Satan, Lucifer and Jaweh, who had many other names, has factually been overcome, has seen the error of his ways and actions and has joined the FORCES OF LIGHT, TRUTH AND GOOD. . . . Satan has given up, he has exchanged his strong ego and erroneous beliefs for Truth, and now is a servant or server of the Light! So fear no longer this evil-doer! He no longer does evil works but rather, he channels Light—clear and pure and has become a Way Shower![45]

To be sure, the Unarius Foundation is not representative of the UFO-New Age movement; in fact, their beliefs and outlandish publicity-seeking events are embarrassing to some in the movement. And I would be remiss if I didn't mention that many people who are UFO enthusiasts—even some of those steeped in New Age occultism—believe in the reality of a real, evil devil. Some tend to do so (despite New Agers' tendencies not to believe in any moral absolutes) because they know, deep down, that we live in an evil, fallen world, a world in which one dictatorial leader of a small, two-bit nation can thrust the world into a near global war as almost happened in August 1990, when Saddam Hussein's army invaded Kuwait.

Many inside the UFO field don't want to face the strong possibility that aliens, or visitors as Strieber calls them, may be trying to enter our unconscious mind to change the way we think of reality.[46] And UFOlogists are often reluctant to face up to a similar possibility that UFOs and the contactee phenomenon may be directly related to demonology, that the aliens may really be fallen angels.[47]

Here is some food for thought from the introduction of Lynn Catoe's UFO bibliography she completed for the United States Air Force. Catoe, who has reviewed some 1,600 articles and books in her role as a bibliographer for the Library of Congress, wrote: "Many of the UFO reports now being published in the popular press recount alleged incidents that are strikingly similar to demonic possession and psychic phenomena which have long been known to theologians and parapsychologists."[48]

A Night in the King's Chamber

The king's chamber at the center of the Great Pyramid of Giza opens up to reveal a large room containing an open crypt. One night near the beginning of the twentieth century the chamber became the site of a strange occurrence. A young man and woman obsessed with the occult chose to spend the night there. By candlelight the man began to read an occultic invocation designed to bring forth "spirits." But as he was reading, and doubtless as his voice was echoing down the long hall leading to the chamber, a strange purplish glow began to fill the chamber. Finally the "astral light" was so bright that he blew out the candles and continued to read on.[49]

That man was the infamous Aleister Crowley, and many consider him the most famous Satanist in history. He called himself "the Beast" and the "Antichrist 666," and he relished his media reputation as "the wickedest man in the world." But in reality, notes researcher Jon Trott, he "did not believe in Satan's existence and did not call himself a Satanist, though he seemed to fit the bill."[50] Rather, he considered himself a magician,[51] and he fused that with his belief in a lack of moral restraint. He combined this philosophy with his search to learn and practice hard-core occultic spells and rituals to communicate with spirits and evil entities in his lifelong quest to become as debased as possible. He practiced sex magic, witchcraft, and called upon the devil's name in ceremonies. Once he even claimed to have "subdued" a high-ranking demon during a strange ritual.[52] Although from his youth he maintained an obsessive hatred of Christianity, he freely practiced mystical rites of other traditions that included yoga, Buddhism, the Cabala, and Free Masonry.[53]

In a sense, although Crowley died in 1947, he still cuts a larger-than-life figure in both today's occult and heavy-metal rock-and-roll subcultures. Crowley's bald-headed photo appeared on the cover of the Beatles's *Sgt. Pepper* album; black metal king Ozzy Osbourne wrote a song in his honor; and Jimmy Page, lead guitarist for the rock group Led Zeppelin, purchased a mansion in Scotland once owned by Crowley. Several sensationalistic books have been written about Crowley's life and antics, and biographers usually agree on the following about his life.

He joined the Order of the Golden Dawn, a magic and mediumship group founded in 1900 that had been influenced by its founders' ties to Helena Blavatsky.[54] He eventually founded his own occult groups, The Order of Thelema and a secretive, magical society called the Ordo Templi Orentis (or O.T.O.) that continues to operate in cities throughout the United States and Europe. He practiced masochistic and perverted homosexual and bisexual sex, and during one bizarre incident forced his mistress to submit to intercourse with a goat, then slit its throat.[55] He also allegedly sacrificed animals from time to time, and he was accused of enlisting his Thelema group to participate in infant sacrifices while they operated at an abbey in Sicily, Italy.[56]

Although some say Crowley may have embellished details of his life in his autobiography, *The Confessions*, no one has challenged his claim that a short time after his night in the Great Pyramid, he and his wife, Rose, based then in Cairo, had another significant experience: contact with an alien.

It occurred at midnight, March 19, 1904, when his wife went into a trance, and an entity named Aiwas began speaking through her in a strange voice. That entity told Crowley that he was to create a new religion and had been chosen as the new messiah.[57] The entity, whom Crowley said was his guardian angel, a "messenger from the forces ruling this earth at present,"[58] gave him instructions concerning further transmissions of a new bible that he called *The Book of the Law*, which was to supplant all other religions.

Today, Kenneth Grant, Crowley's successor as head of the O.T.O., said the entity was "an extraterrestrial," and that his mentor "was the first modern occultist to demonstrate the existence of superior alien intelligences." More strikingly, Grant says, these contacts coupled with Crowley's death in 1947 (the same year that kicked off the modern UFO era) may be related to the apparent increase in modern UFO sightings.[59] In his way of thinking, Crowley's death may have unleashed the heaven, allowing UFOs and other assorted entities to come to earth and begin to communicate more readily with humanity.

Whether or not we believe Grant's explanation is irrelevant; the fact is that Crowley claimed contact with a variety of otherwordly entities during his lifetime. While with the Order of the Golden Dawn he was among the few who claimed success in contacting angels via magic[60] (some of whom identified themselves by names), and he claimed to have contacted Lam, an alien from Sirius and Andromeda.[61]

Brad Steiger notes that in July 1973, New Age-occult writer Robert Anton Wilson was dabbling with one of Crowley's magical books and decided to perform Crowley's invocation of the holy guardian angel. He "received an expansion of consciousness" and new wisdom about the universe, and the next day he wrote in his diary: "Sirius is very important." He searched through his occult books for information on Sirius, which is the brightest star in the sky located in the constellation Canis Major, and found Crowley's claim to have been in touch with a Sirian alien. Wilson noted that the star had been an object of veneration to the ancient Egyptians, the Zoroastrians, the Australian bushmen, and other groups.[62]

The Whitley Strieber Connection

Interestingly, Crowley once had tea with twentieth-century mystic George Gurdjieff, for they both allegedly knew about "strange powers of the will," the ability to control people by suggestion, and to communicate telepathically, according to Wilson.[63]

As mentioned earlier, Whitley Strieber's occult belief system was influenced by Gurdjieff. Strieber, in both *Communion* and *Transformation*, makes much of his long-time relationship with Gurdjieff mysticism, particularly during his attempts to use its principles in out-of-body experiences and to contact others through telepathy.

When Crowley, prior to 1945, contacted Lam, the entity from Sirius, and allegedly drew an image of him, an interesting "coincidence" turned up. The painting, noted Conroy, "depicts an eggheaded face characterized by a vestigial nose and mouth and two eyes in narrow, elongated slits. Its resemblance to the image on the cover of *Communion* is remarkable, save for the dimensions of qualities of the eyes."[64]

What kind of material is in *The Book of the Law,* the book that the entity Aiwas dictated to Crowley in Cairo in 1904?

It's a lot of gobbledygook, but it states that "every man and every woman is a star,"[65] and it gives Crowley in a sentence the law that apparently governed his life: "Do what thou wilt shall be the whole of the Law."[66] It affirmed Crowley as the leader of a "new Aeon" that would last 2,000 years ("the term 'New Age' hadn't yet come into currency," noted Conroy).[67] Contemporary followers continue to look to Crowley as their New Age leader. The December 22, 1977, "Newaeon Newsletter," published by one Crowleyan group, states "Jesus shall never return for it was never meant to be. But the Christ, the Logos of the Aeon, the New World Teacher hath come already and his name is Aleister Crowley, the Beast 666."[68]

Aiwas also instructed him to "take wine and strange drugs . . . and be drunk thereof" and promised him that his "death shall be lovely—whoso seeth it shall be glad."[69] But Aiwas turned out to be a liar, just as Ashtar, Molech, the Baals and countless other extraterrestrial beings have been. Crowley abandoned his wife and daughter in Hong Kong, and when they tried to return to England his daughter died of typhoid in Rangoon.[70] "He became a heroin addict, and his son mysteriously died during a private ritual that only the two attended."[71] He lost his mind during the last several years of his life, became very sick, and died a horrible death at age seventy-two.

9 Channeling Fallible Gods

The sun ricocheted off the blue waters of the swimming pool and glimmered through the blinds at the Clarion Hotel in San Diego one March day. Although the small conference room was darkened, the bright daylight seeped in and interfered with some strange happenings.

In that small room I joined about ten other people in plunking down forty dollars to attend an intensive workshop in which Robert Short, a veteran in the UFO field, would talk to the space brothers.

I didn't like being there. I was mindful that channeling in reality is divination and spiritism, condemned by God in Scripture. But I reasoned that if I was to be fair in my investigation of the modern UFO movement, I had to at least come to hear one of the best-known alien channelers.[1]

Short, a man of average stature with white curly hair, dressed in his typical blue outfit that seems to match the name of his organization, the Blue Rose Ministry of Joshua Tree, California, is a likable person. He talked slowly with the small gathering of people, weaving stories of how he got into the UFO movement and his experiences with channeling.

He told of how he became involved with George Van Tassel in the 1950s and how automatic writing led to his contact with a space creature named Jan-al and then directly into channeling. He said it was at Van Tassel's place in Giant Rock (at the site of Van Tassel's Integratron) that he amazed a gathering of Van Tassel's disciples by channeling an alien in a booming voice. And then, just as he does now when he goes into a trance and allows strange voices to come through him, he never remembers anything that the space brothers have said after they have spoken. It's as if he leaves his body and an entity enters, he said.

The most common entity Short claims he channels is Korton, a highly evolved being from Mars.

When his chatting with the audience was over, Short announced that he was ready to channel Korton. The gathering of people, most of whom were already into occultism and who had gone to other channelers for insight, were thrilled to get to this part. Some of them had paid their forty dollars because they believed Korton had answers to their current dilemmas and they looked to him for guidance.

Into an Altered State

Short started by very firmly reading Psalm 23 in a slow, mysterious way. Then he sat down, closed his eyes, braced himself with hands on knees, and grunted. The color left his face for a moment, he shook, turned a bright red, then almost purple. Suddenly a voice not his own reverberated from his mouth.

"This is Central Control . . . This is Central Control . . . Stand by, information to follow," he gasped in a hesitating voice. "Stand by. Information to follow. Five, four, three, two, one. Mark. This is Central Control calling Eddie . . . Central Control calling . . . We are standing by on Frequency 250 . . . Standing."

Short, still with his eyes closed, was interrupted by a high-pitched voice coming from his mouth: "Central Control this is Eddie. We are ready to transmit. We are ready to transmit. One moment please."

Seconds later a booming low voice, distinctively different, spewed: "This is the voice . . . orange spark relay automatic . . . From the manual the earth calls Jupiter. On behalf of the honorable Korton, r-r-r-r-representative. We are ready to begin with the information which we have records for the individual in this time period. Let us begin with the individual on the left."

Korton spoke to the first man, who told him that he was uncertain over his life's direction and needed advice. Korton responded by telling him in a halting vibrato voice that he had to watch a middle-aged woman in his family and it would come clear what he had to do. The man seemed satisfied.

But the next questioner was definitely not satisfied after Korton told him to pack up his belongings and move to an impossible location—out in the middle of the Pacific Ocean.

The mustachioed young Californian, Eddie, looked to be a professional man in his early thirties, dressed in designer jeans, grey Nike sneakers, and a blue shirt. Unknown to Korton, the man lived near the beach in San Diego. Following is a transcript of part of the session.

Eddie: "I have a second question. What other information might you have for me?"

Korton/Short: "There, uh, will be, uh, change with respect to your present location. Uh, within 120 of your earth days. You may begin to consider, perhaps it would be more conducive to . . . both in your activities . . . in another area that would appear to be more conducive to your activities, rather than in your present location where you feel somewhat more limited, uh, or restricted in your movement and also in what may be shared with others, uh. . . . You might wish to consider a movement of locations in that time period. . . . Is that understood?

Eddie: A physical move?

Short's wife, who was assisting her husband in tape recording Korton's sessions with each participant, then turned to Eddie. "Have you thought of that?" she asked. Then turning to Korton/Short she asked, "How far?"

Korton/Short: "You sir, uh, would be, uh, perhaps within 100 to 150 of your earth miles from your present location. It would be toward, uh, south and west of that present location. Is that understood, uh?"

Eddie: "I don't see how. That would put me over the [Mexican] border. I would be over the water."

Korton/Short: "A southerly direction, perhaps not so much westerly. It could be out there where there'd be more open space. You would be freer in your movements and perhaps there would be. . . ."

Eddie: "If I moved south and west I'd be out in the middle of the water."

According to my tape recorded transcript, when Eddie pushed the fact that the all-knowing Korton advised him to move out into the Pacific Ocean and into Mexican territory, the voice began to change its tune. Korton concluded the session with him by saying that his sense of direction is different from ours and that what he really meant was to move east off of Interstate 8, which flows easterly from San Diego into Arizona—the exact opposite from his original advice. And if that were the case, Korton was advising the baffled guest to move into the desert, somewhere between Mexicali and Yuma, Arizona. The young man looked troubled. He seemed to be concerned about his job.

I came away from the workshop more convinced than ever that channeling should be rejected from a logical point of view and because of the heavy weight of condemnation God places on the practice (and related practices) in Scripture.

Korton/Short's statements of "wisdom" dispensed to everyone in the room were so vague that they could have been gleaned from the pages of the local newspaper's astrology column. And there was the issue of the false information given to Eddie. What went wrong there? Logically I can think of two possibilities: (1) Robert Short was simply guessing, under the guise of Korton, with his eyes closed and an altered voice to sound like he was receiving messages. His motive could have been to make money. (2) An entity, perhaps one that was evil and not all knowing, could have possessed his body and guessed wrongly, or it deliberately could have given wrong information to Eddie for unknown motives.[2]

No matter what the solution to the puzzle, clearly the channeled messages that afternoon were not truthful and could not be trusted. Korton/Short or whoever the entity was lied to the young man.

But more telling to me as I listened to the others interact with Korton that day was that he proclaimed a New Age worldview, and his teachings were in opposition to God's Word. To the next man, who sought advice on how to develop himself spiritually, Korton quoted Christ out of context to make him appear to say, just as Shirley MacLaine said on the Malibu beach, that we are all gods. "The master," presumably Jesus, Korton/Short said in a booming voice, "said, 'Know you not that you are gods?'"

You Are Gods

This assumption, the New Age idea that we are all gods, was also a theme I ran into repeatedly during my investigation of the UFO movement. In conferences across America during the past several years, and in many books written by New Agers, I found New Age leaders and UFO speakers repeatedly referring to the notion that Jesus affirmed godhood for all. Where did they get this notion, and did Jesus really affirm that?

Certainly not.

What they are talking about is a crucial passage in John 10 in which Jesus was so firm about his claim to divinity that the Jews picked up stones to try to kill him (v. 31). In verse 24, as Jesus was walking in the temple area, some Jewish leaders asked him if he was going to admit that he was the promised Messiah. Christ instead launched into a dialogue about his miracles speaking for themselves and that only his people would believe him anyway. Speaking about his followers he said:

> "I give them eternal life, and they shall never perish. . . . I and the Father are one." Again the Jews picked up stones to stone him, but Jesus said to them, "I have shown you many great miracles from the Father. For which of these do you stone me?"
>
> "We are not stoning you for any of these," replied the Jews, "but for blasphemy, because you, a mere man, claim to be God" (John 10:28, 30–33).

And here is the passage that New Agers misrepresent: "Jesus answered them, 'Is it not written in your Law, "I have said you are gods"'" (John 10:34)?

The problem is that New Agers always seem to stop there. They don't read the related passage Christ was referring to (Ps. 82:2–7) that helps explain what he meant. They don't read any farther in John where Jesus explained what he meant. Edwin A. Blum, writing in *The Bible Knowledge Commentary,* lays it out for us:

> Psalm 82 speaks of God as the true Judge (Ps. 82:1, 8) and of men, appointed as judges, who were failing to provide true judgment for God (Ps. 82:2–7). "Gods" in Psalm 82:1, 6 refers to these human judges. In this sense, God said to the Jews, You are gods. *In no way does this speak of a divine nature in man* (emphasis mine).[3]

Jesus developed this argument in the verses following. He said, in effect, that since the Bible called their judges gods, they could not accuse him of blasphemy for calling himself God's Son, since he was under divine orders (set apart) and on God's mission (sent into the world).[4] In developing his brilliant argument further in verses 37–38, Jesus told the people if they didn't believe his words, that he was God in human flesh, to at least believe him for the miracles that he performed "that you may know and understand that the Father is in me, and I in the Father." Their response? They tried to stone him again, but he escaped.

Again, this is one of the biggest lies of the New Age movement: that humans can become divine or like God. The Bible, cover to cover, never affirms the divinity of man. For man to declare himself God is blasphemy and idolatry of the worst kind. It is among the sins for which the coming Antichrist will be thrown into the lake of fire, for he will force humankind to worship him as God (Rev. 13:15). And it is the original lie of the devil in the Garden of Eden (Gen. 3:5).

Humankind is separate from God, just as God's creation is separate from him. The apostle Paul said humankind is under the curse of sin, and those who reject God he gives over to their own degrading passions. Among them is the worship of created things. "They exchanged the truth of God for a lie, and worshiped and served created things rather than the Creator—who is forever praised" (Rom. 1:25).

Paul, in this same section, is more specific about God's curse upon humankind. He said it is because humans know the truth about God and his identity, yet they've suppressed the truth by their own wickedness.

> The wrath of God is being revealed from heaven against all the godlessness and wickedness of men who suppress the truth by their wickedness, since what may be known about God is plain to them, because God has made it plain to them. For since the creation of the world God's invisible qualities—his eternal power and divine nature—have been clearly seen, being understood from what has been made, so that men are without excuse (Rom. 1:18–20).

Who Is Jesus?

Jesus is not an alien in charge of a spaceship or a fleet of ships in our sector of the galaxy. Jesus is God in human flesh, and he will not share his position with anyone. Even the most exalted view of Jesus that appears in UFO literature (that Jesus was a great master leading the world into better ethical standards) denigrates the biblical revelation of who Christ really is.

> For by him all things were created: things in heaven and on earth, visible and invisible, whether thrones or powers or rulers or authorities; all things were created by him and for him. He is before all things, and in him all things hold together. . . . he is the beginning and the firstborn from among the dead, so that in everything he might have the supremacy. For God was pleased to have all his fullness dwell in him, and through him to reconcile to himself all things, whether things on earth or things in heaven, by making peace through his blood, shed on the cross (Col. 1:16–20).

Imagine what Paul is saying in that passage by inspiration of the Holy Spirit. All things hold together in Christ. The protons and the neutrons are held together by his power. Without him everything would fall apart. Your very next breath, life itself, is in his hands. Yet I don't know of a single UFO enthusiast who gives Christ his total due. They misrepresent his words, and they especially misrepresent his mission. Almost all teach reincarnation, not God's judgment, and none that I know of teach, as the Bible clearly affirms, that humans can be saved from judgment except, as Scripture says, "by making peace through his blood, shed on the cross."

Not only does the New Age-UFO movement reject a complete understanding of Christ's death on the cross and of his mission, some leading figures in the movement hate Christ. No other known religious figure is the object of such hatred, only Jesus. (Oddly enough, the name of Jesus Christ is among the few personal names used as an expletive worldwide.) Here are the words of Robert C. Girard, publisher-operator of the Arcturus Book Service of Stone Mountain, Georgia, one of the largest distributors of UFO books in the world. In a book exploring an alleged link between rock star David Bowie and aliens he comments:

> Grotesque, sleazy geeks like Bowie, Presley, the Beatles and other such "culture heroes," will earn places in the history of this cycle of human "civilization" very near to—or perhaps a bit below—the scum at the bottom: among such negative and destructive presences as Jesus, Idi Amin, Caligula, any number of Catholic popes, Pizarro and Cortes, Jim and Tammy Faye Bakker, Ronald Reagan, Saddam Hussein, Frank Lorenzo and as many others as readers would like to add for themselves.[5]

Robert Short's "Ministry"

Short claims his ministry is Christian. He is unusual among UFO cultists in his frequent quotations of Scripture and his claimed affinity with the Jesus Christ of the Bible. But in reality, Short cannot be counted on to teach any spiritual truth at all. Not only is he deeply involved in spiritism, he is involved in many other occultic practices, and he believes strongly in universalism, the belief that it doesn't really matter which faith one follows as long as one is sincere. "There are many names for Israel's Holy One," said Short, and that includes Mohammed, Buddha, and others.[6]

For example, during his workshop he said he was into occult dowsing and the use of divining rods and believes in reincarnation to the point of his having been a close friend of sixteenth-century French astrologer-occultist Nostradamus in a previous life. During his major speech at the National New Age & "Truth about UFOs" Conference[7] he affirmed his belief in astrology, which is also condemned by God (see Deut. 4:19; 17:1–5; 18:9-11; 2 Kings 17:16, 17; 23:5; Jer. 8:1, 2; 19:13; Ezek. 8:16; Amos 5:26, 27; Isa. 47:13, 14). He distorted the gospel of Christ by declaring that it is simply "peace and love" to humankind and he denied the physical return of Christ that is clearly proclaimed throughout the Bible, while at the same time he engaged in unscriptural date setting. He claimed that Jesus will come spiritually to earth in A.D. 2032. The Bible warns that he who denies Christ's coming in the flesh is a deceiver and an antichrist (2 John 7), because on the day Jesus ascended into heaven two angels said, "This same Jesus, who has been taken from you into heaven, will come back in the same way you have seen him go into heaven" (Acts 1:11).

Robert Short has not told us the truth about God, and if he is in contact with alleged aliens, they are beings who also lie and twist Scripture. But, as we have already seen, lying is a way of life in the gospel according to extraterrestrial messengers.

Points of Origin

Today most people who claim to be in touch with extraterrestrial beings claim they come from other star systems. My guess is that the leading stars suspected to be the origin points for sending aliens to Earth in the 1990s are Zeta Reticuli and the Pleiades. As we noted, the trend to place alleged visiting aliens outside our solar system did not start until the mid-sixties when NASA and Soviet space probes began their tours of the neighboring planets that made clear the impossible living conditions on each one.[8]

I remember in the 1960s watching excitedly when the first closeup photographs of Mars taken by an earlier *Mariner* mission were about to be revealed to the nation on television. But when the photographs finally appeared, I was just as disappointed as the scientists to know the truth that Mars could not possibly support life. I wanted to believe in life on Mars, but instead I realized that Mars was only moonlike. The pictures showed large areas of the red planet pounded with craters.

Today as I write, the United States' space probe *Magellan* is busy at work, mapping Venus's surface as it reports hellish, 900 degree conditions on the surface of the poison-gas-cloud-shrouded body. The beautiful, radio-transmitted pictures in computer-generated color show a jagged, tortured rocky surface without a hint of life.

Yet in the history of modern UFOlogy no planet has been cited more often than Venus as the alleged point of origin for the space brothers. Some have even claimed that the "space brother" Jesus lives there. How have the contactees gotten around the fact that Venus is lifeless? As previously mentioned, a few have changed their tunes to indicate the aliens live underground on Venus and the other neighboring planets, but by far most of them who continue to stick by their claims say that aliens are still there but exist in another dimension or in the "etheric," or spiritual, realm.

Short, for example, claims that Korton and other Martians "are from a parallel universe." "They used to come from Mars," he explained, "but they blew up a [nearby] planet and destroyed the atmosphere of Mars."[9]

But more serious questions are these: Are the space brothers giving us bum information as to their origins? Are the contactees attention-getting liars? Either way, lies are being told about their origins. Let's look at UFO history for a roster of other sites, mostly outside the solar system, that are suspected of being homes to extraterrestrial beings. All of the following planet and star systems have been seized on by UFO enthusiasts as homes for aliens visiting earth.

From the planet UMMO from the Wolf 24-star system;[10] from a planet in the Arcturus system; from Selo[11] and Centurus,[12] the alleged third and second planet in the Alpha Centauri star; from Clarion, a mythical parallel planet to Earth in our own solar system that allegedly avoids detection by traveling on the other side of the sun on Earth's same orbit; from the planet Iarga; from the star Capella; from the planet Korender in the Andromeda galaxy; from the stars Tau Ceti and Episolon Eridani;[13] from stars in the constellation of Orion and Bernard's Star;[14] and from the star Apus.[15]

Parallel Reality

Although some UFO enthusiasts claim aliens may be coming from all of the above locations and even more, logic indicates they are not. As the "from our own solar system" claims have collapsed since the 1960s, will these new, other star-galaxy claims evaporate during the 1990s?

I believe the best explanation for the aliens' origin is that they are malevolent spiritual beings from a parallel reality with their own agenda for humankind. They want to hurt humankind. They want to keep us tied up wasting precious time on the unsolvable UFO riddle one UFOlogist jokingly referred to as "the mother of all mysteries." But most of all, the UFOnauts, proved on almost every contact, want to change the way we think about God.

Under a Curse

These beings are all under a biblical curse for distorting the gospel of Christ and deceiving people into rejecting the salvation the gospel brings. "But even if we or an angel from heaven should preach a gospel other than the one we preached to you, let him be eternally condemned" (Gal. 1:8).

The Bible says that Jesus Christ is the hope of glory (Col. 1:27), our only chance of eternal life. The Bible's message is the same from Genesis to Revelation. The God of the Bible is consistent, "who does not change like shifting shadows" (James 1:17). It teaches resurrection of our bodies, not reincarnation, which is no salvation at all. The Christian message offers salvation as a free gift, not as the result of our good works. Reincarnation, on the other hand, offers the hopeless promise of having to work harder and harder over many lifetimes until you get it right, and then you return to the great nothingness, losing your individuality.

The Bible affirms the value of humans, who were made in the image of God. Each person is loved by God individually. On the other hand, the space beings and the New Age movement denigrate the value of people, demoting them to animal status as mere advanced evolving beasts on a never-ending journey to nowhere. The theory of physical and spiritual evolution promotes racism and bigotry toward the supposed less-evolved creatures, those deemed closer to the jungle and our primate ancestors. This sort of worldview discourages helping the underlings of this world who must work out their karma. Just take a look at India's Hindu caste system.

Along the same vein, I wonder why the humanoid-type space brothers (not mythical grays) are usually white Nordic types. In fact, I don't know of a single instance where humanoid aliens have resembled blacks.

People are of more value than sparrows, Jesus said (Matt. 10:31). But God even looks after the birds and all the creatures he made for us to enjoy (Gen. 1:26).

The gospel of the extraterrestrial messengers gives humankind no hope but instead draws people away from their only hope. They bring the same doctrines of demons with which they have deceived humankind for centuries. Scripture warns us of this very thing occurring in the end times: "The Spirit clearly says that in later times some will abandon the faith and follow deceiving spirits and things taught by demons" (1 Tim. 4:1).

The messages channeled from extraterrestrial beings as well as their attempts at predicting future events are no different from the fallible "knowledge" attained through other occultic methods. It makes no difference whether one uses a Ouija board, tarot cards, psychometry (psychic messages from personal articles), palm reading, handwriting analysis, bumps-on-heads readings, seances, automatic writing, aura reading, crystal ball gazing, or astrology. The message is the same. Therefore, it can be deduced that they all stem from the same source. The Bible calls it spiritism and condemns the practice repeatedly.

For anyone who has dabbled with the occult, Jesus Christ is the only way out of its consequences. His is the only name used for casting out and fending off demonic attacks. One can learn a lesson from the early Christian converts who had been practicing magical arts; when they believed on the Lord they brought their occult books and burned them publicly (Acts 19:18, 19).

I have heard testimonies from UFO contactees who turned their lives to Christ and renounced their occult practices and were not contacted by the demons again. In my investigation I have seen that Christians are not good subjects for the space brothers to tamper with. In fact, I've never known it to happen.

10 A Swiss Man Meets a Different Jesus Back in Time

The folks in the crowded northern Virginia hotel room, near Washington, D.C., were laughing.

"Look at the drunken UFO pilot!" a dark-haired woman said, sending the small gathering of mostly UFO skeptics into fits. I was among the twelve or so people.

We were watching a Japanese documentary about the Eduard "Billy" Meier UFO case, which has been trumpeted as the most documented UFO case in history. But instead of the film convincing us that Meier's claims were valid—that indeed aliens from the Pleiades constellation flying "beamships" were visiting the one-armed Swiss man—the film convinced every one of us that Meier was a fraud.

The film displayed Meier's footage of a Pleiadian beamship doing aerial demonstration maneuvers for his benefit as he photographed it. But what Meier's "proof" turned out to be was a metallic disk going back and forth in rhythmic motion, swinging like a pendulum near a tree. Each time it reached the end of its swing the disk fluttered uncontrollably, which would have shaken up anyone who was inside. And this evoked more laughter from the spectators.[1]

The scientific UFO community with few exceptions has thoroughly trashed Meier's claims. One author called it "the most infamous hoax in ufology." Dennis Stacy, editor of the prestigious *MUFON UFO Journal,* wrote that "photographic analysis [of Meier's photographs] . . . reportedly revealed that Meier's amazing array of flying saucers consisted of small models suspended from strings."[2]

Even more telling is the very real evidence that Meier had faked his story of being a long-time UFO contactee. According to Gary Kinder's book *Light Years*, Meier's wife, Popi, became angry at her husband and confessed her role in having helped perpetrate a long-running UFO scam. According to European investigator Martin Sorge, Popi Meier showed him many color slides that she allegedly pulled out of a fire before her husband could dispose of them. They showed models of Pleiadian beamships that Meier made and superimposed on prints of the Swiss countryside.[3]

"I saw pictures of a UFO and it really was a model," Sorge told Kinder. "In the first place I saw that it was a model, and in the second place I learned it from his wife. She said, 'Yes, he is working with models.'"[4]

In another case Meier announced that Semjase, his beautiful, blonde Pleiadian, who had an uncanny resemblance to actress Sandra Dee, took him on a beamship trip into the future and allowed him to take a picture of San Francisco as a heap of ruins following a huge, future earthquake. However, the picture he proudly displayed was faked; the same picture appeared later in *GEO* magazine. It was an artist's lifelike painting of what a massive earthquake might do to the city.[5] Apparently Meier took a picture of the painting and claimed it as his own.

Meier Still Has Many Followers

Despite these problems with this case, and many others we will see later, the Swiss man has many, many followers (outside the scientific UFO research community), and his incredibly clear pictures—several hundred of flying saucers hovering above the ground near his home near Hinwil, Switzerland, have been circulating worldwide. Major European magazines and international television crews have thoroughly covered the Meier story, mostly because of the clarity of his still shots of the saucers. In some of the shots, not one but a handful of the saucers is seen in the photograph.

The gist of his story is that Meier claims to have been selected as a young boy as a contactee from a superior, benevolent, group of extraterrestrial beings from the Pleiades constellation, about five hundred light years from earth. Although the Pleiades is a cluster of several thousand stars in the constellation Taurus, it consists of seven bright stars that can be seen with the naked eye and are sometimes called the "seven sisters." There are many ancient references to the Pleiades, including two references to the constellation in the Bible's Book of Job (9:9, which also mentions Arcturus and Orion, and 38:31).

Meier claims that in 1944 he began receiving telepathic messages from an entity known as Sfath, an old man who would periodically appear to him and who eventually took him up into the sky in a pear-shaped flying machine. Sfath tutored him in matters of wisdom and the universe, but he "never told me his origin and what my mission essentially was," Meier said.[6]

When Sfath's voice disappeared from his head a new female entity named Asket, who claimed to come from an unknown parallel universe called Dal, began talking to him.[7] For the next nineteen years she continued to teach him, Meier said. His relationship with Asket led him more deeply into occultism, and she continued telepathic teachings imparted to his "greater spiritual awareness." This led to Meier becoming a world traveler, studying various religious philosophies. He traveled to Jerusalem, Bethlehem, Jordan, West Pakistan, the foot of the Himalaya Mountains, India where he learned Buddhism, and then to Turkey.[8]

Tracing Jesus' Steps

Why did he travel in these areas? He was retracing Jesus' (Meier called him Emmanuel) footsteps. It didn't matter much to Meier that Jesus, except for his flight to Egypt as an infant, never traveled farther than seventy miles from the place of his birth. What mattered to Meier was that these telepathic voices and occasional teachers told him that Jesus was a mystic globetrotter.[9] During these travels through Turkey in 1965 he lost his arm in a freak bus accident.

Meier claims that in India in 1964 Asket let him photograph her flying saucer, which turns out to be his first saucer picture. Even though she claimed to be from a parallel universe, she still needed a flying saucer to enter our realm. At that time she also confided to him that earth's forefathers came from the constellation called Lyra.[10]

It wasn't until January 28, 1975, that Meier had his first contact with Semjase, and she promptly gave him an alternative history of the human race. The blonde-haired woman affirmed that most of the human race descended from aliens from Lyra and that her race also descended from the same source. She added that Pleiadians mated with primitive earth beings thousands of years ago and then colonized it again later. Despite their efforts, earthlings still destroyed the planet twice in its history, and that's part of the reason she was here talking to Meier, she said. She wanted to use Meier to help lead the world into a new age.

> Semjase and the Pleiadians who had chosen to return again to Earth were descendants of a peaceful Lyrian faction that now felt responsible for guiding Earth in its spiritual evolution, so the earth humans could avoid the setbacks long ago experienced by their Pleiadian ancestors.[11]

What Kind of Proof Do We Have for Meier's Claims?

The truth of the Meier case is that we cannot document much of anything he says, even though he claims he has given the world proof. On the contrary we have evidence, as MUFON director Walt Andrus has stated, that a fraud is being perpetrated on the public. Andrus even added that in several of Meier's photographs investigators spotted a balloon that supported a model of a Pleiadian saucer on a string while Meier moved it through different angles.[12]

Meier's chief supporter in the UFO field is Wendelle Stevens of Arizona, but most UFOlogists consider Stevens' support for

Meier's claims a conflict of interest. Why? Because not only has Stevens claimed to have investigated the Meier case, he has also been making money off it. His Genesis III Publishing Co. markets Billy Meier books, tapes, and other assorted materials.

In Stevens' book *UFO...Contact from the Pleiades*, Stevens makes claims that various elements of the Meier case, including metal samples the Pleiadeans allegedly gave Meier and photographic evidence, have all been verified by large testing labs, but he cannot name who they are and therefore cannot back up his claims.

> Unfortunately, though we have used very large and well known industrial and plant laboratories and even the most advanced government research facilities, we must accede to their specific precondition (because of the nature of the subject) that we not reveal the true location of the work, the laboratory or research facility used, or the names of contacts or scientists, leaving the option of such release and its timing to them.[13]

But Kinder's book, though sympathetic to Meier in certain areas, notes that the identification of the testing laboratories was never given, and that a University of Arizona study had already determined that Meier's metal samples were simply potmeal, which is used to make tin items.[14] Furthermore, another metal sample Stevens claimed proved the authenticity of Meier's story disappeared from another laboratory, and although Meier took hundreds of pictures of the alien ships, no one could say whether the photographs were legitimate or not since Meier claimed the originals had been either lost or stolen.[15] Meier also claims he took several pictures of the aliens, including a fuzzy picture of Semjase, but a leading UFOlogist claimed that the woman in the picture was actually Meier's wife in a blonde wig.[16]

Those who still support Meier usually assert an argument that Meier doesn't have a motive or the means to pull off such a fantastically complex hoax. How can a one-armed man do it? some of them ask. But there are plenty of motives, from a need for attention, to a more practical one: material possessions. As

Kinder noted, Meier, a lifelong vagabond who had trouble holding down a job, became so popular that those visiting him are put to work tending his farm.[17] Shirley MacLaine even visited him and she was put to work. According to Kinder, she spent five days with him "helping to weed the garden and trim tree branches by day, and at night probing Meier for answers about the universe."[18] His followers even bought the farm for him at a cost of about $240,000.[19]

Meier's Occult Powers

Meier also has a reputation of having strange powers that some link to the occult. Kinder reported that with Meier's mind power he was able to make a table shake and to melt metal with his bare hands.[20]

But most telling to me, and perhaps it is not so unrelated to his mind powers, is Meier's hatred of orthodox Christianity and his attempts to alter Christianity. Kinder reported that in 1976 Meier began to attack all religion and argued against the "need for worship or belief in God."[21] According to Randolph Winters, a Meier devotee from Los Angeles who produces videos, audio tapes, books, and seminars on Meier's alleged contacts, Meier believes that: "Nowhere else on the planet is there as much negative and hostile energy as there is coming from the Vatican state. The Earth people should know that even though the papacy talks of peace, they have been the major cause of death and suffering on the planet for two thousand years."[22]

But even more to the point is Meier's attitude toward Jesus. Meier basically denies every tenet of the Christian faith, and claims he got his information directly from Jesus in his trip back in time arranged by the aliens.

This happened in 1956 when Meier was nineteen years old, according to a seminar booklet given out by Winters's organization, the Pleiades Project. His guide, Asket, brought him back to the year A.D. 32 when they met with Jesus. "Jesus" allegedly told Meier the following.

1. Judas Iscariot was not a traitor. He was actually Christ's scribe whom Jesus chose to write down the "truth" about his teachings. Judas was instructed to bury his writings, with the hope they would be discovered someday.[23]

2. Jesus explained that he had never been called Jesus Christ. He claimed he knew he would be called that, because his teachings would be falsely rewritten by others to further the religious aims of the apostle Paul.[24] Therefore, what would be written in the Bible about him would be "deceitful lies."

3. He never died on the cross.[25]

4. He denied his virgin birth and told Meier that his father was a man called Ishwich Gabriel, who was apparently trained by the Pleiadians.[26]

5. He denied that he was the Creator or the Son of God.[27]

After Meier returned to 1963, he began to learn more things about Jesus and his "true" mission. What really happened is that Jesus didn't die on a cross; he was in a coma. People from India and Joseph of Arimathaea helped nurse him back to health. Christ then moved to Damascus where he lived for two years and had a dangerous run-in with his bitter enemy, Saul of Tarsus. He then moved on to India with his mother, Mary, his brother Thomas, and Judas. There he spread his "true" teachings, and when he was about forty-five he married a pretty Indian woman who bore him many children. He then settled in Cashmere, India, and died at age 110. Later one of Jesus' sons took the true story of his life back to Israel and hid it in a tomb, where it was finally dug up with Judas's writings in 1963.[28]

Meier claims he knows these matters are true, because he visited the grave site of Jesus in India three times, and during one of the visits he dug into the ground near the grave and found objects that Jesus had left for him to find twenty centuries later.

It's hard to fathom how anyone can believe Meier's story, yet many do. Meier, in fact, has been selling his alternative story of Jesus to the public along with many other booklets of his experiences. For one hundred dollars one can purchase from Winters *The OM*, the book of books; for twenty-five dollars, the prophecies; and for fifteen dollars, the "true" teachings of Jesus.

A False Prophet

Billy Meier is a false prophet who has not only been exposed in the secular media, but his words don't stand up to the Word of God. There is no evidence that anything by way of scrolls confirming what Meier says was uncovered in 1963. Moreover, the way of Billy Meier leads to a denial of the historic person of Jesus Christ, a mistrust of the Bible, an affirmation of Hinduistic ideas including reincarnation, and eventually the occult. I find it extremely interesting that Stevens ties Meier's Pleiadians to the construction of the Great Pyramid, the Parthenon in Ancient Greece, the Devil's Tower in Wyoming, the Great Pyramid of the Sun in Mexico, Machu Pichu and the Nazca Plains in Peru and to other artifacts of the ancient world that attract many occultists.[29]

Could it be that part of the reason the Pleiadians are linked to ancient humankind is they are a part of an ongoing assault on the God of the Bible? The gospel according to Billy Meier is one of reincarnation and faith in the Pleiadians, not to save us from our sins but to show us a more peaceful way to live. Meier even claims that Adam was fifteen feet tall and was seeded on earth by his Pleiadian scientist father.[30] In Meier's view of things, every major biblical truth from creation to the new Jerusalem is radically altered.

Objections Aired Out

I once had the opportunity to discuss my concerns over some of the main teachings of Meier with Winters on a Christian radio show in southern California. Immediately Winters used the platform that day to attack the Bible. Here are some excerpts of that show that aired on KBRT Radio on August 27, 1990, hosted by Tim Barrends.

Randolph Winters (when asked what Meier's aliens say about Jesus): They were quite confused why we spent so much time arguing and fighting over him. That puzzles them a lot, because they regarded him as being, not only one of them, but a very, very highly developed person, and that we had misused his information. . . . As far as the overall general information [being] anti-biblical, I guess, [that] would be a way of saying it, because there is some information coming through Meier from the Pleiadian beings that would challenge common biblical thinking for sure. . . . It's very difficult to get any sort of exacting information on what's really been happening centuries ago. The Bible, of course, has been regarded as our best source, and that is being challenged by the Pleiadians that Billy Meier talks to. And they did draw several references to areas where it's inaccurate, where it's been rewritten, and they even, as far as reincarnation, they pointed out that it was in the Bible for years and provided Meier with copies of earlier documents which show the way it was written years and years ago. Meier has in his possession a book written by Emmanuel at the time when he was alive, stating as they said what he really had to say. And there are some strong differences in there. I have a copy of that, and that definitely goes against many of the things that are in the Bible, so it certainly opens your mind up and starts challenging you. . . .

Bill Alnor: Let me just respond to something that Randolph said which makes people who are apologists a little upset when we hear that the Bible has been rewritten many times. The evidence of history just doesn't accept that whatsoever. In fact, we have the Dead Sea scrolls that were unearthed in the 1940s that showed that the version of the Bible that we had during the time of Christ, the Old Testament, is exactly the same as we have today. And there have been many New Age sources that have tried to say that, and they've been decisively debunked, not only debunked today, but debunked for centuries about this whole concept that the Bible once taught reincarnation and that it had been rewritten over the centuries. It's a bunch of garbage.

Randolph Winters: They said that Jesus was a man who lived and was born just like us, and that was one of the areas where we had taken some liberties historically with who he was. He was not Lord of the universe. . . .

Bill Alnor: At one point he (Meier) claims that aliens took him back in time to talk to the real Jesus, and that real Jesus affirmed the fact that he claimed he wasn't God. Now when you look at this and compare it with the Scripture, what we have here is that the Jesus that Billy Meier and the aliens have is not the Jesus of the Bible, because Jesus said, I am the way. . . .

Randolph Winters: I was raised in a family. My mother was one of the directors of the Episcopal Church and my two brothers are ministers. I certainly grew up within it and am well versed; I could probably still recite the Nicene Creed if I thought about it for a second. I spent my years as an acolyte. I found just for myself in growing up that it was not satisfying to me, that the Scripture itself, I had too many doubts. I frankly did not believe the concept that Jesus Christ was Lord. It never made too much sense to me from the scale of the universe. I had a lot of trouble with that personally; probably that alone is one of the reasons for my own unrest to search things out and look for things. . . . Now personally, for me the Bible is not satisfying.

Bill Alnor: I think that perhaps he's been influenced by a dead kind of church life. He hasn't experienced the real Jesus in his life, and if he had he wouldn't say that.

Stuart Goldman (the Christian who investigated Whitley Strieber): The new interest in UFOs is really just a by-product of the general acceptance of New Age kind of thinking. . . . I know it sounds funny for people to say, Don't keep an open mind, but keeping an open mind has become a catch-all phrase for accepting false doctrine.

Final Thoughts

Billy Meier has ignored some of the most remarkable aspects about Scripture and about the nature of Christ. To attack Scripture as Meier has done is to attack God's very words. "All Scripture is God-breathed," according to 2 Timothy 3:16, "and is useful for teaching, rebuking, correcting and training in righteousness."

Scripture demolishes the concept of reincarnation, not affirms it, and despite New Agers' claims, there is no evidence at all that reincarnation was ever written out of the Bible. We have extensive historical records from the church fathers, such as Justin Martyr and others, and from church councils that show them rejecting reincarnation as "contrary to the Christian faith." Many New Agers today (including Shirley MacLaine), claim reincarnation was written out of the Bible at the Second Council of Constantinople in A.D. 553, but a close look at the facts indicates that the New Testament canon was closed, at the latest, in the fourth century and that the council "had nothing to do with reincarnation."[31]

And the implication that Jesus' "true" teachings had been lost for almost 2,000 years until Meier and his associates recovered them is a malicious attack on Christ's faithfulness to his church. The last thing Jesus said to his disciples in the Gospel of Matthew was, "I am with you always, to the very end of the age" (28:20). Burying scrolls in the ground in Israel for recovery 2,000 years later (leaving humankind in spiritual darkness for that period) is not the work of the Jesus of the Bible, who calls himself the Light of the World. Only Satan operates in darkness, seeking to confuse and devour.

Meier's Jesus is a different Jesus preaching a different gospel.

The Attack on Christ Comes Through Other Channels

As far out as Billy Meier's theories are, he does share common roots with many others in the New Age-UFO movement. In fact, almost across the board the gospel according to extraterrestrial messengers attacks the nature of Christ and the authority of God's Word. In almost every channeled message I've seen from the space brothers from around the globe, they immediately attack Christ, Christianity, and God's Word. Let's look at more examples.

The Bible

A 1990 issue of Timothy Beckley's *UFO Review* ran a prominent article called "A Message to Earth from Space Brother

Tibus." It was channeled through Diane Tessman, a fairly well-known New Ager popular with the UFO crowd. As is usually the case, it doesn't take long (the third paragraph of the message) for Tibus to criticize Christians and the Bible. Here are some excerpts from Tibus's message:

> The breaking down of thousands of years of Earth's spiritual level will allow a new, higher vibration to wash in and cleanse this troubled world. A new rush of higher consciousness will raise the spiritual level to new heights, never before experienced on planet Earth. . . .
>
> Many people, however, are hesitant or afraid to work with the spirit anew. They feel secure and comfortable in their old watered-down, dogmatic explanations of spirituality. They blindly accept the old definitions given by organized religion of what the spirit is. These people accept that Biblical writings are psychic channelings but they will not listen to the current space channeling which is being done by enlightened men and women the world over. . . .
>
> What makes these 1990s different is that Earthers can no longer hold onto outdated, unusable beliefs nor can they cling to the dogmatic definitions and perceptions of spirituality. The old definitions and beliefs simply will not work anymore.
>
> We stress that the basic channeled messages of the Bible are wondrous and valid. It is thus with the holy writings of other religions. However, it is the MISUNDERSTANDING of such writing which has proved very detrimental to the human race for hundreds and hundreds of years now.[32]

Other contactees and UFOnauts have other things to say about the Bible. Dr. Fred Bell of California, who also claims to have had many contacts with Semjase the Pleiadian, announced at the Whole Life Expo in New York that the Bible had been edited, which resulted in its original meaning being altered.[33]

Raphael, the extraterrestrial being behind Ken Carey's "Starseed Transmissions," claims that the second coming of Christ proclaimed in the Bible has been widely misunderstood. "It is the event that primitive civilizations have looked forward to as 'the return of the gods,'" Raphael said. "The Mayans went so far as to pinpoint its actual occurrence in what you would call the year 2011 A.D." He then implies that the Bible may have been responsible for the misunderstanding. "You must realize that God did not invent the words used in scripture. He merely arranged them in the order most approximating His meaning."

The Aetherius Society is another UFO group working on its own bible. They, too, believe the Bible that has come to us has been altered. Locked in underground vaults in Los Angeles and London are a collection of 620 "transmissions" founder George King received from various "cosmic masters" sources. The tapes are there, according to a *Los Angeles Herald Examiner* article, so that "future generations will not have to rely upon the . . . inaccuracies of secondhand reporting of great events."

"Imagine if we had a videotape of the Sermon on the Mount," an Aetherius Society official told the newspaper. "This is the equivalent."[34]

The space brothers told contactee John Dean that we should trust some of the ancient books that were rejected for being part of the Bible. They also told him reincarnation was a fact and two of the extraterrestrial beings sending him messages, Laskon and Zagga, claimed to be immortal. "Spacemen have told us that many of our prophets were, at one time, members of the solar tribunal on Saturn—masters and doubtless immortals," Dean wrote. "We may learn much from the rejected books of both the Old and New Testaments, but those approved as 'canonical' barely suggest reincarnation."[35]

This issue of accepting books long rejected by various councils in both Christianity and Judaism is a hot one to extraterrestrial beings. What they usually refer to as books worthy of consideration alongside the Psalms, Genesis, and Matthew, Mark, Luke, and John, are various ancient mystical occult books. Some UFO enthusiasts even believe the mystical Jewish Cabala is on a par with Scripture. But all the books they believe should be part of the Bible were rejected for various reasons, the main one being that scholars did not believe them to be credible or inspired by God. In UFO literature today many go to a somewhat modern source, *The Aquarian Gospel and Jesus the Christ,* by Levi Dowling (1844–1911), and they urge its acceptance, despite the fact Dowling was not alive in the first century to write about Christ. Dowling got his information between two and six every morning, and he received it via "an occult form of subjective (nonverifiable) illumination," notes Ron Rhodes.[36]

Attacking Christ's Words and His Mission

Reinhold Schmidt, a popular contactee in the 1950s, had a lot to say about Jesus. One day, he claims, an alien named Mr. X took him aboard a flying saucer, took him to Egypt, and told him that spacemen had built the Great Pyramid. Inside the Pyramid the alien took him into a secret room containing a small flying saucer, and inside the saucer he spotted the cross Christ was crucified on, along with a crown of thorns, sandals, and a robe. Schmidt said the alien told him that the saucer was the vehicle through which Jesus ascended to his home planet Venus. Mr. X told him that the saucer and relics would someday be shown to the world when people are more willing to accept "Universal Laws and Truths." Schmidt claims he was also shown new sacred writings and new prophecies of the future that indicate 1998 will mark the beginning of a new era that will be a "preparation for the coming of the Master."[37] Jesus was not identified as the master.

Today in the world of the space brothers even lying messages from counterfeit Jesuses are commonplace. In fact, Jesus, or Sananda as most New Age-UFO enthusiasts call him, is right behind Ashtar as the entity most commonly channeled. And these supposed messages from "Jesus" all have several things in common: They attack the person, nature, and work of the historical Jesus Christ. They especially attack Christ's death on the cross 2,000 years ago to save people from their sins. This counterfeit Jesus always attacks Christianity and claims the Bible is not reliable.

In Winfield Brownell's channeling session from Jesus dated November 29, 1978, Jesus says that the early church simply taught ethics, the golden rule, but the church later warped his true teaching; claims he is beginning an outpouring of his "holy spirit" that will help bring in the new age; claims the Bible was wrong in many places, that he didn't die on the cross to forgive sins and instead his mission was to show humankind the truth of reincarnation; claims that he never taught about the existence of hell and that to believe in it is a "blasphemous insult"; claims that no more evil exists in the world today, for he took it all away. He concludes by pushing the Aquarian gospel as an "accurate . . . excellent account of my life on Earth."[38]

I could easily cite more than a dozen channeled messages from the space brother Jesus in these pages, but to do so would prolong the point. The Jesus of the UFOnauts is not the Jesus of the Bible. It's a different one, and as mentioned before, Jesus himself warned us not to accept anyone else coming in his name, no matter what the source. Jesus said that in the days leading to his second coming many false christs would deceive the world.

Additionally, those UFO enthusiasts who channel lying messages from the counterfeit Jesus are directly tied in to occultism and the New Age movement. Sandra Michael of San Diego, who claims to practice Huna Kane (Hawaiian) shamanism, says that the Pleiadeans taught their advanced mysterious occultism to the dwellers of the lost continent of Lemuria from where the secret knowledge was transferred to Hawaii. Using Huna Kane principles, she channels various entities, including a counterfeit Jesus. In a tape of her channeling "Jesus," the entity says that many have done a "great disservice" over the centuries by misrepresenting his teachings. He further goes on to declare God as "the father and the mother," that humans "are perfect Christ beings," and that the planet itself is a "living being."[39]

Along the same vein, Benjamin Creme's Lord Maitreya, who he claims is the messiah, the Islamic Mahdi, Buddha, Krishna, and the Christ, has also given us lying messages. According to Creme's Fall 1990 newsletter published before Desert Storm, which features Lord Maitreya's "forecasts," Maitreya claimed: "The Iraqi leader [Hussein] is not as bad as he is painted by the Western media. . . . He is a man with a generous heart. . . . He is also being made aware that it is against the sacred law to invade another country. He will quietly hand Kuwait back to the people."[40]

But the messages of all the counterfeit Jesuses being channeled from space are the same as the messages allegedly received from Jesus by automatic writers and occultists. The Jesus who allegedly channeled the popular *Course in Miracles* book, an alternative New Age religious movement, said he did not die on the cross, and he did not claim to be exclusive. The Jesus who revealed himself through automatic writing to two Connecticut women who wrote the 1979 book *The Jesus Letters* (which carried with it an endorsement from Norman Vincent Peale on large advertisements in at least one New Age catalogue)[41] affirmed reincarnation and monism: "Be one with the universe for all are one"; declared that abortion is acceptable because it's the fetus's fault he is aborted: during pregnancy the reincarnated soul planted in the mother changes his mind about wanting to come back to earth for another incarnation, so the baby tells the mother he doesn't want to be born, and the mother then follows through to abortion; said that the New Testament is not to be taken literally and the Bible is not the final authority.[42]

Most telling, however, is that the Jesus of *The Jesus Letters* says the same thing about the cross—the very thing that makes it possible for us to have peace with God—as the space brothers' Jesus: that the cross is not needed:

> The doctrine of vicarious attonement [*sic*] of letting Jesus pay for your sins by dying on the cross is a misunderstanding. The idea that Jesus could die for your sins before you have committed them implies that man is going to be evil. That is not true. Man does not need to be evil. Man is born a god.[43]

The Gospel According to a French Race-Car Driver

A blatant attack on Christ and the Bible also forms the centerpiece of the rapidly growing Raelean movement founded by French writer and race-car driver Claude Vorilhon (allegedly renamed Rael by the space aliens).

In a booklet entitled *Help Us Welcome Extraterrestrials*, Voril-hon claims that on December 13, 1973, "in a volcanic crater located in the center of France," he "met with a space-craft from which emerged a small human-like being" that looked like a child. Vorilhon said the space being chose him as the one to spread "the greatest message ever revealed to human-ity," and that he would be an apostle of a new world order.

The message was that he was to prepare humanity "for the Age of Apocalypse to the Age of Revelation," which was kicked off by the explosion of the first atomic bomb in 1945. The space being also told him that life was created by aliens from the ELOHIM planet in a DNA laboratory.[44] According to Raelian theology, people from the Judeo-Christian tradition have been mistaken in referring to God as monotheistic and singular. What they have mistakenly been referring to in the singular is the ELOHIM, which in reality is the plural for many space aliens who helped create humanity.

Vorilhon, like other contactees, has rewritten the Bible to give us an alternative account of the life of Christ, his purpose, and variant readings of some of the biblical stories, including the creation story. Jesus was part alien, he asserts, who was revived by other aliens called the ELOHIM after his crucifix-ion. Rael, however, leaves out the essential element of Christ's death on the cross—the sacrificial payment for the sins of the world. Instead Vorilhon writes in his book *The Message Given to Me By Extraterrestrials* that Jesus' purpose on earth was to help us advance scientifically and medically to make room for the return of the ELOHIM to the planet.[45]

Vorilhon has also claimed to have been transported to the ELOHIM planet where he received many new revelations. He said that he met Satan while on the ELOHIM planet, and that he is actually a good guy, "the bearer of light" who first revealed to humankind that the gods were not divine but simply people like themselves.[46] Satan was also a scientist who helped cre-ate humanity in a laboratory.

The Raelian movement is surprisingly large and organized. It claims 30,000 members worldwide and has more than a dozen offices throughout the world—including ones in Japan, Africa,

Switzerland, Mexico, Canada, and three in the United States in Los Angeles, Las Vegas, and Miami.[47]

I went to a workshop headed by the Raelians in New York recently and was struck by the sect's logo (a swastika inside a star of David), as well as the hippylike demeanor of most of their members. At the seminar attended by about twenty people we were told that the number 666 referred to in the Bible is the number of generations, since humankind was created in a laboratory, before the ELOHIM return to Planet Earth.

"Six-Six-Six . . . is not a beast," said Marie-Helene Parent of the sect's Canadian office. "It's not a monster." What it refers to is the number of generations they would let pass before the ELOHIM would come back to earth around 2025.[48] Accordingly, the Raelians have been pooling their resources to "build an embassy in Jerusalem, to accommodate extraterrestrials when they eventually return to this earth."[49]

UFO writer Jacques Vallee has a dim view of Vorilhon's movement. In *Messengers of Deception* Vallee notes that Vorilhon has written that the ELOHIM told him that they "want us to destroy democracy after selecting as a prophet a man born in France"[50]—himself!

11 Ancient Tall Tales from the Ruler of the Air

One of the most prevalent misconceptions stemming from the modern UFO movement is that the flying saucer phenomenon is new. Most of today's UFO enthusiasts would have us believe that after Kenneth Arnold's 1947 sighting extraterrestrial beings stepped up their visitations of earth and are trying to help us join them in a new era.

But the evidence is overwhelming and inescapable that UFOs, even waves of UFOs, have been with us since time itself, even coexisting with us. A long tradition of alien contact with humans dates into the ancient past.

Whitley Strieber is among the few modern writers to make this ancient connection. It made sense to him, since he never came up with clear answers to the identity of "the visitors" who would kidnap and experiment on him in the middle of the night. Near the end of *Transformation* he wrote:

> The "visitor experience" is old. Two hundred years ago a farmer might have come in from his plowing and said, "I saw fairies dancing in the glen." A thousand years ago he might have seen angels flying. Two thousand years ago it would have been Dionysus leaping in the fields. Four thousand years ago he might have seen the goddess Earth herself walking those old hills, her starry robe sparkling with the pure light of magic. . . . We hide from the visitors. We hide in beliefs. They're the gods. They're gentry, dwarfs, elves. They're demons or angels. Aliens. The uncon-

scious. The oversoul. Hallucinations. Mass hysteria. Lies. You name it. But what they never are, what we never allow ourselves to face, is the truth.[1]

Brad Steiger also knows about an ancient historical connection between aliens and people, and he affirms a strong link among today's star people, ancient Native American and Incan legends, and legends of fairies in the British Isles of old. In fact, he says, many of today's star people "have had continuing series of episodes with 'angles,' 'elves,' 'fairies,' 'masters,' 'teachers,' and openly declared 'UFO intelligences.'"[2]

They Change Shapes

One of the most interesting things about UFO sightings throughout history is that they change speeds and shapes, depending upon the era in which we are living. The end result is total confusion and an assurance that humankind will never get to the bottom of the UFO mystery. One of the most interesting contemporary changes UFOs have gone through during this century is a gradual general change from cigar shapes in the early to middle part of the century, to a disk shape following Kenneth Arnold's 1947 sighting, and now a triangular shape.[3]

This is not to say people don't see flying disks or saucers anymore; many claim they do. It's just that the flying triangle is now the most often reported shape of the UFO. A striking example of this is the tremendous amount of triangular UFO sightings seen over Belgium. According to the October 10, 1990, *Wall Street Journal*, more than 2,600 sightings of triangular UFOs were reported there the previous year.

And the enigma of the triangle has been with us in recent contactee experiences as well. Whitley Strieber claims the visitors placed a triangle figure on his body to symbolize a new trinity that could be formed when humankind merges with the visitors.[4] Barbara Schutte, the former contactee who became a Christian, says that a triangle mark was also placed on her neck, and she knows another contactee branded with the same mark.

She now believes, however, that the marks have a satanic or New Age significance.[5]

The Prince of the Power of the Air

I believe that the triangles appearing in the sky and on people in recent times are part of a delusion to keep us looking into the sky for hidden occult meanings rather than to God who has revealed himself clearly to humanity. I also believe most, if not all, the UFO sightings and actual contacts with alleged aliens are more evidence that humankind has been toyed with by evil forces for a long, long time.

In Ephesians 2:2 Satan is referred to as the "ruler of the kingdom of the air, the spirit who is now at work in those who are disobedient." And we know from various parts of the Bible that Satan has the power to manipulate matter at times, sometimes physically, and at other times by causing people to see strange things. When Jesus was tempted in the wilderness for forty days, Satan caused him to see intricate visions in his failed bid to alter Christ's mission. Perhaps this ability is one reason why Christ so firmly warned his disciples about religious deception even to the point of "great signs from heaven" (Luke 21:11) in the era of his return.

Ancient Lies from the Ruler of the Kingdom of the Air

I believe that Satan has been preparing humankind for confusion throughout history, and as we get even closer to the time of Christ's return, many of Satan's centuries-old occult lies are coalescing, making it easier for people to accept false religious ideas even within the Christian church. In the same way, he has induced people through pagan religions to build triangular pyramids on divergent sites throughout the ancient world, such as in Mexico's Yucatan Peninsula and in Egypt, to make humankind today believe there is something significant in pyramids.

Christianity stands alone among all the world's religions. It is not one religion among many that is valid. It claims to be the only valid way to God. And that truth is precisely the main point the gospel according to extraterrestrial beings will deny every time.

The Descent of Sky Gods

The forces of evil and the gods of the UFOnauts were there with the formation of the false religion of Shinto in Japan, an ancient religion that fuses ancestor worship with mysticism. The early source books that reinforced the mythology behind the religion are the *Kojiki,* "Record of Ancient Things" (A.D. 712), and the *Nihongi* or *Nihonshoki,* "Records of Japan" (A.D. 720). These books emphasize the divine descent of the imperial house, "but," wrote religious historian Robert S. Ellwood, Jr., "they also exemplify the main theses of Shinto myth in general—the descent of sky gods to marry earth goddesses."[6]

Today in Japan UFOlogy is big business. The Japanese public eagerly follow many of the recent developments of UFOlogy, and some UFOlogists believe the Shinto traditions are part of the reason for its popularity. As one UFO conference attendee recently noted, many Japanese are interested in the possibility they could find, through UFO research, certain windows in the atmosphere that serve as a link between the world of the gods and our own. In November 1990, a large international UFO conference took place in Hakui, Japan, which was attended by a number of government officials. Prime Minister Toshiki Kaifu's message declaring that it was time to take the UFO phenomena seriously was read to the large gathering.[7]

Likewise, in the ancient *Bhagavad-gita,* one of the primary texts of Hinduism, are references to beings from other realms coming to Earth. A. C. Bhaktivedanta Swami Prabhupada, who gained a great number of followers in the 1960s as the founder of the Hindu-based Hare Krishna movement, even released a widely read translation that inserted the word *planets,* meaning alien planets, to describe other realms as origin-travel points of the gods.[8] While some would, no doubt, argue with Prabhupada's choice of the word *planet* in the text, early Hindu literature that predates Christianity by a millennium contains various references to flying "celestial and aerial cars" and even flying disks.[9]

Other ancient religious traditions contain references to "the gods" coming to earth to mingle with humankind. Brad Steiger tells us that the legends of the Eskimos tell of their ancestors being flown about by "god-like beings with metallic wings." Steiger is among a growing number of New Agers who are being attracted to Native American and South American shamanistic religions, and he, along with many others, is quite willing to link them with aliens. Steiger claims that the bible of the Quiches tribes in Guatemala talks about visitors coming from the skies, bringing with them unusual knowledge.[10]

When Brad and Sherry Steiger returned from their September 1990 tour of the ancient cities of Peru they claimed they had found new evidence that the Inca Indians were really *Inkas*— visitors from the stars who are returning to earth today to help usher in a new age of shamanism. The Steigers claim that the Inka visitors' alien powers enabled the Incas to build many of the dramatic ancient ruins in South America including the Nasca Lines, the Pyramid of the Sun of Pachacama, the Sun Temple in Cusco, and the mountain city of Machu Picchu. Steiger, who claims that the mythology of Peru verifies their origin, told *UFO Review* this about the Inka aliens:

> [They] came to our planet as part of a well-designed scientific plan, a plan that has remained in ritual outline in the teachings of the wise ones, the shamans, of many cultures. Understand the true meaning of the ancient rituals, and one receives a much clearer understanding of the actual purpose of the UFO intelligences.[11]

The UFOnauts Trifle with Western Man

While there is reason to doubt many ancient myths from Far Eastern and Indian cultures on alleged visitations from space, the factual chroniclers of other traditions, including those from the Western world, have also given us ample evidence that someone, or something, has been toying with humanity for a long time through strange happenings in the sky.

Kenneth Arnold wasn't even the first person to coin the term *flying saucer.* According to Jacques Vallee, John Martin, a farmer from Texas, saw a flying disk cruising high in the sky at an enormous speed on January 24, 1878, and he used the term *saucer* to describe it.[12]

But in past centuries they have taken on many other forms. "It is interesting to find that reports were made, and in practically the same terms as the modern ones, concerning strange vehicles flying across the sky long before the advent of Christ," notes Vallee.[13] In Vallee's book *Anatomy of a Phenomenon* he notes that he has on file reports of more than three hundred UFO sightings prior to the twentieth century.

In the annals of Thutmose III of Egypt, who reigned about 1480–1450 B.C., it is recorded that a circle of fire appeared in the sky, and after a time "these things became more numerous in the sky than ever. . . . the army of the pharaoh looked on with him in their midst" when the first circles rose higher in the sky.[14]

Vallee notes, quoting ancient books, that in 218 B.C. there was a UFO wave in the Roman Empire. Strange men in white clothing appeared in various places, a "shield" flew through the sky, two moons appeared at night, ghost ships appeared in the sky, and at other places "luminous lamps" appeared in the heavens.[15] Other Roman writers such as Pliny, Seneca, Julius Obsequens, and Joannes Lydus, also wrote of "flying columns and flying shields" that allegedly zoomed throughout the empire.[16]

In Scotland in A.D. 60 a ship was often seen speeding across the sky.[17] Vallee lists other sightings.

In 919, in Hungary, spherical objects shining like stars, bright and polished, were reported going to and fro in the sky. Somewhere at sea, on July 29 or 30 in the year 966, a luminous vertical cylinder was seen. . . . In Japan, on August 23, 1015, two objects were seen giving birth to smaller luminous spheres. At Cairo in August 1027, numerous noisy objects were reported. A large silvery disk is said to have come close to the ground in Japan on August 12, 1133.[18]

Similar reports continued through the Middle Ages to the twentieth century. John Weldon and Zola Levitt document that just four hours before he discovered land in 1492, Christopher Columbus, standing on the deck of his wooden ship, reported lights moving up and down in the distant sky.[19]

Cases of Alien Visitors Are Also Old

Not only is it a myth that UFOs and their passengers have recently become interested in man and began showing up in large numbers during this century, it is also false that alien beings have been contacting people primarily during this century. According to W. R. Drake, "Agobard, Archbishop of Lyons, wrote in "De Grandine et Tonitrua" how in A.D. 840 he found the mob in Lyons lynching three men and a woman accused of landing from a cloudship from the aerial region of Magonia."[20]

Weldon and Levitt also told the story of how a fifteenth-century European was confronted by seven "men" who appeared to him. They wrote:

> They claimed to be made of air, denied the immortality of the soul, and also denied that God had made the world for all eternity. They seemed interested in theological matters, and they described a system wherein God is constantly recreating the world.[21]

In fact, prior to 1947, a whole body of occult literature discusses creatures from other dimensions contacting humankind. But the difference between earlier times and today is that they were not usually seen as aliens from other planets but were associated with "religious beliefs, and were treated as manifestations of supernatural forces."[22]

Coming into this century they were known by a variety of names, including elves, fairies, goblins, gnomes, "wee folk," and many other titles, depending on the culture. Legends grew up about them. In medieval folklore they were seen as coming from a mythical land above the clouds known as Magonia, or the land of the fairy. In fact, some argue that these fairies, long associated with the occult, are in reality demons posing as aliens today in an attempt to trick humankind. According to occult literature fairies and elves have a long history of being tricksters. To understand how prominent fairies figured into folklore one has to read no further than Shakespeare's *A Midsummer Night's Dream* to find Puck, the mischievous fairy, trying to manipulate circumstances in people's lives.

Historically fairies have also been linked to building mounds in the fields and dancing in crop fields making circles. Some have suggested that the crop circles showing up in increasing numbers throughout the world could really be these "fairy rings."[23]

But one thing is certain: Fairies, elves, gnomes, goblins, sylphs, and other entities have always, until the UFO enigma of today, been associated with evil, satanic forces, and not with the God of the Bible. Some varieties of these otherwordly beings have been directly accused of being demons.

Some of Whitley Strieber's experiences with the visitors, for example, are sexual. He admits having been sexually attracted and aroused by one of the visitors and to being in love with them. And in light of the fact that many contactees talk about being afflicted by the visitors with strange sexual rituals and "operations," he talks frankly about the possibility they may be incubi or succubi, demonic creatures who allegedly rape humans.

> It is terrifying, of course. But reflect also that mankind has had a sexual relationship with the fairies, the sylphs, the incubi, the succubi, and the denizens of the night from the very beginning of time. Nowadays men find themselves on examining tables in flying saucers with vacuum devices attached to their privates, while women must endure the very real agony of having their pregnancies disappear, a torment that I, as a man, doubt I can really imagine.[24]

But instead of accepting the traditional view of the incubi and succubi as evil demons bent on destroying humanity, Strieber again lapses into illogical reasoning and writes that he sees them as saviors, and hints that their lives may be linked to our own. One astounding thing is that he lists the horrors these beings are allegedly engaged in, then makes the statement about them being saviors. He claims they may be "trying to save us from ourselves," because without humans their lives may be "less exciting. . . . Maybe there really is another species living upon this earth, the fairies, the gnomes, the sylphs, vampires, goblins, who attach to reality along a different line than we do, but who know and love us."[25]

There Is Nothing Good about Demons

"According to many Church Fathers," writes Rossell H. Robbins in *The Encyclopedia of Witchcraft and Demonology*, "an incubus is an angel who fell because of lust for women. Essentially the incubus is a lewd demon or goblin which seeks sexual intercourse with women. It is also termed *follet* (French), *Alp* (German), *duende* (Spanish), and *folletto* (Italian). The corresponding devil who appears to men is the succubus."[26]

Robbins writes that many church figures, including Thomas Aquinas in the thirteenth century, believed such beings existed, and that later demonologists believed that the "lowest order of devils functioned as incubi." Reports of these demon lovers are of "such universal appeal" that the incubus, "in the literature of the demonologists, takes first place."[27]

Aside from UFO literature, the idea of human-raping demons is still widely referred to. In a top-secret tract released by Moses David (a.k.a. David Berg) the reclusive leader of the Children of God ("Family of Love") cult, he talks about how such spirit lovers come to him on occasion, and sometimes they were physically so rough on him sexually he feared they would hurt him. It's interesting to note that not a word of such beings was ever uttered in Children of God literature until after the cult became one of the most debased, morally degenerate cults in the modern world. In recent years Berg has moved far away from the Bible and has tolerated homosexuality, religious prostitution, mass orgies, and has promoted experimenting sexually with children. He has even redefined the concept of the Holy Spirit as a near-naked woman who was God's lover.

The Church of Jesus Christ of Latter Day Saints

If Joseph Smith, founder of Mormonism, were alive today, he would be considered a contactee, wrote Jacques Vallee.[28] At one time during the advent of the religion in the nineteenth century most people rejected Smith's beliefs, but today the church has grown to include 7.3 million members throughout the world.[29]

In 1823, in an era when more people believed in angels than in visitors from space, an "angel" named Moroni allegedly appeared at Smith's bedside in upper New York State and recommissioned him as a prophet to launch a new dispensation of Christianity that would restore the apostate church. In 1820 Smith allegedly received a vision claiming that he was God's new prophet. Moroni allegedly told young Joseph, who had a habit of digging for lost treasure in the nearby hills utilizing magical stones for guidance, that he would find golden plates with a new message for humanity.[30]

Walter Martin writes:

> In 1827 Smith claimed to receive the golden plates upon which the *Book of Mormon* is alleged to have been written. Shortly after this historic find, unearthed in the hill Cumorah near Palmyra, New York, Smith began to "translate" the "reformed Egyptian" hieroglyphics inscribed thereupon by means of the "Urim and Thummim," a type of miraculous spectacles which the always thoughtful angel Moroni had the foresight to provide for the budding seer.[31]

The end result of the Book of Mormon is a new religion that denies some major tenets of orthodox Christianity, and like the ancient religions that talk about life in space and otherwordly visitors, is very much a space-based religion. And just as contemporary New Agers declare that humans are actually gods, Mormonism teaches a similar doctrine, although this concept is not found in the Book of Mormon, according to cult expert

James Bjornstad. In Mormon theology the Christian concept of heaven is redefined to state that believers will preside over their own planet upon death.

James Walker, a former fourth-generation Mormon who now directs the Texas office of the evangelical watchdog group, Watchman Fellowship, said this of Mormonism:

> Mormonism is in a whole different family. . . . Mormonism is based on polytheism. They believe God used to be a man named Elohim on another planet on a star named Kolab and because he was such a good man the other gods allowed him to become one of the gods. He lives on this planet with his goddess wives having billions of offspring. Everyone of us on this earth today were born first to our heavenly father and heavenly mother and Mormonism teaches that if we join the Mormon church and attend the secret Mormon rituals and obey all the commandments, we too will have a chance of godhood . . . over another planet somewhere.[32]

It turns out that Mormonism has many links with space. Smith taught that the moon was inhabited and that he would someday preach his gospel there.[33]

The Church of Scientology

Just after World War II two of the most ardent members of Aleister Crowley's Ordo Templi Orientis (O.T.O.) branch in Los Angeles were propulsion engineer Jack Parsons and L. Ron Hubbard, a science fiction writer. Parsons claimed he "met a Venusian in the desert in 1946." Later Hubbard, who died in 1986, founded the Church of Scientology.[34] Today church officials try to downplay Hubbard's connection with Crowley, who called himself "666, the Beast," but it is not reciprocated by the O.T.O. Kenneth Grant, Crowley's successor as head of the O.T.O., proudly wrote that Crowley was the "first modern occultist to demonstrate the existence of superior alien intelligences." Grant also stated that Hubbard was somehow connected with subsequent contact with extraterrestrials.[35]

An article in *Cornerstone* noted:

Alexander Mitchell, an *English Sunday Times* journalist, claims
that Hubbard was once practicing witchcraft with John Parsons
[and that] Parsons says Hubbard acted as high priest during several occult rituals which included acts of sexual perversion.[36]

Even though Hubbard wrote science fiction novels, his life
also revolved around science fiction themes. *Cornerstone* said
that Hubbard "claims to have visited Venus, the Van Allen Radi-
ation Belt and heaven twice. Of course, this happened in his
other lifetimes many trillions of years ago."[37]

Speaking before a writers' conference in New Jersey in 1949,
Hubbard said, "Writing for a penny a word is ridiculous. If a
man really wanted to make a million dollars, the best way
would be to start his own religion." After the publication of
his 1950 book *Dianetics: The Modern Science of Mental Health*,
that's exactly was he did; he founded Scientology.[38] To this day
critics worldwide have accused Scientology of not being a religion at all but rather a moneymaking scheme and personality
cult fashioned around the legacy of Hubbard.

As many other religions have done in the past, Scientology
projects outerspace mythology (that sounds like it comes from
the pages of science fiction) directly into its doctrine. A Spiritual Counterfeits Project fact sheet on Scientology reports this:

> Ultimate reality, Hubbard has come to teach, is populated by
> "Thetans," or gods—eternal, uncreated, omnipotent, omni-
> scient, personal beings, free from all laws, all cause-effect rela-
> tionships, and all other Thetans. However, by collective agree-
> ment, the spiritual Thetans submitted to one another and
> created the Material-Energy-Space-Time (M-E-S-T) universe
> external to themselves.[39]

Later these Thetans reincarnated into the bodies of animals
and plants and eventually, through evolution, they ascended
into man. However, by the time of the advent of man, the omniscient Thetans forgot about their divine heritage and they had to
be awakened. In the 1960s Hubbard added new twists to his
religion: The Thetans were actually banished to earth seventy-

five million years ago by a "cruel galactic ruler named Xenu." A person who wanted to follow his religion faithfully had to audit those Thetans (for a large monetary fee) so he or she could eventually achieve a state of "clear," which is equivalent to the godhood promised by New Agers.[40]

Ralph Lee Smith, writing in *Today's Health,* said that this space-based theology led to myths of incredible ingenuity.

> One preclear [student of Scientology] said that this Thetan . . . had inhabited the body of a doll on the planet Mars, 469,476,600 years ago. Martians seized the doll and took it to a temple, where it was zapped by a bishop's gun while the congregation chanted "God is Love." The Thetan was then put into an ice cube, placed aboard a flying saucer, and dropped off at Planet ZX 432, where it was given a robot body, then put to work unloading flying saucers. Being a bit unruly, it zapped another robot to death and was shipped off in a flying saucer to be punished. But the flying saucer exploded, and the Thetan fell into space.[41]

The serious student wishing to go higher in Scientology would also have to have some "body" Thetans released, which are negative spiritual beings that have "been asleep or unconscious inside you for millions of years." Total cost for the step-by-step process, according to *Time*: $200,000 to $400,000.[42]

Today, although followers of both Mormonism and Scientology in their early days were regarded as crackpots from the lunatic fringe, so far out that they didn't deserve a hearing by the average person, both religions have become international organizations with fabulous wealth, bent upon achieving worldwide dominance. And it is this concern over growing extraterrestrially based religious movements that has Jacques Vallee concerned that they might be part of a conspiracy by "manipulators" to "change our belief systems."[43]

He adds, writing from a secular perspective, that society may be vulnerable to UFO manipulation because some institutions have been weakened. "In the eighteenth and nineteenth centuries," Vallee writes, "a group leader attempting to start a new cult based on revelation was likely to be opposed by the combined powers of church and state." But today an attitude exists in society and in the media of tolerating groups with extreme beliefs.[44]

Vallee has a very chilling view of UFOs:

> UFOs are real. They are an application of psychotronic technology; that is, they are physical devices used to affect human consciousness. They may not be from outer space; they may, in fact, be terrestrial-based manipulating devices. Their purpose may be to achieve social changes on this planet.[45]

The Urantia Book Is Revealed

Another growing religion firmly linked to the stars follows the teachings of the over-two-thousand-page *Urantia Book* which purports to have been penned (through channeling) by "numerous supermortal (angel-like) beings" working in accord with a small group of people headed by a Chicago psychiatrist in the 1920s.[46] According to Urantia literature the true identity of the person used in the channeling sessions would never be revealed, which would help the book speak for itself.

But in 1991 Martin Gardner, a columnist for the *Skeptical Inquirer,* completed some six months of sleuthing and announced in his column, even offering good proof, that the *Urantia Book*'s channeler was Wilfred Kellogg, son of Rev. Charles Kellogg who was related to W. K. Kellogg, the founder of the Kellogg Company in Battle Creek, Michigan.[47]

Wilfred Kellogg died in 1956, but he was a founding trustee of the Urantia Foundation, and he was business manager of another key figure in the movement, Dr. William Sadler, whose building served as the headquarters of the Urantia Foundation. (Today followers of the *Urantia Book* may also belong to another organization called the Jesusonian Foundation, based in Boulder, Colorado.)

The *Urantia Book* is at far variance with the Bible by teaching that God is a "trinity of trinities," that the human race never had a fall, and that humans are moving forward through progressive revelation to become fused with God. The book also gives a detailed "account" (or gospel) of the life of Jesus Christ that perverts the truth enough to help send a person to hell. It declares that Jesus did not die to satisfy the Father's justice and wrath.[48]

Despite the book's knowledgeable flavor, the discerning Christian easily can see through it. In Gardner's column in the Winter 1990 *Skeptical Inquirer* he ridiculed it, calling it possibly "the largest, most fantastic chunk of moonshine ever to be found in one volume."[49] He may be right. Here's how he further described it:

> The book's first two thirds concern cosmology and the history of Urantia (pronounced you-ran-sha), the name for Earth. We live on the 606th planet in a system called Satania, which includes 619 imperfect, evolving worlds. Urantia's grand universe number is 5,342,482,337,666. Satania, with its headquarters at Jerusem, is in the constellation of Norlatiadek, part of the evolving universe of Nebadon. Nebadon in turn belongs to a super-universe called Orvonton. Orvonton and six other superuniverses, each unfinished and still evolving, revolving around the central universe of Havona. At the core of Havona is the flat, timeless, motionless Isle of Paradise. This is the dwelling place of the Great I AM, the ultimate, eternal, infinite Deity.[50]

Gardner adds that Urantia claims Paul, Peter, and others "outrageously distorted" the history of Christ on earth, but "records supplied by the guardian angel of the Apostle Andrew have set matters straight." Like Billy Meier's revelational ravings from Switzerland, the *Urantia Book* portrays Jesus as a globe-trotting wanderer who even reached India at one point. And he wasn't God's only son, as Scripture declares. Urantia says he was "Michael of Nebadon, one of hundreds of thousands of Sons of the Eternal Son," who created our local universe.[51]

Aside from these obvious heresies propounded by Urantia, it is one of the most complex religions to understand—and that's probably one of the main reasons the devil helped create it. To be a loyal Urantia follower, much effort, indeed an individual's life's blood, must be poured out in endless hours of trying to understand the basic message. Quite simply, the true religious message of the *Urantia Book* is an exercise on how far it can get a person to chase his tail in never-ending facts and intrigue on God's creation, the planets, and the universe, instead of on God.

Urantia runs contrary to the simplicity of the gospel, which is just as clear for the most sophisticated man or woman as it is for the simplest. The true gospel of Jesus Christ is easy to understand; Jesus died for our sins so we can have peace with God by accepting his free gift. Jesus said he is easy to follow. He said, "Come to Me all who are weary and heavy laden, and I will give you rest" (Matt. 11:28 NASB).

12 The False Origin of the Species

Very slowly, but most certainly, Zecharia Sitchin has become one of the most influential figures in UFOlogy. Last summer he reached a high-water mark in his career: he was one of the main speakers at the most influential gathering of UFOlogists in the United States: the annual Mutual UFO Network's International Symposium.

In his speech at a Chicago hotel, the Russian-born and Palestine-reared Sitchin told the gathering that UFOs are really identified flying objects and he was offering solutions as to their identity. Furthermore, he said, ancient Sumerian texts tell us all about real extraterrestrials who once visited our planet, created humankind, and helped form all the world's religions. And, he claims in his voluminous writings, many ancient texts, including the Bible, back it up.

Sitchin is today's Erich von Daniken. (Von Daniken, of course, is the Swissman, whose book, *Chariots of the Gods?,* sold more than forty-five million copies since it was first published in the late 1960s.[1]) Sitchin has clearly emerged at the top of the heap of ancient astronaut theorists. Not only has he been at the center of a revived interest in studying ancient artifacts to find clues pointing to our alleged ancestral being from other planets, he may also be more influential than von Daniken ever was. And so far he hasn't faced a serious scholar who is challenging his work.

He has gained more stature in the UFO community with the publication of each book, both with the serious side (groups like the Mutual UFO Network, or MUFON, that study the UFO phenomenon from a scientific perspective) and also with the New Age side. These two factions within UFOlogy make strange bedfellows; MUFON makes little secret of its distaste for mystical New Agers like Brad Steiger, Shirley MacLaine, Ruth Montgomery, and Whitley Strieber that see UFOs as part of a worldwide transformation into a New Age, yet they are quite willing to accept Sitchin and his alternative theories of the creation of the world and the alleged seeding of the earth by aliens as one of their own. Yet the UFO-New Age mystics, who are already sold on the idea of ancient extraterrestrial visitations accept him too. He has spoken at various New Age and UFO conferences (including one at the Great Pyramid in Egypt in January 1992). He has been photographed chatting with Shirley MacLaine in her apartment, and many New Age-UFO enthusiasts are readily testifying of their belief in Sitchin's theories.

Sitchin's first book, *The Twelfth Planet,* was released by Stein and Day in 1976, and it was slow to catch on at first because of its scholarly nature. But by the time his next book, *The Stairway to Heaven,* was released by Avon in 1980, he had a following and it became known as book II of Sitchin's Earth Chronicles series. Book III, *The Wars of Gods and Men,* was published by Avon in 1985, and in February 1990 book IV, *The Lost Realms,* was released. In October 1990, Sitchin summarized many of his writings and gave us an alternative view of the Bible's Book of Genesis in his latest work, *Genesis Revisited.*

Sitchin's theories are original—and astounding. I will summarize them later, but let me say they are better reading (in a fanciful way) than most science fiction novels; they're filled with wild conjecture and amazing conclusions that, if true, will shake the foundations of the world. But it's not just his theories that are making Sitchin King of the Ancient Astronaut Teachers, there are at least three additional reasons for his popularity:

(1) His books resemble scholarly treatises. They are packed with diagrams from the ancient world and loaded with details

giving the impression he knows what he is talking about. They are also long books: two, three, and four are over 295 pages; and book one is well over 400 pages. And Sitchin, unlike von Daniken, has credentials. He is well versed in ancient languages and archaeology and was educated at the University of London.[2]

(2) They are hard to debunk since Sitchin claims to get his source material from ancient clay tablets and ancient sources—items the average layperson does not know how to work with.

(3) His books explain away almost all ancient myths, and they especially attack the Bible, and specifically the God of the Bible, which sits well with the New Age crowd.

They don't, however, directly attack the person of Christ, which could be one of the reasons Christians and other culture watchers have not done significant research into Sitchin.[3] It is also true that Sitchin did not have to attack Christ to discredit the Christian message. The whole point of his books is to demolish the foundations of every ancient tradition in favor of his notion of ancient astronauts coming to earth. In the case of the Judeo-Christian tradition, he cleverly asserts that the Bible may not be wrong; it is simply misunderstood. The Nephilim the Bible talks about in Genesis 6, he asserts, were simply the gods of all the cultures, aliens from the mysterious planet Marduk.

Crash Went the Chariots

Sitchin filled a void left by von Daniken, a high-school dropout, who was thoroughly discredited on all fronts for playing fast and loose with the truth. Additionally, von Daniken's theories were not sophisticated enough to wash with the intellectual community. But his basic ideas were expressed with such power and vitality that the Swissman left an indelible mark on the modern world and in the media. In less than a decade after publication of von Daniken's *Chariots* the book had been translated into dozens of languages and spawned the *Chariots of the Gods?* movie and two television specials. It also generated a literal worldwide spate of other related books as entire ancient astronaut organizations formed overnight dedicated to finding out more about our alleged ancient visitors.

In *Chariots,* von Daniken deduced that a mysterious series of markings (called the Nazca Lines) in Peru were actually the landing strip of our ancient ancestors; that a mysterious flying object in the Book of Ezekiel was really a spaceship; that the ark of the covenant of the Bible was really a radio transmitting information to aliens who were helping to mold the young Hebrew nation.

Von Daniken was thoroughly rebutted several years later by Dr. Clifford Wilson, a Christian archaeologist from Australia, in a book called *Crash Go the Chariots* (Lancer Books, 1972). In it Wilson showed how von Daniken engaged in unwarranted speculation and at times he deliberately twisted the truth to "prove" his theories about ancient astronauts. One of Wilson's criticisms was that von Daniken should have posed his speculations as questions instead of presenting them as exclamations of fact.

Wilson's rebuttal book sold more than one million copies, but that didn't stop von Daniken from continuing to speculate. His next two books, *Return to the Stars* (later retitled *Gods from Outer Space*) and *Gold of the Gods,* continued on the same theme and added more unwarranted speculation to the picture. Wilson responded with another well-written book, *The Chariots Still Crash* (New York: Signet, 1976), that states on page 1: "Despite von Daniken's theories and speculation, visitors from outer space were *not* responsible for the pyramids, the Easter Island statues, the Piri Re'is map, the so-called electrified ark, the destruction of the cities of Sodom and Gomorrah or Ezekiel's 'space vehicle.'"

Later Wilson added what I think is the crux of the issue, and what is still the bottom line of today's influential ancient-astronaut teachers like Sitchin: von Daniken's theories on ancient astronauts are not part of a scientific probe at all; they are part of a new religious movement. Wilson wrote:

In a sense von Daniken *is* a prophet. Rather subtly, a change has come and the new order has demanded a fresh "revelation.". . .

History has shown that often there seems to be a vacuum, and then pseudo-science and cultism take over. Once the vacuum has been created, a new prophet soon emerges. Some members of a gullible public will be waiting to follow the leader, even though it involves the wearing of a mental blindfold. . . .

Von Daniken had fulfilled most of the requirements for establishing a new cult, especially by his theories about spacemen breeding with earthwomen (or their predecessors).[4]

Wilson added that in reality von Daniken's theories, even if true, did not solve anything. They only pushed the problem back "one more step." "Where did the spacemen themselves come from: What was the explanation as to the being behind the spacemen? And what could be known about the origin of life itself?"[5]

Playboy Goes after von Daniken

Although Wilson's book helped inform many about inconsistencies of von Daniken, an unexpected boost to his argument came from Hugh Hefner's *Playboy,* which published a very critical interview with von Daniken in August 1974. That interview was followed up by another critical article in January 1975 in the then-counterculture (but influential) *Rolling Stone.* Both articles, which were written by reporter Timothy Ferris, highlighted the fact that von Daniken, prior to his adventures into the archaeological arena, had multiple convictions in Swiss courts for fraud and embezzlement, and during one of the proceedings a court-appointed psychiatrist pronounced him a "pathological liar" and a "psychopath."[6] The *Playboy* article added that he spent a year in prison for these crimes, which included forgery, and that when von Daniken was age nineteen and a school dropout another psychiatrist said that he displayed a "tendency to lie."[7]

Among the things *Playboy* uncovered (pardon the pun) is that von Daniken admitted the vast tunnels of gold in Ecuador he claimed he had visited in *Gold of the Gods* were fictional, because he really hadn't been there but had mentioned them for "theatrical effect."[8] When Wilson found out about the nonexistent tunnels, he wrote, he wasn't surprised. Von Daniken's "'new' . . . discoveries . . . have the habit of dissipating when investigated," he wrote.[9] It also came out that the most convincing piece of evidence presented in the *Chariots of the Gods?* movie—a so-called ancient Russian cave painting that showed what looked like an astronaut—was a well-known hoax.[10]

Where Did von Daniken's Ideas Come From?

The most revealing thing about von Daniken's theories is their origin. He got all of his early ideas from the occult in the same manner many UFO enthusiasts claim to receive messages from extraterrestrial beings—through telepathy from an unknown source and from out-of-body travels. "I know that astronauts visited the earth in ancient time," he said in a widely published interview in 1974. "I was there when the astronauts arrived. Why should anybody believe I am able to leave my body whenever I desire and observe the past, present and future—all at the same time? Nonetheless, it is true. It has been true for many years."[11]

Wilson, quoting the August 1973 *Encounter* magazine in his book *The Chariots Still Crash*, adds:

> Under the heading, "From Jesus to the Astronauts," it states that von Daniken's conversion from the faith of Jesus to that of the astronauts "began with a vision—or a process of extrasensory perception—which he subsequently christened *Esspern*, a German verbalization of the initials ESP." Daniken now submits that it was his first ESP experience in spring 1954 which convinced him of a prehistoric earth-landing by astronauts from outer space. From then on, he was enabled, in fact impelled, to go in search of the traces left by his gods.[12]

Von Daniken has admitted that in his second book, *Gods from Outer Space*, he quotes at length from *The Book of Dyzan*, purportedly a mystical book that "originated beyond the Himalayas in Tibet" that tells about the ancient world and the evolution of humanity over millions of years. The problem with this is that no one has a copy of the book, and the first mention of it came from none other than Helena P. Blavatsky who quoted from it in her magnum opus, *The Secret Doctrine*, which she claims she received from the Tibetan mahatmas.[13]

According to L. Sprague de Camp, Blavatsky's mahatmas (or masters) showed her a manuscript of the *Book of Dyzan,* which was originally written in Atlantis in a forgotten language, while she communicated with them in trances. She claims it was written on palm leaves.[14]

But far from being unknown, the book from which Blavatsky quoted was actually plagiarized from other books, de Camp reported. Part of the *Stanzas of Dyzan* she cited in *The Secret Doctrine* was stolen from the *Hymn of Creation* in the old Sanskrit *Rig-Veda*, he said, quoting the scholar William Emmette Coleman who died in the early part of the century.[15] Besides, as previously mentioned, Blavatsky was exposed as a fraud who had never visited Tibet.

People Want to Believe It

The bottom line is that the entire ancient-astronaut theory is based on lies, plagiarisms, and the occult. Virtually all of today's ancient-astronaut advocates have followed the path blazed by the lying and very rich pioneer from Switzerland with a criminal background. Logic would dictate, considering von Daniken's record and occult sources, that there is no validity at all to ancient astronauts. But in spiritual matters, logic seldom rules without the convicting power of the Holy Spirit. As Pastor Joe Focht of Calvary Chapel of Philadelphia has said, "If I wasn't a Christian, I'd probably believe we were placed on earth by aliens." Focht is pastor of one of the largest evangelical churches in the Philadelphia area, but prior to his conversion he followed Eastern mysticism. Speaking from experience, he says people want to believe in ancient astronauts, because it absolves them of their responsibility to their Creator. It gives them an out, and most people will take it every time. As Jeremiah said: "The heart is more deceitful than all else and is desperately sick; who can understand it?" (Jer. 17:9 NASB).

Ancient-Astronaut Teachers Exposed

Probably the most forceful thing the writers about ancient astronauts push is a rejection of the Judeo-Christian religion and its Bible. However, Vallee sees a nonreligious danger in the ancient-astronaut theory. He says it "undermines the image of man as a master of his own destiny." These theories give people the impression that many of mankind's greatest achievements could not have happened without alien intervention. Things like the building of ancient structures, agriculture, mining and other things are credited to the aliens, which "encourages passive expectation of another visit by friendly space creatures to solve current human problems."[16]

Following is a brief look at some of the anti-Bible teachings in some of the popular ancient-astronaut books.

Jesus was criticized for his "intolerance" in Gerhard R. Steinhauser's 1975 book *Jesus Christ: Heir to the Astronauts*. He also declares that Christ was not God, that the resurrection never happened, and that Christ never said much of what was attributed to him in the Bible. To top it off, Steinhauser wonders why the belief in Satan as "the true lord of the Earth" is such a wicked and evil position as Christians claim it is.[17]

In *First Man, Then, Adam* (1975) Irwin Ginsburgh claims that God sent spaceships from the Pleiades with Adam on board, that the serpent of the Garden of Eden could have been the cave man (not necessarily evil), that Enoch and Noah also could have been aliens, and that the Garden of Eden was a spaceship.[18]

In *The Lost Tribes from Outer Space* by Marc Dem, which was a 1974 French book translated into English and published by Bantam in 1977, *YHWH* (an ancient Hebrew name for Jehovah) was not God; flying saucers parted the Red Sea; the second coming of Christ will be a UFO landing; and we should not believe the Bible, especially not the four Gospels, which recount Christ's life. (Even though there were eyewitnesses,

Dem says, they can't be trusted, because they were trying to push their own agenda for Jesus.) He also denied the virgin birth, using the same argument neo-Nazis and identity "Christians" use—that Jesus was the "offspring of Mary and a Roman soldier." But most troublesome of all, Dem alleged that Jesus was not the Messiah but simply claimed that role as a "ruse" in order to thwart *YHWH*'s plan for the Jews.[19]

R. L. Dione in his works *God Drives a Flying Saucer* and *Is God Supernatural?* asserts universalism; aliens sent "father images" for humans which were found in many religions (Jesus being one); UFOs made Jesus walk on the water; Jesus never died on the cross; and "not one of the four Gospel writers says point-blank that Jesus died on the cross. Check it yourself."[20] He also denies the virgin birth of Christ. He claims the angel Gabriel hypnotized Mary and artificially inseminated her.[21]

Dione's charge that not one of the four Gospel writers said that Jesus died on the cross is false. All four clearly said it. Matthew 27:50 states: "And when Jesus had cried out again in a loud voice, he gave up his spirit." Mark 15:37: "With a loud cry, Jesus breathed his last." Luke 23:46: "Jesus called out with a loud voice, 'Father, into your hands I commit my spirit.' When he had said this, he breathed his last." John 19:30: "When he had received the drink, Jesus said, 'It is finished.' With that, he bowed his head and gave up his spirit." In all four accounts Jesus was on the cross when he died. John's Gospel continues: "But when [the soldiers] came to Jesus and found that he was already dead, they did not break his legs." Instead one of the soldiers pierced Jesus' side with a spear (John 19:33, 34).

Sitchin Has the Same Agenda

Zecharia Sitchin seems to have the same agenda as the ancient-astronaut theorists mentioned above. His basic theory can be summarized as follows.

Humans are created beings, made in a laboratory of the genes of a superior race of aliens crossed with Earth animals. Humans were created as slaves to help mine gold and precious metals from the earth by the space creatures Freer refers to as the

Nefilim. What's more, the Nefilim came from a twelfth planet in our solar system called Marduk (or Nibiru), which orbits the sun once every 3,600 years in a cometlike elliptical orbit; its path goes opposite the direction of the other planets, which makes it impossible to see at most times.

Sitchin also claims these Nefilim (which are referred to as the Nephilim in Genesis 6) are really the gods of all the ancient religions and traditions, including the ancient God of the Israelites: *Yahweh* or Jehovah. The way he sees it, all the ancient mythological gods of Persia, Egypt, the Far East, Greece, and the early Americas were real. But they were not gods. They were from the planet Marduk and used rocket-based technology (similar to our own space program) to come to Earth for mining purposes. It was in their best interest to give the created earthlings the impression that the Nefilim were gods, as each one of them was responsible for different parts of the world.

Yahweh, or Jehovah, the God of the Jews, was actually an insignificant Nefilim, Sitchin has written. In New Ager Neil Freer's book, *Breaking the Godspell* (foreword by Sitchin), he writes Jehovah was:

> remote, peevish, exacting and quite ruthless . . . [he could] . . . order anyone killed who worked on the day he had declared the day of rest, annihilated whole cities and who was, by his own admission, "a jealous god" even to the point of insecurity, to Ishtar. Ishtar was put in charge of the third center of civilization built by the Nefilim in northern India. She was not beyond playing manipulative politics with her peers or even having one of them killed. But, in contrast to Yahweh, she instituted public sexual rituals, once a year with her foreman (king) and kept male human consorts in her palace and was the source, the institutor of a sexual "religion."[22]

Thus, Freer added, Ishtar was Yahweh's "female relative." (We discussed Ishtar in chapter 8. Other names for her include Ashtar, Ashtoreth, Athtart, and others.)

Neil Freer, a silver-haired New Age author from California, has become one of Sitchin's most effective propagandists. New

Age heavyweights are also tuned into Freer. Marilyn Ferguson, author of the key New Age book, *The Aquarian Conspiracy*, has raved about Freer's book in her *Brain/Mind Bulletin.* Seattle guru J. Z. Knight has had Freer speak to her many students. At the Whole Life Expo in New York City in October 1990 Freer delivered several talks based on Sitchin's theories entitled "Beyond the New Age." "No valid reason is ever advanced by historians or prehistorians why," he writes, "at the same time we take the [ancient] kings lists as valid and accurate, the list of gods is rejected as myth."[23]

It forms the centerpiece of his belief system and he believes— he hopes—this "revelation" will help change humanity forever. In explaining his Sitchin-based theories in *Breaking the God- spell* he declares that "every word of this book is meant to cause a revolution, a gentle revolution in the way we conceive of ourselves individually and as a planetary race."[24]

Sitchin's books are likewise meant to cause a revolution.

Each book he writes tears away at the fabric of the Judeo-Christian tradition. For example, at the end of his *Wars of Gods and Men* (book III) Sitchin published a "Time Chart" that turns even more of biblical history on its ear. Following are some details from his scenario. The Nefilim arrived on earth about 450,000 years ago and began mining gold. About 49,000 years ago they plotted humanity's demise, because some of them were marrying the daughters of men, their genetically created beings. Due to the close approach of their planet Marduk, they knew it would cause huge tidal waves that would wipe out the earth by flood around 11,000 B.C. But a friendly extraterrestrial messenger told Noah (who was also known as "Ziusudra") to build an ark—a submarine in which he and his family could survive the flood.

After the flood the Sinai Peninsula was chosen as a space port, and a control center was placed in the future Jerusalem and at about 8300 B.C. Jericho became an outpost to the space facility. At about 3450 B.C. languages were confused (paralleling the biblical Tower of Babel incident). At 2041 B.C. a war broke out, and Abraham, the biblical patriarch, blocked a military advance near the gateway to the space port.[25]

Some Inconsistencies

Without delving too deeply into Sitchin's teachings we find inconsistencies in his theories that include the failure of key archaeological scholars familiar with Sumerian tablets to endorse him, and the distortion of accepted interpretations of certain Sumerian myths that have, for a long time, been pored over by Bible scholars. It is also troubling that Sitchin can so readily accept the myths of the ancient world (and add to them guesses about rocket ships and space travel details) as true fact, and especially how he can accept certain ancient deities such as Ishtar (whom he also referred to as Inannai and Irnini) as among the Nefilim partly responsible for creating humanity.

Along the same vein as the good-and-evil reversers mentioned thus far in this chapter and throughout the book, are those who keep referring to Satan as good, and the Judeo-Christian God as bad. Isaiah 5:20 warns us about men like Sitchin: "Woe to those who call evil good and good evil, who put darkness for light and light for darkness." He distorts the story of the serpent in the Garden of Eden beyond recognition when he suggests that the serpent was right after all by telling Eve that "you will be like God, knowing good and evil" (Gen. 3:5) if she ate the forbidden fruit. "The Biblical Serpent surely was not a lowly, literal snake," wrote Sitchin, ". . . he knew the truth about the matter of 'knowing,' and he was of such high stature that he unhesitatingly exposed the deity as a liar." Instead, the serpent could have been the honest Nefilim, Enki, who told Eve the truth against the wishes of Enlil, the ruling Nefilim at the time. And that truth was that she was every bit as much a god as he was.[26]

Sitchin's argument that we should take the ancient-gods lists seriously as we do the kings lists also doesn't wash. Are we supposed to believe our modern folklore, using Freer's same criterion? That would mean believing that Paul Bunyan dug the Grand Canyon with his axe, that the headless horseman of Sleepy Hollow was real, and that butter was created by a tiger chasing Sambo around a tree so fast that its stripes melted.

The Babylonian Flood

Perhaps more disturbing to scholars is Sitchin's reinterpretation of ancient texts to fit his purposes, many of which scholars had long translated with differing results. Scholar Arnold Rhodes, for example, gives us the traditional rendering of the ancient story of *Enuma elish*. He says it tells the story of how Marduk, the elected champion of some of the gods, did battle with the dragon goddess Tiamat. Marduk won the battle by enmeshing Tiamat in his net, then pierced her heart, split her carcass in two, and formed the heavens and earth out of it.[27]

Sitchin, however, redefines Marduk as a planet (or at other times, when convenient, as a Nefilim leader) that collided with the planet Tiamat, which he says used to be between Mars and Jupiter, and created the asteroid belt. In Sitchin's theory twelve planets were originally in the solar system. The moon was considered one of them along with the other nine plus Marduk and Tiamat.

Also for many years historians and Bible scholars have known about the existence of ancient flood stories in many cultures. One of the most interesting stories that has some parallels to the biblical story of Noah and the flood is the Babylonian *Gilgamesh Epic*. But Sitchin makes Gilgamesh the protagonist of a sci-fi soap opera. Taking wild liberties with the text, which at times is displayed near Sitchin's commentary, he claims Gilgamesh was two-thirds divine (Nefilim), that he flew on a rocket ship, and others rocketed away to escape the deluge.

Who Were the Biblical Nephilim?

Sitchin is not the only one talking about the biblical Nephilim today. Many channeled messages from extraterrestrial beings talk about them, and theories abound within the New Age-UFO communities about their identities.

Were the biblical Nephilim mentioned in Genesis 6 really a super race that once lived on earth? The truth of the matter is that scholars are divided on the issue. The Bible says: "The Nephilim were on the earth in those days, and also afterward, when the sons of God came in to the daughters of men, and they bore children to them. Those were the mighty men who were of old, men of renown" (Gen. 6:4 NASB).

One Christian author who discusses the various theories is I. D. E. Thomas in *The Omega Conspiracy*. Thomas favors the theory that the Nephilim were fallen angels who came to earth and committed "carnal acts with the daughters of men," which almost caused the annihilation of the human race via genetic impurity.[28] God flooded the earth and imprisoned them, he says. But in Thomas's highly speculative book he suggests that in these last days these demonic entities could be working against humankind again and may be using UFOs in their plan to conquer the earth by setting up a new super race that will help set the stage for the Antichrist.[29]

Although Thomas's book makes interesting reading, I'm not sure the Nephilim were fallen angels. They could have been large men or warriors.[30] Clifford Wilson also considers Thomas's position on their identity a possibility, but he suggests another interpretation: They could have been those from the godly line of Seth taking wives from the ungodly line of Cain.[31]

I'm not sure what to make of this obscure passage in the Bible. But I do agree with Wilson on this point concerning the Nephilim: "Certainly the Bible does not endorse the breeding experiments to which von Daniken points."[32] (Von Daniken, like Sitchin and other ancient-astronaut teachers, claims aliens created humanity via genetic experiments with animals.) And the Bible does not endorse the possibility of breeding experiments suggested by Sitchin, other ancient-astronaut teachers, UFO cultists, and New Agers.

It Leads Us to the Occult

At the Whole Life Expo in New York Neil Freer was ending his speech. The lights of other Manhattan skyscrapers glowed through the lecture hall's windows in the early evening. He told us we had a wonderful future if we would "break the god-spell"—these ancient controlling mechanisms the Nefilim placed on us to control us—and start realizing our own divinity.

We should learn more of the ancient occult myths the Nefilim left behind, Freer said, because through the occult myths humankind may learn to become immortal like the Nefilim. Perhaps they left the secret of immortality. Perhaps we simply have to "decode" it from the ancient occult rituals.[33]

In a friendly question-and-answer session Freer's fans crowded around him asking excited questions about the Nefilim. I approached and asked him one question: "How do you explain the New Testament, and Jesus and the spread of the Christian church, in light of your theories on *YAWEH?*"

Freer looked at me, smiled, and recited the same line about Jesus that almost all UFOnauts and New Agers teach: that Jesus may have indeed been sent to earth, but his mission was simply to give us ethical direction.

"That's a whole different topic in itself . . . but let me give you some definite objective conjecture," he said. Mary may have been approached by a "rocket ship pilot" he said, (under the guise of an angel) "to create a virgin birth . . . for the sake of genetic manipulation." The purpose, Freer said, may have been for the Nefilim to instill into humanity some "advanced teaching . . . to carefully upgrade our thinking away from 'an eye for an eye, tooth for a tooth' to a more benevolent type on society."[34]

But Freer blatantly contradicted the actual eyewitnesses of the Bible who heard directly from Jesus himself on the nature of his mission both before and after his resurrection. Jesus did not come the first time to create a more benevolent type of society (although that will happen if enough people are Christians in a society). Jesus came to earth as a sacrificial gift to die in our place for our offenses against God. In exchange for our accepting his free gift, he has already granted us that evasive immortality that occultic signs and wonders and the mythical Nefilim can never give.

"I am the resurrection and the life," the apostle John recounts Jesus saying, "he who believes in Me shall live even if he dies" (John 11:25 NASB). These words he spoke to Lazarus's sister Martha just before Jesus raised her brother from the dead four days after he was entombed. Jesus always backed up his words with his actions to demonstrate to us all who he is: the only begotten Son of God and the only door into eternity (John 10).

John would hardly misquote or misrepresent one whom he had seen do the things he recorded, and the words that he penned were "God-breathed" (2 Tim. 3:16). Besides, Jesus promised that the Holy Spirit would bring to remembrance all that he said to them (John 14:26). And John (as well as the other New Testament writers), being well acquainted with Old Testament Scriptures, knew the warnings given by God: "You shall not add to the word which I am commanding you, nor take away from it" (Deut. 4:2 NASB).

Every ancient-astronaut theory and every alternative creation story channeled from the space brothers or any other source either adds to or takes away from God's words.

Tail Chasing with Wolves

Dozens of people got up from their chairs in the conference room and after several minutes of confusion formed a circle around the chairs, holding hands. The workshop leader, Rev. Frank E. Stranges, began to lead them in prayer.

"Eternal Father," the crowd piped in unison, "Creator of the universe, hear this day my petition. Surround me now, with your divine protection, your divine ring of fire, the fire of your abundance, the fire of your complete healing, the fire of divine abundance. I now command the hand of almighty God on my behalf.

"Let it be so . . . this very moment: in the blessed name of our Lord and Master, Jesus Christ."[1]

But the gathering was not a prayer time at a charismatic conference. It was the ring-of-fire ceremony prayer at the 1991 National New Age & "Truth about UFOs" conference in San Diego. Each of the forty-two persons forming the circle had paid forty dollars to hear Rev. Stranges, president of International Evangelism Crusades of Van Nuys, California (who was also master of ceremonies at the conference), talk to them for several hours on how God wants them to be healthy and rich.

Stranges, a slightly heavyset man with graying hair, is a compelling, witty speaker and was one of the favorites of the conference. He is a friendly, "full gospel minister," as he describes himself, who sounds very much like a preacher when he talks, constantly bringing biblical images into his messages. He is also a veteran in the UFO field. His first book, *Flying Sauce-rama*, was published in 1959. But perhaps he is best known for his books *My Friend from Beyond Earth* (1960) and *The Stranger at the Pentagon* (1967), which tell the incredible (but undocumentable) story of how he got through the Pentagon's security in December 1959 and was ushered into a room for a prearranged talk with Val Thor, a Bible quoting, sinless man from Venus who had no fingerprints. In conjunction with meeting the Venusian, Stranges writes about his experience aboard their spaceship and his meeting with other Venusians.

Stranges's emphasis on Jesus makes him an anomaly among the UFO crowd. In *My Friend from Beyond Earth* he wrote that Val Thor, short for Valiant Thor, photographed as a young man with dark hair, "came in order to help mankind return to the Lord. . . . He said that Jesus Christ would not force men to be saved from their sin, even though He made a way for mankind to be redeemed through His shed blood when they crucified Him on the cross."[2]

Stranges quotes Val Thor as telling him:

> I know that Jesus is the alpha and omega of your and everyone's faith. He today has assumed His rightful position as the ruler of the universe and is preparing a place and a time for all who are called by His name to ascend far above the clouds where His Power and Authority shall never again be disputed.[3]

In a 1968 Christian Research Institute booklet, *UFO: Friend, Foe or Fantasy*, CRI was not critical of the Stranges story, perhaps because of his emphasis on Jesus. It says of his book, *The Stranger at the Pentagon:* "an interesting and intriguing story, suggesting that our government is working in collaboration with beings from outer space."[4]

Emphasis on Jesus

Today, however, as evidenced by recent publications from Stranges and his organization, it is apparent that Stranges is a wolf in sheep's clothing whose teachings and life are full of contradictions and whose doctrine shoots wide of biblical

Christianity. We've already discussed briefly how Stranges now claims Val Thor, his Venusian otherwordly visitor, comes from the interior of Venus, now that it's known the planet has a hellish, poisonous atmosphere with temperatures in the nine-hundred degree range. But in the introduction to *The Stranger at the Pentagon,* allegedly written in 1967 by Val Thor himself, he states: "I am a native of the planet you call Venus. It is not too unlike your Earth, in fact, we still enjoy the air-conditioned atmosphere that Earth had before the great flood.[5]

More Inconsistencies

More inconsistencies have blossomed. At the March 1991 conference in San Diego Stranges claimed that Val Thor and other Venusians were really God's angels, even guardian angels, which is at variance with his previous accounts (and with God's Word). Val Thor's testimony in the same book states that when their Venusian ships first came to earth many years ago, they were surprised to find life on Earth. Prior to that time "our most powerful detectors indicated it was not capable of sustaining life," he said.[6] But according to God's Word, not only did all the angels know about Earth, "all the angels shouted for joy" (Job 38:7) when God created it.

Other inconsistencies surfaced in 1978 when Stranges reissued a book allegedly written by Val Thor under the pen name Frater VIII in 1932. In the book *Outwitting Tomorrow* Val Thor prophesies that the millennium will begin on January 1, 2000, and he delves into date setting for future events using questionable calculations allegedly gleaned from the Great Pyramid of Giza.[7] Of course, all date setting is unbiblical and wrong, which was the final thing Jesus told his disciples as he ascended into heaven. "It is not for you to know the times or dates the Father has set by his own authority," he said (Acts 1:7).

But before publication of this book question marks surrounded parts of Stranges's message. In *Stranger* he writes that Val Thor is also here "to encourage a One-World Government under the control of God-loving scientists and not professional politicians, prior to the establishment of God's Kingdom."[8] As

many are well aware, God seems to forbid the formation of a
one-world government until the second coming of Christ, when
he will rule the world from Jerusalem.[9] And even when Christ
is ruling, Scripture declares, there will be national sovereignty.
Isaiah talks about Christ during the millennium settling dis-
putes between the nations (Isa. 2:4). It's interesting to note that
the Book of Revelation talks about an imposter, the Antichrist,
leading a one-world government and that God will throw him
alive into the lake of fire at the Battle of Armageddon (see Rev.
13:7; 19:20).

Suspect Credentials

More troubling things about Stranges's ministry center
around his educational credentials. He is never at a loss to provide information about his credentials by including biographical sheets about himself with each new publication. He claims
he is director of the National Investigations Committee on UFOs
(which few, if anyone, outside Stranges's own organization
identifies as a national UFO study group). He claims his International Evangelism Crusades, which he directs, are a "worldwide Christian Denomination,"[10] yet fourteen years earlier he
identified it as "a world-wide ministerial association."[11] But
few, if anyone, in the Christian world have ever heard of it. He
doesn't say who ordained him as a pastor, and veracity of his
degrees is fuzzy.[12]

To top it off, perhaps, is his claim that he is founder and
president of the International Theological Seminary of Van
Nuys, California. His very unprofessional catalogue of the seminary, published in 1984, states that his International Evangelism Crusades organization issues ministry "licenses" and "ordinations." (I.E.C. ordinations "must be renewed each year,"[13] a
sure sign of an unorthodox ordination-by-mail business. Real
ordinations don't expire.) Even more telling are Stranges's
degree requirements at his seminary. It takes but twenty-four
hours of study (as contrasted to well over 120 semester hours at
most colleges in America) for a bachelor's degree, thirty hours
to receive a master's degree, and thirty-four hours to receive a

doctor's degree. And for those seeking a Th.D. or a D.D. at Stranges's "seminary," it is not even required that they have completed their master's degree.[14]

The catalogue mentions that enrolling in the program is a chance to earn an accredited, earned degree, but accredited by whom? More organizations that few ever heard of. It is not accredited by the recognized accrediting agency in California, the Western Association of Schools and Colleges.[15]

According to the catalogue's statement of faith, the seminary purports to be evangelical and orthodox Christian. It clearly affirms the Trinity and the vicarious atonement through Christ's death on the cross, as well as other orthodox Christian doctrines. But in the masters' programs section was perhaps a slip up. "The Master of Divinity program," it says, "deals with the Divinity of Jesus Christ along with the possibility of mankind rising to the point of higher spiritual experience that will make him as God is on that appointed day."[16]

Is this a simple slip of the tongue? Or is it actually a foretaste of what Stranges really believes?

What Stranges Really Teaches

I paid my forty dollars for Stranges's workshop partly because I really wanted to see what he taught behind closed doors. The truth of the matter is that Stranges, the "Christian" minister, teaches occultism and Hindu-New Age concepts. And he fuses his teaching with the false gospel of prosperity and word-faith, which is taught by a number of television evangelists. He also perverted various Scripture verses and misquoted others, not a very good record for a so-called full gospel minister.

Take Stranges's ring-of-fire prayer, for example. "I now command the hand of almighty God on my behalf" is clearly unbiblical. When Jesus taught his disciples to pray the Lord's prayer, he said nothing about commanding God to do his bidding. "Thy will be done," is a revealing phrase from the prayer. But what was just as unbiblical was what led up to the prayer that day. He said God wants everyone to be rich.

"Are you aware as a disciple you have the right to ask for the very best in civilization?" he asks. When it's time to buy a new car, don't settle for any vehicle; go for a "Lincoln Town Car or a Cadillac." If you use your five senses, "your faith begins to bubble up in you to the point that the car will be yours," he said.

Go to a showroom, he said, and exercise your gift of sight and look at the one you want. "Open the door and walk around the car," he instructed. "Smell the car, touch it and say 'I have a right as a child of God to this.' Think it," and pretty soon the car will be yours.

Of course, Stranges also applies this type of thinking to physical health as he proposes the false belief that Christians can simply confess away illness and disease. Evangelical critics call this "prosperity teaching," "name it and claim it," or "blab and grab" theology. Although it's popular with certain television evangelists, it's alien to the Bible. One needs to look no further than the Book of Job or to the New Testament where the apostle Paul himself suffered sickness, near starvation, persecution, and at times poverty (2 Cor. 11:23–27). Yet he saw them as trials that he should rejoice in because his difficulties came through his work for the cause of Christ. They also helped to build his character and to exact more of a dependence on God. "That is why, for Christ's sake," Paul said, "I delight in weaknesses, in insults, in hardships, in persecutions, in difficulties. For when I am weak, then I am strong" (2 Cor. 12:10).

Stranges Delves into the Occult

But after the prosperity message, Stranges's real colors came out as he advocated pyramidology, out-of-body experiences, the divinity of man, occult aura reading, and how to activate the chakra points, including the "third eye" (a popular Hindu concept) by activating the "kundalini serpent power" at the base of the spine. Stranges had taken us from aberrant Christianity into New Age Hinduism during the workshop. Russ Chandler defines kundalini in his book *Understanding the New Age*: "Psycho-spiritual power thought by YOGI(S) to lie dormant at the base of the spine. *Believed to be a goddess,* kundalini is referred to as "the serpent power" (emphasis mine).[17]

At the end of the workshop Stranges handed out forms. For sixty-five dollars you can receive his monthly "Interspace-Link," a "confidential" UFO newsletter that contains a personalized message for you alone from Val Thor. Val's saucer, he told the conference a day earlier, is anchored on the bottom of Lake Mead, and each year Stranges meets with the Venusian and friends for a three-day "council meeting," he said.[18]

Of course, nothing Stranges says about the visitors can be verified, and as we have seen, besides his story being so far out that it is, well, unbelievable, there is a wealth of evidence that Stranges is not believable about much of anything. He also showed the crowd an obviously doctored NASA photograph of the earth from space with a large black hole in the North Pole region that Stranges claims is "proof" that the world is hollow. The crowd gasped with delight. "I don't give a damn who believes me," Stranges said defiantly to the crowd that day, which produced some clapping.

Stranges is a man who uses his questionable affinity with the Christian gospel and the Bible as a calling card for his UFO business. But despite his popularity in UFO circles, he is easy to see through.

A More Subtle Preacher

In 1968 the groundbreaking book *The Bible and Flying Saucers* was published. Its author, Presbyterian minister Dr. Barry H. Downing, unlike "Dr." Stranges, has impressive credentials. Downing, though his approach is not one of a Bible quoting preacher like Stranges, is quite willing to delve deeply into the works of Christian theologians, and he does so often in his book.

Downing's book continues to sell. Avon Books reprinted it in 1970 and 1973, Sphere Books Ltd. picked it up in 1974, and in 1989 Berkley Books reissued it as a paperback containing the complete text of the original edition.

Downing has a bachelor's degree in physics from Hartwick College, a theology degree from Princeton Theological Seminary, and a Ph.D. from the University of Edinburgh. He is pastor of Northminster Presbyterian Church (Presbyterian Church U.S.A.) in Endwell, New York. At times he comes down on the conservative side of the denomination. In March 1991 Downing wrote a report for his denomination that denounced an attempt to allow acceptance of practicing homosexuals into the clergy and conditional approval of other-than-marital sexual activity. In the UFO field he is a heavyweight. He is on the editorial staff of the Mutual UFO Network (MUFON) journal and was a sixteen-year consultant for MUFON in theology.

His approach, even before Erich von Daniken emerged on the scene, was to look at various events of the Bible and place them in the context of possible UFO involvement. But in this area, Downing, to his credit, has not been dogmatic. Along with his assertion in *The Bible and Flying Saucers* that a UFO might have caused one of the most dramatic miracles of the Jews during the exodus, he points out other possibilities:

> I have frequently been asked, "Do you yourself believe that the parting of the Red Sea was caused by some sort of UFO?" My answer is "Yes, about 80 per cent." I say this because I believe that I must leave room for doubt, so that I will be open to new evidence.[19]

Downing also lists other biblical events as probable miracles caused by UFOs, and he adds that the biblical angels were probably aliens from another planet. He claims extraterrestrial beings might have appeared to Abraham, that Moses' burning bush could have been caused by such beings, that UFOs (the pillar of cloud by day) could have led the Israelites out of Egypt, and that Ezekiel's vision of wheels within wheels (Ezek. 1:4–28) was a UFO. In the New Testament, UFO activity could have caused the transfiguration of Christ (Matt. 17:1–8), the star of Bethlehem, the Spirit descending like a dove on Christ at his baptism, Christ's ascension, and the light that blinded Paul on the Damascus road.

But his approach is also one of a theological liberal in most areas. To expound the Bible he uses the basic ideas of scholars like Thomas Altizer (who became famous for his "death of God" theology in the 1960s), Paul Tillich, Rudolf Bultmann and others in a greater company of Bible destroying theologians. He suggests, citing Bultmann's term, that we must demythologize the Bible, "which means to recognize the supernatural events described in the Bible (e.g., the ascension of Christ) as mythological rather than historical; we must then proceed to reinterpret such myths in terms modern man can understand."[20]

In taking such an approach, Downing has put himself at odds with biblical conservatives who believe, as I do, that we have no right to take liberties with the Bible (2 Peter 3:16). We would adamantly disagree with Downing's statement: "We have to admit immediately that there is much historical evidence to support the view that much of the Biblical material is mythological."[21]

The facts show the opposite. Downing does not list what historical evidence he is talking about; he only cites Bultmann, a scholar conservatives have taken to task for many years. To the contrary, there is no historical evidence to support that view, and the more archaeological evidence from the ancient world that surfaces, the stronger the conservative case gets.

Downing Is the One Espousing Myths, Not the Bible

To accept Downing's ideas means to accept fables and retranslations of God's revealed Word. Peter, who was at the mountain of transfiguration with Christ, said: "We did not follow cleverly invented stories when we told you about the power and coming of our Lord Jesus Christ, but we were eyewitnesses of his majesty" (2 Peter 1:16). I do not believe that God has a hidden agenda with us in using angels from another planet and UFOs to carry out his purposes. The Bible lists the dwelling place of angels as heaven (not another planet) and the Bible teaches that God is not from another planet. Solomon lamented the fact that "the heavens, even the highest heavens, cannot contain him" (2 Chron. 2:5, 6). Orthodox Christian theology affirms that God is "a personal, transcendent Creator, . . . distinct from creation."[22]

Handle with Extreme Caution

Perhaps it was because of Downing's approach that the same year *The Bible and Flying Saucers* was published the Christian Research Institute, then located in New Jersey, issued a strong note of caution over the book:

> In many respects, he [Downing] is very orthodox in his approach, but in his discussion, he fails to delineate clearly the exact person and nature of Jesus Christ, whom he connects with UFO's. Although this book is very stimulating, extreme caution should be exercised as to the nature of the people to whom it is recommended, e.g., persons who are not grounded in the Christian faith, or who are emotionally unstable may find this book distressing, or stress producing.[23]

In Downing's introduction to the (1989) Berkley edition of his book he states that he still believes his original thesis. "We need to explore the possibility that what we now call UFOs carry the angels of God, and that these angels were active in the development of the biblical religion."[24] But he states that this approach, though not popular with the religious community, is worth the risks involved.

> Certainly there are risks for Jews and Christians in a study that links UFOs and the biblical faith. I cannot promise that this is all going to work out in a way religious leaders would prefer, but it should be remembered that neither Jews nor Egyptians liked Moses very much during the heat of his confrontation with Pharaoh. Likewise the "good news" that Jesus brought was not received as good news by the religious leaders of his day.[25]

The risks Downing referred to were a mystery. But speaking at MUFON's 1990 International UFO Symposium in Pensacola, Florida, he gave us plenty of clues. In a transcript of Downing's speech he argues that "the Judeo-Christian tradition can mostly be saved by going in the direction I have gone."[26] And what direction is that? Toward the possibility that today's UFO contactees may give us new revelations from extraterrestrial beings on par with Scripture itself. He cites the incredible story of Betty Andreasson in Raymond Fowler's *The Andreasson Affair* (New York: Bantam, 1980) as possibly being new divine revelation. It wasn't; it clearly contradicts God's Word.[27] He claims that "divine revelation progresses. . . . Jesus was the last word, yet he wasn't, the Apostle Paul had more."[28]

But in this crucial area Downing is wrong. Paul did not give us new revelation. He simply testified of the words Jesus had spoken while continuing to carry out his part in preaching the gospel as Christ had ordered his disciples to do in the Great Commission. Christ himself told Ananias, whom he later used to heal Paul of blindness, that Paul "is my chosen instrument to carry my name before the Gentiles and their kings and before the people of Israel. I will show him how much he must suffer for my name" (Acts 9:15, 16).

Downing says "we need a UFO canon" to decide whether new UFO spiritual revelations are to be believed. But the canon is closed. God's Word says there won't be any new revelations until Christ returns in power at his second coming. As Hebrews puts it, Christ is the final revelation: "In these last days he has spoken to us by his Son, whom he appointed heir of all things, and through whom he made the universe" (Heb. 1:1, 2). Peter, speaking of Christ, adds, "And we have the word of the prophets made more certain" (2 Peter 1:19).

But perhaps what was more troubling in Downing's speech was the implication that the same UFOs that may have helped form the biblical religion "may also have stimulated other world religions." "That is my UFO creed at the present time," he said.[29] He then attacked Christian leaders as possibly being unwilling to accept new truth about UFOs and charged that they may to be to blame for the government's reluctance to give us the truth about UFOs. "No political leader wants to face the wrath of religious leaders," he said.[30] He added that "Eastern religions—Hinduism and Buddhism in particular—are less likely to be socially traumatized by extraterrestrial contact than the Western religions of Judaism, Christianity and Islam."[31]

Later he rejected the theory that UFO visitors may be demonic and he misrepresented the position of Christians, such as Clifford Wilson, John Weldon, and Zola Levitt, who have proposed this. He claimed they are in the same camp with fundamentalists who believe it's fine for American jet fighters to fire on UFOs. "If UFOs are demonic they deserve it," Downing said, misrepresenting their position.[32] However, none of the Christians he mentioned have ever advocated in speech or writing this course of action.

Could the Angels Have Been UFOnauts?

Should we take Downing's (and von Daniken's) theory seriously—that many of the miracles of the Bible were actually performed by UFOnauts? Some Christians have proposed the same thing. But I don't think they have a leg to stand on. Let's take the story of Ezekiel's wheel within a wheel (Ezek. 1), the vision of heaven God gave the prophet Ezekiel of the actual throne of God being carried along by four cherubim. This picture of God's glory was also described by the apostle John in the Book of Revelation. The Israelites were given instructions to make a prototype of this heavenly throne in the form of the ark of the covenant. Ezekiel got to see the real thing. This was a vision for the prophet alone. No one else saw this, and when Ezekiel beheld it he fell on his face as if dead, it was so awesome. The Spirit of God had to set him back on his feet again.

Unlike today's UFO phenomena where many people report sightings, Ezekiel's vision was seen only by him, because it was a vision, not a sighting. One would have to take a lot of liberties with the text to read a flying-saucerlike object into that account. Even Jacques Vallee, writing from a secular perspective, has commented on it.

> This is a type of interpretation commonly found in the literature that deals with our problem. The terminology also should be noted. The words "ship," "craft," "engine" are used without

justification. The scientist, obviously, will not be guided by situations thus presented. But the explanation given by Dr. Donald Menzel (that Ezekiel observed a sun dog) is equally unconvincing.[33]

Walter Martin also comments on Ezekiel and tells us what the Bible really has to say about UFOs.

First, does the Bible talk about UFOs at all? Theologically, categorically, flat out, no! You can try and read a UFO into Ezekiel's wheel within a wheel [but] wheels within wheels with eyes running around them are not necessarily portals on revolving saucers. The Bible doesn't mention UFOs by name. The Bible doesn't infer or deduce their existence. The Bible isn't concerned with them at all unless UFOs are not just mechanical craft. Perhaps they are from another dimension. . . . Perhaps we are dealing with something from a supernatural nature and that being the case, it might be very profitable to analyze this phenomena in light of the Bible.[34]

Today Downing is still giving an unclear view of the person and nature of Christ, and his theology only brings mistrust of God's Word. We should reject him thoroughly.

Another man whose work we should reject thoroughly is G. Cope Schellhorn, author of *Extraterrestrials in Biblical Prophecy* (1990, Horus). The book is featured in various UFO magazines and has the back-cover endorsement of Downing. The heavyweight book purports to be a theological look at the Bible (it comes equipped with a Bible verse index in the back), but what it really advocates is a New Age world view and an assault on the person, nature, and work of Christ, whom he claims was probably an astronaut. Written by a long-time associate of the late occultist Edgar Cayce, it relies heavily on the work of Zecharia Sitchin in forming a revised view of the gods' dealings with man. The book feeds us the lie that reincarnation was edited out of the Bible,[35] and it affirms, using Christ's words, that "greater works than these will he do" (John 14:12) to teach the false view that men can grow into perfect god-men.[36]

Faulty Proof Texts

At the end of his speech in Pensacola, Downing said that "the Book of Revelation sees divine knowledge as dangerous, and only those who have met the divine test are found worthy to have divine knowledge."[37] The biblical text he used to prove it, however, did no such thing. He used Revelation 5:1–5, where an angel in heaven asked who was worthy to break the scroll, and no one in heaven or earth was worthy. John the apostle cried because of that. Then suddenly one of the elders said that "the Lion of the tribe of Judah, the Root of David" was worthy.

Far from proving divine knowledge as "dangerous" with only a few worthy enough to have it, this passage clearly shows us that Jesus "had already achieved victory, and that He alone was able to break the seals and open the scroll."[38] One might ask how a Protestant minister can make such an exegetical error with God's Word, but I have discovered that citing faulty proof texts is a pattern for many of those in the UFO movement. Sometimes I suspect it is done to justify their belief that UFOs are good, and so they look for various Bible verses to try to back that up.

For example, after a recent television appearance on UFOs, a representative from MUFON on the show with me didn't like what I had to say about most UFOs being evil and even demonic. In a discussion afterwards he asked me how I knew they weren't really of God. He said when people were abducted in the middle of the night and brought to spaceships it was biblical. "He will come when you least expect him," the man told me. But just as Downing had done, the young man used a very clear verse out of context. Matthew 24:44 states: "So you also must be ready, because the Son of Man will come at an hour when you do not expect him." This verse clearly speaks of Jesus' second coming; his next visit to Planet Earth will be with the eyes of the world watching (Acts 1:11; Rev. 1:7). It has nothing to do with alien abductions.

Another example is early contactee Daniel Fry who was told by the aliens not to hide his light "under a bushel." The aliens then referred him to the Bible, claiming that he needed to get the word out about his UFO experiences to the world.[39] But what Jesus said in Matthew 5:15, 16 was that his disciples are to be a light to the world by doing good and being witnesses of the good news of Christ, so "that they may see your good deeds and praise your Father in heaven."

They Want to Believe So Badly That . . .

There's something addictive about flying saucer watching. As we've just seen, some people will twist the facts—even Scripture—to sustain their theories about UFOs. And that's one of the grave dangers of getting too heavily involved in UFO research. The mystery behind them, coupled with the strange and incredible stories of abductions, government conspiracies, and the like sometimes causes a "suspension of disbelief," according to UFO investigator-writer John Keel.

"I'm seeing more and more excellent UFO investigators going off the deep end," he said during a panel discussion on hoaxes near Washington, D.C.

"They take in any strange theory, because they've been desensitized by all the strangeness for so long," he said.[40]

Indeed, I agree with Keel. I've seen this "suspension of disbelief" during my investigation of the UFO community. On many occasions I wondered about the sanity of various contactees and UFO speakers. What is one supposed to think of a speaker who claims that three times a week UFOnauts bring him (naked) to their base on the ocean floor of the Bermuda Triangle? What about one conference speaker who produced incredibly obviously doctored NASA photographs of the moon to "prove" the existence of alien bases there?

I could cite many more examples. But I suspect that many intensely involved in UFOlogy have gone off the deep end. Barbara Schutte says there's great danger in getting deeply involved in the UFO phenomenon:

> Just like the proverbial TV plot, the UFO story is much the same plot with changing names and places. Yet this mystical

phenomenon lives on despite all the rehash. After all, the unknown is intriguing.

Therein lies the danger of involvement. Intrigue feeds on intrigue and the more intriguing, the deeper you get in. The decision to stay or leave the phenomena has to be made early in the game. The longer you are into it the harder it is to get out.[41]

I call this intrigue tail chasing. It's part of the UFOnauts' plan to keep us tied up focusing on intrigue, wasting our lives until we have no more time left. The longer one makes a commitment to UFO research, the closer he or she is to dying and giving the God who made the planets an account of his life. It is a sin to waste time on unprofitable things. Jesus said, "As long as it is day, we must do the work of him who sent me. Night is coming, when no one can work" (John 9:4).

Take the example of Bo and Peep's UFO cult. The two continually dictated to the followers of the sect that they sacrifice more and more and more to proceed to the next higher level. Key doctrines of the sect were changed, members were asked to move repeatedly and break contact with their families, until finally the sect went underground and broke up.

And there is Fred Bell of Laguna Beach, California. Semjase of the Pleiades gave him the idea of building a "pyradyne receptor," a medallion, which he claims helps in his life-extension work. She also told him about some of the "secrets" of pyramid power.[42] Today there is no evidence Bell's medallion does anything, yet he wears it frequently, and there is nothing to so-called pyramid power. But that didn't stop Bell from founding his own business creating pyramid hats for people (some of his models cost more than $100). At his booth at various New Age conferences gullible people were buying Bell's products at a brisk rate.

Of course, part of the tail-chasing phenomenon is that we can never get to the bottom of what these signs in the skies are. In many cases people began seeing UFOs after they became interested in the topic. And often UFOs will come in a form somewhat familiar to their frame of reference. According to the

"Rain*Maker Newsletter," a defunct publication that explored UFOs and strange events from a Native American point of view, the late famed contactee Chief Frank Buckshot claimed his grandmother almost two hundred years ago saw a "flying canoe." "She saw people in it," the newsletter states. "As it flew low, it had colors."[43]

Ed Conroy, the investigator who wrote *Report on Communion*, said he became the target of tricks and unexplained phenomena when he began researching Strieber's story. According to *UFO Universe* strange helicopters began conducting surveillance on him, and soon "strange messages appeared on his answering machine, including what sounded like mechanical voices."[44] Conroy noted:

> This phenomenon, whatever it is, has a direct link with human consciousness. It is indeed trickster-like, here one moment, gone the next, dazzling us with amazing shows and feats of derring-do. Has it served any purpose to benefit me—or has it been some kind of demonic interference in my life? While my initial response to much of it was alarm, I have come to see this trickster phenomenon as a friend in one sense: It has kept me on my toes.[45]

But the record shows that some UFO contactees, and those involved with channeling, are sometimes given elaborate instructions on complex building or scientific projects that they believe will revolutionize the world. New Age writer Jon Klimo cites one instance where the late Waynesboro, Virginia, artist and scientist Walter Russell received channeled messages from "God" which could have foreshadowed laser and holography technology.[46] But it's questionable that this "knowledge" served any purpose at all, since it was so vague.

Today, UFO contactees are receiving similar messages about building devices, and I don't know of a single case where the extraterrestrially originated projects have ever worked. They all seem to have the same end result as George Van Tassel's nonworking life extension machine, the Integratron. Ruth Norman of the Unarius Foundation, for example, gives complex instructions on how to build machines that draw power from higher dimensions.[47] No one takes her seriously enough to build one, though.

Saucer Construction

But in the annals of UFO history many teams have worked on building their own flying saucers and related machines by following instructions given to them by the space brothers. Yet none of the devices have ever worked and none of the saucers have ever flown. These have not been fringe elements of the UFO movement, either. Some big names have gotten involved, including Howard Menger who went on television to demonstrate his "free-energy motor" that never worked,[48] and Wayne Aho, Warren Goetz, and Charles Gaiffe, who worked on the "Bluebird" flying saucer.[49]

The Crop Circles

England's mysterious crop circles, whether they are being placed there by UFOs or not, seem to have the same demonic purpose. They focus people's eyes away from God and cause people to waste time. Literally thousands are now involved in investigating the mysterious circles and they, in many cases, are quite willing to attribute meanings to them. Not that they shouldn't be investigated, but they have become an obsessive curiosity for UFO enthusiasts everywhere. Even respected professional organizations like MUFON run numerous stories trying to uncover the secret of the circles. If any one force is behind them and is orchestrating many more circles throughout the world, it is not to give people any clear answers as to the cause.

As we discussed earlier, in 1990 many of the circles began to form strange shapes in the fields that some said could have been an ancient alphabet. Circles expert Sandy Mitchell gave some possible interpretations prior to the multinational Desert Storm action against Iraq. It could be some kind of warning about the Middle East crisis, she said, or it could be related to the holy grail legend and the eucharist, she said. But one thing she felt certain of, it was somehow related to the coming new age.[50]

Jon Erik Bekjord, curator of the Crypto-Phenomena Museum in Malibu, had a different opinion, one that he announced at a national UFO conference by issuing a news release. He said he "decoded" four of the circles by using "two ancient Norse/Celtic pictographic languages." "This is the place of the Devil; an evil place," says one. "This is an evil place to camp," says the second, and the last two say "Thor—the God of Thunder" and "Mars—the God of War."[51]

But Bekjord, who said he bases his interpretation on the research of Dr. Barry Fell, an internationally known scholar who often writes about ancient history, said his findings are only tentative. It doesn't help that Dr. Fell doesn't accept his interpretation.

Our Lady of Fatima

If the crop circles really are signs sent from the prince of the power of the air to deceive and confuse us, it won't be anything new. Many UFOlogists speculate that the famous apparition of Our Lady of Fatima in 1917 could have been an alien, and the three shepherd children, Lucia, Francisco, and Jacinto, contactees. The apparition bears no resemblance to Bible accounts of angelic messengers. The entity was described as a "celestial being" that came from the sky in a globe of light. One witness was quoted as saying that "it looked like a disc, of a very definite contour . . . [it] possessed a clear, changing brightness, which one could compare to a pearl."[52] The globe of light in these accounts is reminiscent of the way the good witch Glenda looked in the movie *The Wizard of Oz*.

If such a phenomenon occurred today, the lady could be construed to be a visitor from another planet. But I contend that the being was an "angel of light" (2 Cor. 11:14) masquerading as the exalted queen of heaven in the tradition of the superstitious Roman Catholic Church of that day. The demon was quick to confirm the erroneous doctrines of purgatory, the mass, and Mary worship, thereby gaining acceptance by the pope and even adding to the false teaching of Mary as a factor in salvation. The term the three children gave to her was *Immaculate Heart,* a term that Catholics still use today and offer prayers to.

Today the Roman Catholic Church is abuzz with constant rumors about the contents of certain letters pertaining to Fatima, and in some quarters what has been written about Fatima is more believed than the Word of God.

The Simplicity of the Gospel

Of course, all this tail chasing contrasts directly with the simplicity of the gospel.

> Don't be deceived, my dear brothers. Every good and perfect gift is from above, coming down from the Father of the heavenly lights, who does not change like shifting shadows. He chose to give us birth through the word of truth, that we might be a kind of firstfruits of all he created (James 1:16–18).

14 Extraterrestrial Life and the Parallel Universe

In October 1990, near Buenos Aires, Argentina, a very interesting machine the size of two large refrigerators went on line. Called the Megachannel Extraterrestrial Assay II, or META II, it is hooked up to a ninety-eight-foot-wide radio-telescope dish and is capable of listening to 8.4 million channels in a quest to hear life from outer space in the southern hemisphere.[1]

Its "brother," META I, went on line in 1985. It is hooked up to an eighty-four-foot radio telescope at Harvard's Oak Ridge Observatory in Massachusetts. Both machines are part of SETI, the Search for Extraterrestrial Life project, and are financed by the Pasadena-based Planetary Society, which got the money from contributions (including $100,000 from filmmaker Steven Spielberg) for the project.[2]

But these are not the only attempts to listen for radio waves from space in search of intelligent life. In 1959 scientist Frank Drake used an eighty-five-foot-diameter radio dish in West Virginia and focused it at nearby stars, and for the past twenty-one years the Ohio State University observatory has been doing the same. Elsewhere around the globe huge radio telescopes in Puerto Rico, New Mexico, California, Spain, and Australia have listened to the stars.[3]

Today a large percentage of scientists believe life may exist elsewhere in the universe, and Carl Sagan is one of the leading cheerleaders for this view. Two other big names advocating this view are astronomer Robert Jastrow and Clyde

Tombaugh, who as a twenty-three-year-old Kansas wheat farmer discovered Pluto in 1930. Tombaugh said he thought it likely there are "trillions" of other civilizations outside our solar system.[4] Jastrow, like Tombaugh, bases his view on evolutionary probabilities.

Jastrow and Malcolm H. Thompson are more cautious, however. They note that "neither theoretical calculations nor laboratory experiments can yield an answer" to the question of life, but they add:

> There are 100 billion stars belonging to the cluster we call our Galaxy. Ten billion other galaxies, each with 100 billion stars— and probably a like number of planets—are within the range of the largest telescopes. Perhaps only a small fraction of them are earthlike planets, but that would mean millions of earthlike planets in our Galaxy alone.[5]

What if life does exist on other planets? Will that shake the faith of Christians? It shouldn't. Writer David Wimbish, a critic of today's flying-saucer prophets, said that "God isn't wasteful, and since He created all the planets and stars of the universe, it wouldn't surprise me at all if He put living creatures on many of them." But he cautions us from believing any anti-Christian messages from any alien sources, even "if a flying saucer landed on the White House lawn" and gives us new "truths" about Christ.[6]

So far, scientists have found nothing. The search goes on.

But There Are Sure Signs of Alien Life

As I've demonstrated, there are sure signs of nonhuman life in the skies over Earth. Many people, even evangelical leaders, have testified to seeing UFOs. But what are they?

I believe they are beings from a parallel universe, or a parallel dimension, to our own. We cannot see them under normal circumstances, but they can see us. To me, this hypothesis makes the most sense. Experienced researchers Allen Hynek and Jacques Vallee say this:

If UFOs are indeed somebody else's "nuts and bolts hardware," then we must still explain how such tangible hardware can change shape before our eyes, vanish in a Cheshire cat manner (not even leaving a grin), seemingly melt away in front of us, or apparently "materialize" mysteriously before us without apparent detection by persons nearby or in neighboring towns.[7]

In the Spiritual Counterfeits Project's 1977 journal on UFOs, Mark Albrecht and Brooks Alexander explained how UFOs could be orchestrated by beings from another dimension. They produced drawings of a two-dimensional world called "Flatland" and demonstrated that objects from there that contact the world of three dimensions (height, depth, and width) would cause them to seem to be strange distorted shapes that appear and disappear and even change shapes. Since we live in a three-dimensional world, Albrecht and Alexander take this one step further: How would objects from the fourth dimension appear to us?[8]

I believe the Bible clearly teaches that the heavenly realms exist, not in space somewhere but on another dimension. It would answer many questions such as why Paul, who besides not being permitted to describe his trip to the third heaven, added that it was "inexpressible" (2 Cor. 12:4). In the same vein, if someone from the third dimension were transported into the fourth dimension, there would be no way to describe it, since no one in the third dimension could understand it.

Spiritual Dimension

I also believe the fourth dimension is described in Scripture as a spiritual dimension that is just as real as our physical world. The Bible, I believe, supports this. "God is Spirit," said Jesus, "and those who worship Him must worship in spirit and truth" (John 4:24 NASB).

Likewise, the Bible explains the demonic realm. There are numerous references to evil spirits throughout God's Word, and God forbids us to engage in contact with them. Rather, we are told to "test the spirits," and the test is the measure of what they think of Christ:

Dear friends, do not believe every spirit, but test the spirits to see whether they are from God, because many false prophets have gone out into the world. This is how you can recognize the Spirit of God: Every spirit that acknowledges that Jesus Christ has come in the flesh is from God, but every spirit that does not acknowledge Jesus is not from God. This is the spirit of the antichrist, which you have heard is coming and even now is already in the world (1 John 4:1–3).

My investigation of the UFO movement has come to a close. In more than 20,000 miles of travel, in reading thousands of messages from aliens, and from listening to many contactees, I don't know of a single case where an extraterrestrial message has passed the "Jesus test." Therefore, my responsibility to God, since I know the truth, is to "Have nothing to do with the fruitless deeds of darkness, but rather expose them" (Eph. 5:11). This book is part of that process.

Perhaps this other-dimensional explanation is also the real answer to why UFOs and extraterrestrial beings do not show themselves to the world. Contact is typically made through the spiritual world. Weldon and Levitt write: "Contact with the UFOs often seems to be by occult means. Our visitors have rarely responded to any standard approach, whether it is by aerial pursuit or a ground confrontation. By contrast, the standard tools of the occult have reportedly established contact in innumerable cases."[9]

Apparently time is not the same dimension in the spiritual world as it is in our world. Everything in our universe is oriented around time. Everything, living or not, has a beginning and an end. But in the spiritual realm, we read, are "everlasting torment" and "eternal life." Perhaps when the first man and woman fell into sin in the Garden of Eden, God placed our universe away from his; the Bible says that is when death entered the picture (Gen. 2:17).

Are thousands of contactees and abductees flying off to other worlds with their extraterrestrial friends? Was Whitley Strieber really abducted and saw strange beings? Was Sherry Hansen Steiger really shown a beautiful golden city? I believe they all think they did. And perhaps by dabbling with demonic powers they actually did. In the reported story of Uri Geller claiming that he once disappeared and went into "another dimension" for an hour, his friend told him he never disappeared at all and that it happened during two to three seconds. "It was so real," he kept saying.[10]

He Rolls Out of His Body

It was quite possible, through his occult background and through additional teaching from "the visitors," that Strieber learned he could leave his body and enter the spiritual realm. Or was this simply a demonic delusion? Strieber wrote:

> My many years of meditation made it a familiar condition for me. I began attempting to roll out of my body.
> For an instant, I was very confused and disoriented because the sheet I was lying on had just slid past my field of vision. Then I found myself in the air above my body. I was hanging there, floating effortlessly. I saw my face down below, the eyes partly opened, the lips parted. It did not look like me, not quite. Later, I think, I understood why; I had never before seen myself except in mirror-image.[11]

I believe all these experiences were real enough for God to warn us about their dangers. Albrecht and Alexander point out that since many scholars believe the Tower of Babel (Gen. 11:1–9) was an occult enterprise, God realized that humankind was on the verge of gaining dangerous, unlimited power ("nothing they plan to do will be impossible for them") and he put an end to it. They add:

> The scriptural description of Egypt's "court sorcerers" treats their accomplishments as more than mere conjuring tricks. The apparent manipulation of matter/energy to produce frogs and serpents (Exod. 7:9–12, 8:7) is described, without sensationalism, as a simple, matter-of-fact reality. Likewise the Lord's scathing denunciation of Babylon (Isa. 47) specifies her "many sorceries" and acknowledges the "great power of [her] enchantments" (Isa.

47:9). In the same way, he affirms that her wisdom and knowledge were real enough, in their own fashion, but ultimately deceptive (Isa. 47:10). Such occultic powers are normally held in partial check through the will and for the glory of God (Exod. 8:18, Dan. 2:27). However, at the "end of the age," many of these restraints will be removed, and the human race will experience unexampled manifestations of supernatural power; like the sorceries and enchantments of the Babylonians, they will be utterly real, but finally untrue—their purpose and result is to deceive and mislead mankind.[12]

Followers of the new gospel of the extraterrestrial beings will, no doubt, scoff at this. Brad Steiger, for example, says there's nothing wrong with receiving channeled "guidance from UFO intelligences." It may be part of a "recovery of personal shamanism."

"There is nothing of the occult, the satanic, in such a declaration," Steiger asserts. "There is nothing in the innate ability to channel personal guidance that conflicts in any way with organized religion. There is nothing in the manifesting of creative revelation that offends in any way orthodox science."[13]

But Steiger is wrong. Having anything to do with shamanism is not only wrong, it's satanic. *The American Heritage Dictionary* defines shamanism as "the religious practices of certain native peoples of northern Asia who believe that good and evil spirits pervade the world and can be summoned or heard through inspired priests acting as mediums." It also states that a more primitive form of this "spiritualism" is practiced by certain North American Indian tribes.

Dave Hunt and T. A. McMahon add that connecting with spirit guides is always part of it. "Shamanism involves the development of alleged mind powers, which are always connected with a 'spirit guide' contacted through an altered state of consciousness," they write.[14] Therefore, a modern shaman would fall under the category of a spiritist, which is an umbrella term that can be used to cover New Age channelers, UFO channelers, mediums, and those receiving messages from other worlds (even inter- or multidimensional worlds through various means).

What Does God Think of It?

But it only really matters what God thinks of spiritism which includes Shamanism. And he despises it so much that he, when dispensing the law to Moses, said, "Do not allow a sorceress to live" (Exod. 22:18). In Leviticus God said that the spiritists were defiled and unfit to appear before God to worship him (Lev. 19:31) and he reaffirmed the death penalty by stoning any man or woman who practiced it (Lev. 20:27). It didn't change in the New Testament, either. Spiritism is listed along with adultery, witchcraft, and other offenses that will prevent people from receiving a heavenly reward (Gal. 5:19–21). (The Bible has much more to say about occult spiritism. See Lev. 20:6; Deut. 18:10–12; 1 Sam. 28:6; 1 Chron. 10:13; 2 Chron. 33:6; Isa. 2:6, 8:19; Acts 13:6–12, 16:16–18, 19:19; 1 Tim. 4:1, 2; Rev. 22:15.)

Are They Angels?

We have seen many in the UFO community who claim to be in touch with angels. The Bible does affirm not only the existence of demons and evil forces dedicated to destroying us but of good angels as well, who work throughout the world on behalf of God's chosen people.

But every "angel" discussed in these pages has failed to affirm Christ came in the flesh as the only way of salvation of humankind. On the contrary, a good angel will bring glad tidings (Dan. 9:21–27) and will speak of Christ or be active in helping God's people fulfill the Great Commission. Jesus said that there is "rejoicing in the presence of the angels of God over one sinner who repents" (Luke 15:10).

UFOnaut angels often come in the middle of night abducting and experimenting on people. Their messages lead people away from Christ.

Fallen Angels

The angel theory, however, would not be entirely incorrect, either. The spirit guides, the UFOnauts, the entities from Lemuria and Atlantis and from every other location from here to the mythical Clarion who give us new age messages these days are fallen angels. They have repackaged the same old lies they have been perpetrating against humanity from the time their leader, Satan himself, showed up in the Garden of Eden promising godhood to Adam and Eve in exchange for their disobedience to God.

The Bible tells us that when he (the devil) was cast down out of heaven, he took with him one-third of the host of heaven (Rev. 12:4). These powerful beings "disguise themselves as servants of righteousness" the way "Satan disguises himself as an angel of light" (2 Cor. 11:14–15). They are in open rebellion against God and are trying to recruit as many people as they can into their uprising. Through the years their message remains the same, but they change their methods, using powerful, lying signs and wonders to draw people away from God.

They are from the realm of darkness and the occult. They have the power to interject into our minds evil thoughts. They have been linked to poltergeist activity, ghosts, fairies, strange knocks in the night—the same things UFOs are linked to.

They are dangerous.

Sitting at the breakfast table at a UFO-New Age conference in San Diego was an elderly woman who was a lifelong student of the occult, or "metaphysics," as she put it.

She was clearly excited about the conference and was looking for new "truths" to add to her occult repertoire of deeper and deeper hidden knowledge and to hearing from new, exciting entities.

"I have many friends into metaphysics for a long time," she gushed, smiling. "And I don't know any one of them who's ever left. We just want to go deeper."

But people can and do leave the occult. Larry Gianguzzi of New York was abducted by aliens and suffered a crude operation at the hands of small grey aliens inside a flying saucer.

Later he became a contactee, convinced he was chosen as part of a fantastic plan to help the world at the behest of the space brothers. (See appendix 1 for his testimony.)

Today he is a born-again Christian and director of an evangelical ministry that helps people get out of the occult. Larry burst through the deception of the occult and into a new life.

The Lord, who created all the planets and stars, can do anything. He is God. And, as the Good Shepherd he goes after lost sheep. After all, he left his home in heaven to redeem us.

Appendix:
Pursued by Aliens

Lawrence J. Gianguzzi is in full-time Christian ministry reaching out to those who are entrapped in the occult. He is also a UFO contactee and abductee and was at one time active in the UFO community.

The following story is an account of events that took place in Gianguzzi's life during 1988. The things you are about to read are in his own words[1] based on actual experiences and are clearly related to the statement in Ephesians 6:12: "For our struggle is not against flesh and blood, but against the rulers, against the authorities, against the powers of this dark world and against the spiritual forces of evil in the heavenly realms."

The Story Begins

I was twenty-three years old, and like many other guys who grew up to see the first man land on the moon I had always been fascinated with space flight and the possibility of other life existing in the universe. I grew up very interested in science and technology and recently graduated with a B.S. in computer science. I am currently self-employed and develop custom computer software for diverse applications. I had never used or experimented with any kind of drug and had only consumed alcohol on occasion.

A Documentary on Outer Space

In February 1988, I came across a movie on network television. It claimed that some unidentified flying objects were machines being flown by creatures from other planets. These

244

claims were backed up by fascinating photographs, home movies, and actual witnesses who were thought to have been abducted by these aliens. These witnesses were convinced that they had undergone some kind of medical examination on board an alien spaceship. The examinations were conducted by small beings with large heads, big black eyes, and grey skin. Many of the witnesses were left with scars on their bodies and remembered some kind of surgery involving a small device being placed into their brains through a passage created by a needle forced up into their nasal cavities. I thought these claims were ridiculous. All of the witnesses were from east of nowhere and not very convincing.

The next segment of the documentary spoke of the unusual events occurring in a region known as the Hudson Valley in New York State. The narrator told of over 10,000 who observed a UFO over the area in 1983 and several thousand more observers of UFOs since then. Skeptics said the sightings were nothing more than small planes flying in formation. However, very reliable witnesses, such as police officers and pilots, insisted that the objects were very large, performed incredible maneuvers, and made no noise. Home videos were even taken of the UFO by a couple who lived in Putnam County.

At that point I was ready to believe in little grey beings from outer space. Very reputable people in my area had seen this object, and I wanted to know more. I wanted my curiosity satisfied by becoming a witness to this unexplained phenomenon.

The Quest Begins

In the next several weeks I became extremely interested in UFOs and began to watch the skies whenever I was outdoors. I learned of a local hotline run by investigators where a person could call up and hear their neighbors speak of their encounters. I spoke of these events with friends and family, and as the days went on my curiosity grew.

It was now well into February. On one Sunday night a friend of mine who lives in North Salem invited me over to watch television. I had one beer as a social gesture but stopped at that knowing I had to drive home. After a few hours I started my journey along the winding roads near the Titicus Reservoir. I was shocked as I looked up and saw a brilliant series of lights flying by. I stopped the car and watched them disappear over the treetops. I was sure this was not a plane, so I cautiously drove on.

As I looked over the moonlit reservoir, I noticed a huge object come up and over my car. It was at treetop level and made no noise. I rolled down the car window and lifted my upper body through it. I saw a red dome underneath the object with little figures moving around inside. I was terrified! All of a sudden I began to feel very dizzy. My next recollection was that I was back in my car and driving home as if nothing had happened. What did happen? How did I get back in my car? Where was the UFO?

It took me over twenty minutes longer than usual to get home and I didn't know why. I told my parents what happened, and they found it very hard to believe. But they knew that I wasn't a storyteller and saw that I was shaking and looked frightened.

I was afraid to sleep during the next several months, because I had dreams of being lifted up into the UFO and being held down on a table inside. I contacted the UFO hotline and was told that this had happened to others and that they felt sure I was abducted by aliens. According to them, a person's memory is erased in 98 percent of the abduction claims because of the trauma, and the only way to bring back the missing time is through hypnosis. I agreed to this procedure and a hypnotist in New York City was recommended to me. She was a Ph.D. and specialized in UFO abduction cases.

The Mystery Unfolds

The hypnotist was a very busy person, so the investigators met with me several times and verified that I was not lying, and the meeting was set up. My cost was one hundred dollars, and the visit lasted over three hours. During that time, I was placed into a hypnotic trance and the session was recorded on audiotape for my records.

The session revealed that I was taken aboard a UFO. I was placed on an operating table in a dark room with lots of buttons and lights on the walls. Three short grey beings with big heads and large black eyes paralyzed me. I couldn't move as they examined me and stared at me with those eyes. They communicated with me through ESP and assured me that I would be all right. They stuck a long needle up into my nose and broke through to my brain. As I relived this under hypnosis tears streamed down my face, my nose became swollen, and I was terrified. Apparently they had implanted something into my brain. They told me that they would be coming back for me sometime in the future. I was beamed back into my car and was on my way.

When I came out of the trance, the doctor told me that she had heard hundreds of similar stories, so I wasn't unique. She gave me hypnosis tapes to help me fall asleep and told me to keep in touch with her. She was an unusually nice lady but appeared to be in some kind of trance herself. She would often pause before speaking and gave me a big hug before I left.

The next few months were quite traumatic. I felt like I was always being watched and had headaches all of the time. I was told to expect these things, because research had shown that the brain implant was a radio transmitter used for monitoring humans and that this would cause some discomfort. I started spending less time with my friends and more time reading books about other people who had similar abduction experiences.

Some of these people noticed a uniform on the aliens that contained an armband with a symbol of a dragon or serpent on it. Others spoke of being cut and scarred by the aliens. Basically there was nothing good to be said about them. I was scared, felt helpless, and was looking for others who had experienced the same things that I had. My parents told me to forget about my experience, and their friends, who were born-again Christians, told me that these things were the works of Satan. At that time I was a member of the Presbyterian church. I felt that church was a place to go late at night on Christmas Eve to waste some time. The literature that I was reading told me that the pyramids were created by the aliens and that there was strong evidence indicating that Jesus Christ was also created by them. The devil to me was just some kind of made-up being enabling the churches to exist for monetary purposes.

A Mystery Woman

The *Pennysaver* magazine ran an ad which stated that a UFO discussion group was being set up for Westchester and Connecticut abduction cases. I was thrilled that I would finally be able to talk to others who were "in my shoes" and wasted no time in calling the listed phone number.

I spoke with a lady in her mid-forties whose name was Joanne.[2] She was a loner and had met up with so-called aliens many times since she was fifteen. She had a very tough life. Recently she had been in a car accident which left her in a coma. At that time she saw an "angel of light" sending all sorts of healing energy to her. When she recovered it was as if she were a different person.

Joanne claimed that she often traveled out of her body to disaster areas such as where planes were about to crash and earthquakes were in progress. She said she was placed there to help the dying people get to the other side. She said that she had many periods of missing time in her life because of the aliens. She had even visited their planet and was asked to stay there with them but refused because she wanted to come back to Earth.

Joanne believed that she had several past lives and told me that she felt that she knew me from the ancient civilization of Atlantis. She claimed that she was in contact with my mind through ESP and proved it to me many times. She said that she was a good witch, but she had the most evil witch laugh that I had ever heard. She claimed that God was some kind of energy in the form of a white light and that she used crystals along with this energy so as to perform healings on people. She had recently burned her leg with cooking oil and claimed that this power was the source behind the healing that was taking place in her wound.

Our phone conversations went on for a period of about a week. During this time I found myself on the phone at all hours of the day and night. I was often very confused, because the conversations would seem to last for only minutes, but in reality hours had gone by. We both decided that it was time to meet in person and felt that the reason for the meeting was linked to the UFOs.

Introduction to the Occult

Our first meeting took place 11:00 P.M. on a Sunday. Joanne was a very nice, relaxed person. We talked about her UFO experiences and she showed me her crystal collection. She said that we had to surround ourselves with the white light of God to protect ourselves from evil forces. We looked at some books and then she offered to do a crystal healing on me. I told her that I had a nervous stomach since birth, and she decided that this would be a good place to start focusing the energy. She said a short prayer and held the crystal over the troubled spot. I felt warm there as she laid her hands on that spot and told me to relax.

When she finished I felt better, but something was not right. I looked at the clock and over three hours had gone by. When I asked her what had happened, she didn't know either. We assumed since it was a missing-time incident and since we expected our meeting would involve the aliens that we had somehow just been abducted. As we tried to explain the lost time, the room started spinning and Joanne passed out. While her eyes were closed and she was unconscious she began to speak. Her words were sophisticated and her voice was very calm.

I was told that she was being used as a channel for communications with beings from another world. These beings claimed that their spirits were inside her body and that they were controlling her. Their names were Foosjoy and Natas. I was unaware of what the latter name spelled out when the letters were reversed. The so-called alien beings answered many scientific questions I had about the universe. They spoke of their home planet being destroyed in a nuclear war and stated that they could not reproduce. As a result of this they began cross-breeding via genetic experiments with our species thousands of years ago and claimed that many Earth people were in fact their children. They also said that they share the same God as we do and that the white-light energy is throughout the universe. I was told that we were to meet again the following week in the same manner and that it was time for Joanne to regain control of her body. They asked me to use my own judgment as to whom I would tell of these events and to let Joanne know of our conversation.

I spent a few minutes watching Joanne's eyelids for any sign of movement. I was sure that this was just a joke, and I was looking for some kind of proof. Her eyelids never moved, and neither did she. After a short time, I decided to wake her up. She asked me what was going on and why I was looking at her funny. I told her of my conversation with the alien spirits, and she called it channeling. She said that her friends had chan-neled and that she had heard about it but had never done it before. She had no recall of the entire conversation and agreed that we should meet again the next week as they requested. I departed from her house at daybreak.

Powers Bestowed

As I slept that morning I had a very strange dream. I saw an angel in a white robe floating over me throwing streams of elec-tricity at me. I didn't see a face on this angel but was led to believe that it was an angel from heaven.

When I woke up, I felt that my whole body had been charged up and was wide awake as if I had too much energy. I remem-bered that Joanne spoke of this energy having healing powers, so I went up and explained to my parents that I knew about crystals and how God works with them. My mother complained about a headache and backache so I laid hands on her, sur-rounded myself with the white light, and she was healed. By now, I realized that I had a gift, but I didn't know if it was from the aliens or from God.

I continued to speak with Joanne on the phone during that week and noticed that she was reading my mind now more than ever. Before this incident I needed eight to ten hours of sleep but now I was sleeping no more than two hours on and off in the course of a twenty-four-hour day. The energy was keeping me all charged up and awake.

We met again on the following Sunday. After some small talk it was back to business. Once again the room started to spin, but this time I saw a transparent head floating around in mid air. When the head got close to me I noticed a frightening face that appeared to have the characteristics of a Greek statue. All of a sudden, I was being spoken to again by the aliens channeled through Joanne. They informed me that the head I was seeing was a projection from their ship used to inform me of their presence. Because this sounded so incredible I wanted more proof. I asked to physically see the beings, but they said it could not be done at that time. I was suspicious, so they said, "We came with the wind and will leave with the rain." With that a huge gust of wind blew by and it began to pour down rain. This was some proof, but I still wanted to see a spaceship or one of them in person.

Now they began to use prophecy to persuade me into believing. I was told that the earth will face devastating catastrophes in the next ten years and that they were here to help us through them. They told me that Joanne and I, as well as many others, had ancestral roots from their world. They referred to us as their children and said that they were here to give us these powers to help us during the disasters ahead. They said that we were special and that they would not let their children die on Earth. They guaranteed us that they would take us to safety in a starship. These beings were even able to project visions of these end time events into Joanne's mind during these channeling sessions. They said that this was a time of spiritual growth and learning for both of us.

Life Patterns Change

In the next few weeks I began to fall deeper and deeper into the trap. I was so charged up with the energy that I didn't feel that sleeping and eating were necessary. My parents were very concerned and suspicious of the things that were going on. Their Christian friends were giving them all sorts of literature on the powers and deceitful ways of the devil. I was shown this material and pushed it away claiming that it was absurd. I was constantly questioning the validity of the so-called alien beings and was hoping that I would see the proof that I needed in the sessions to come.

I was told during the channeling that I should allow myself to become the channel, but I didn't want to because of my uncertainty. The aliens claimed that while I was asleep my spirit was on their ship being taught about the things that I would need to know in the future. They said that they were training me much faster than usual, because I was special and very powerful. They had a job worked out for Joanne and me. We were to be their Earth representatives. Their plan was to channel information to us regarding the other individuals in our area that they were also interested in. We were to round up these individuals and tell them of their alien heritage. We were to start a so-called end-time crusade to prepare the masses for a full-scale alien landing. They would notify us of the time and place of the landing, and we would all be instructed to gather there and be taken off to safety to be reunited with our true relatives.

We arranged for a meeting one night out by the reservoir, but as usual the aliens never showed up, and again I had no proof. Joanne was very tuned in to my mind and claimed that this was possible because she tapped into God's energy and received my thoughts through it. She always spoke of a distant healing being similar to this. It was a method of tapping into the energy through prayer and sending more of it to certain individuals in need. She did this for my stomach on a daily basis.

One afternoon my hand got very hot as if it were burning. This normally happened at her house when I would be doing a healing on her, but that was ten miles away. I called her up to ask what was happening. She told me that I was doing a distant healing on her leg. I didn't believe that until she told me to move my right hand in random patterns. I moved it in all sorts of confusing directions and to my surprise she somehow felt these movements on her leg and described them to me as they were happening.

I constantly felt as if I were being watched and often saw the floating head even when I was not with Joanne. I continued to experiment with my new powers and read more literature on the crystals. According to the books, if a healer held the crystal or focused the energy on another person that person could also obtain the powers. I asked a friend if he would let me experiment on him and he said yes. I held the stone over his head and prayed for the energy to flow through him. All of a sudden his eyes fluttered and he began to fall. He stumbled into the other room pleading with me to take the crystal away. I stopped praying but he almost passed out anyway. He said that his whole body felt numb and that he was very dizzy. He needed to sit down and asked me to find out what had just happened.

I called Joanne. She said that he was going through a rebirthing process and that he should cry if he felt like it. I immediately told my parents about what had happened and tried the same thing on my mother, but it had no effect on her. My father and the rest of the family were too scared to let me try it on them.

Since I was so new to this, Joanne invited me on a trip to Danville, Vermont, to attend a dowsers' convention to learn more about my powers. She said that it was a meeting of good witches and would be very educational. The aliens said that I should go and if nothing else use it as vacation time.

Confirmed by the Clergy

Obviously my parents said that they would like it if I did not go and recommended that I call up our minister to see if what was happening to me was God's work. I felt that I owed it to them, so I made the call. I explained the circumstances to the minister and told him about everything from the crystals to the angel in my dream. I even told him of the UFO abduction, but I purposely didn't tell him about the channeling. To my surprise he said that these things were all right and that they were indeed a gift from the Lord. He even said that he would speak to my parents if I wished. He told me not to tell others about these things, because they wouldn't understand. My parents valued his opinion and didn't bother me anymore. After all, how could a nice lady like Joanne, who lets insects roam around in her home because they are living entities as we are, be involved in anything evil?

By this time I felt that I should contact my hypnotist and let her know about my abilities to heal and use the white light as an energy source. When I spoke with her, she sounded very comfortable with my situation and told me that I was gifted. She said she also knew of the light and used it as part of her nightly New Age meditation exercises.

The Trek Begins

On a Tuesday we left for Vermont, and because of Joanne's bad leg I had to drive her car. My parents felt they were never going to see me again, but I assured them I would be all right. During the long drive into the country we discussed the UFOs. The aliens had told us that they were also going to be at the convention and that we should look for other people whose ancestral roots were not of this world. The drive was long and boring, and we didn't arrive until 3:00 or 4:00 A.M. We were both very tired but as usual only needed a few hours of sleep.

When we woke up we knew that it was going to be a busy day. I told Joanne I didn't want to be a part of the convention and that she could teach me about what she learned later. I drove her up to a little town in northern Vermont. The buildings were very old but had been restored, and one of the first things I noticed was a church in the middle of the town green. Apparently her first meeting with these people would take place there. I was asked to go in with her and decided that a few minutes couldn't hurt. The people seemed unusual to me. I noticed that they were all in a very calm relaxed mood. The majority were between middle and old age and they all seemed to be mesmerized or fascinated.

Each person was given a package that contained various shaped metal and plastic rods and a wooden pendulum to be used in conjunction with the white-light energy. The instructor tried to give me one but I refused and he seemed upset. Verifiable questions were posed to the universal light. If the pendulum swung clockwise, the answer was "yes"; counterclockwise meant "no." To my surprise, the answers were correct. The disciples were also instructed on how to use the rods to find water, gold, or any other substance. The meeting continued outside where the people had opportunity to experiment with their new-found powers in searching for underground water mains.

I left Joanne there to learn more about these powers while I drove around the country on my own for the rest of the day. I was extremely bored and when I returned to pick her up she asked if we could stay for the opening ceremonies. I agreed to this and once again found myself in a church. There were hundreds of people there and they were all in some kind of trance, as I believe I was myself.

The ceremony began with a prayer to the Lord by a priest. Everyone in the room blessed themselves in the name of the Father, the Son, and the Holy Ghost, and the meeting continued. The instructors briefed the audience on the available seminars. Some had to do with crystals, others with past lives, and yet others with dowsing. Joanne and I both noticed some kind of white spiritual mist over the people. This mist was very intense, and what appeared to be ghosts were entering and leaving the bodies of many of the people there. All of the participants had their dowsing packages with them, and some were even practicing during the meeting.

An Evil Power

When the meeting was over we went back to the hotel room and Joanne decided to show me some of her instruments. She said that she had a great day and learned a lot. She even found out that the instructor engaged in channeling with alien beings as well. The instructor told Joanne that she was very powerful and different from the others. Joanne was in a good mood and started using the pendulum and the dowsing rods. I asked her if I could try them, because I wanted to make sure that she wasn't moving the devices with her hands. I held the pendulum in my hand, and it started to swing and spin. The piece of wood was spinning in a circle as if there were no gravity holding it down. I felt some kind of force tugging on the object and was amazed. I asked it questions that I would only know, and it answered them correctly. Now we each grabbed a pair of dowsing rods and started to play with them. They were spinning around at a good speed and it looked as if a bunch of windmills were in the middle of a hurricane. I was satisfied that this was not a trick and wanted to go to sleep, but Joanne wanted to try channeling the alien beings.

She got comfortable and attempted to make contact with them but was having a hard time. She tried for over an hour and then something started to happen. Her eyes were closed, but something was not right. She started to move as if she were being pushed around in her sleep. It seemed like she was being beaten up. All of a sudden she shouted for me to wake her up. I was terrified and tried to wake her, but she wasn't responding. I slapped her in the face, but still nothing happened. As a last resort I slapped her again, this time with a lot of force. She opened up her eyes, and all I could see were the whites of her eyes. She looked dead, so I continued to smack her, hoping that she was okay. Her eyes closed again, and as they opened she was all right. She told me that some negativity got to her because she hadn't put the white-light shield around herself. She reached to her side in pain, and there were black-and-blue marks along with burns in her skin. These marks were not there prior to the channeling attempt. Once again she blamed herself for not putting up the spiritual shield of light for protection, and we decided to forget the contact for that evening and go to sleep.

On Thursday, I drove Joanne to the convention and spent the rest of the day reading up on the power of crystals. I thought a lot about the night before and was disturbed by what had happened. After all, if this white light was really God, then why did the evil forces get a hold on her? I began to really feel that the things that had been happening were of an evil nature, but I was trapped over six hours from home and had no way of escaping.

I picked up Joanne and once again she spoke of meeting other people who practiced channeling. She said that she also met people who claimed they were not from Earth. She felt that it was once again time to attempt making contact with the so-called aliens. She asked me if I was interested in being the channel, but I said no way because of what I had seen the previous night.

Once again she started to relax, but found it difficult because of unknown forces in the room. Finally her voice sounded more sophisticated, and I was told that I was speaking with the alien beings, but it wasn't really them. Some other being had started channeling through her and lying about who he was. The being was not one we were familiar with, and Joanne sensed this so she woke up.

By this time I was really concerned, but she assured me that the channeling would work. After another try, and she made contact. Foosjoy and Natas were very unhappy with me and said that I should be attending the conference and meeting others like myself. They said that I was resisting them and that I had to trust them. They complained and said that I should stop ignoring the little voices in my head, because it was really them trying to guide me in the right direction. They claimed that their voices in my mind guided me to the specific books that I was reading about channeling. I was told that I had to laugh more often and let my inhibitions go so that the other people at the convention would be drawn to me. I told them that I would attend the next session and said that I would like it if they were there to help me out. They agreed to this, and Joanne woke up.

Her leg was hurting and she asked me to do a healing on it. The healing that I am speaking of involved holding the crystal in one hand which was used to magnify the universal light energy being channeled through me and running the other hand over the area of pain. I had been doing this with her since I found out that I had this ability. My whole body would become electrified and hot and I could feel the energy flowing out of me and into her burn. The wound would start to ooze and begin to close up more and more each time I would do this, but it didn't seem to be getting any better. We finished very late that night, and it was time to get some sleep.

Spiritual Schizophrenia

The next morning after the usual two hours of sleep we were on our way, but something was different. Joanne seemed to be switching the channeling on and off involuntarily. I was told that by my request the aliens were there with me. Each time Joanne spoke, she denied having ever said anything. She requested that we go to a liquor store, because her pain killers were not working and the aliens suggested the use of alcohol as a remedy. We went to the store and she picked up a fifth of vodka, a bottle of vermouth, and a pair of sunglasses, and we were on our way to the diner for lunch.

During the fifteen-minute drive she managed to mix the alcohol and finish a half-bottle of each. Her altered states of consciousness were now extremely confusing. As we entered the diner, she insisted on leaving the sunglasses on, even though I told her it was rude. We placed our order and then she said that she didn't like what she had ordered. However, when the food came she ate it as if nothing were wrong. Then she accused me of eating her pickle and stealing her fries, because she didn't remember eating them just seconds earlier. She ordered me to smile, but I refused and then started to laugh out of control. I had no reason to be laughing, and everyone was looking at me, but I couldn't stop. I was unable to eat or drink, and was very embarrassed. I asked her to stop whatever she was doing, and then I was fine.

When we left the diner Joanne asked me when we were going to eat. I told her that we just came from lunch, but she didn't believe me because she didn't remember it. She continued to drink the alcohol as we drove over to Danville, but it didn't seem to be affecting her. She told me to be happy, because others would be approaching me today. The ride seemed longer than usual, and when we got there the vodka was gone. We went into the town hall, and a lady selling crystals was there with a girl around my age helping her. I was told by the alien beings that I should have sex with the girl, because she was also from the light. They said that sex with a person who was a part of the energy would be the best. This girl was really in a trance. She talked as if she were high on drugs, and I wasn't interested in her.

All of a sudden an older man approached us. He said that he knew we would be there and that he was from Earth. He claimed to have visited other planets and even showed us a meteor he brought back. He did a healing on Joanne, read her mind, and seemed to be a real authority on channeling and alien beings. This man appeared to be a very gentle, kind and loving individual. As he departed it was as if he had disappeared. When we turned around there was no sign of him. We even looked out the windows and all over the building, but he was gone.

An hour or two had gone by since her last drink and Joanne decided that it was time for another round. We left the building, and as we approached the car Joanne started physically pushing me around. She told me not to resist her touch and to let myself go. I questioned her intentions but rather than answering me, she began to cry and accused me of not caring about her. After I insisted that I did care, Joanne finally stopped crying and once again directed her attention to the bottle, but it was empty. She picked up the pendulum and told me to drive. According to her, I was to make my turns correspond to the direction of the pendulum's movement. This whole idea was ridiculous but I decided to humor her anyway. So I started to follow the prompts. As I was driving, I commented on her sunglasses. I insisted that they were not needed because it was beginning to get dark. Once again she refused to remove them because her eyes were hurting. After driving several miles and being led through many intersections, the pendulum stopped. I looked around the general area. To my surprise there was a liquor store across the street. Joanne laughed at me, slammed the door, and went for the liquor. She managed to prove to me that we could be led to a liquor store but I couldn't understand why God would bring us to a place like that to solve her problems. When she returned to the car, Joanne immediately began to drink. She became very angry and told me to take her back to the hotel because she had to go to the bathroom.

Evil Forces Take Over

During the ride back to the hotel, I felt very uncomfortable. It was pitch black outside and Joanne still had those sunglasses on. I told her to take them off, but she refused. She looked over at me and in a strange, evil-sounding voice said, "We are not of this time dimension." I looked back at her and demanded that she take the sunglasses off, because there was something wrong with her. She hesitated, so I pulled the car over and waited for her to do so. All of a sudden she took them off and once again all I could see were the whites of her eyes. She demanded that I continue to drive because she was getting very angry. I did what I was told, and once we were on the road I asked her to speak about God and Jesus. She avoided my request by constantly opening the windows and causing other disturbances.

I asked her if she was evil, but instead of answering, she asked me what I was. I told her not to play games with me and to answer the question, but she wouldn't. I felt that some evil power had somehow gotten a hold on her and that the only way to get her back was to speak of God. At that point I was so confused that I didn't know where God fit in. I didn't know if he was the energy that she spoke of or what, but I did know that I should threaten the evil with the name of God as I had seen in the movies. I told her that when we got back to the room I would use all of the energy in the name of God to force the evil out of her. She replied by saying, "It's a challenge," in a wicked voice.

At that point I was extremely frightened and knew that if I took her up on that challenge that I might end up dead. I then knew that I had been deceived by some evil force. I felt that since I did not know where God fit into all of this, I might be really inadvertently asking the evil energy for help instead of

God. I decided it was too risky. I thought out my options, and even though I was not a thief, I decided to try to steal her car and drive home to New York. I pulled up to a local pizza place and told her that there was a bathroom inside that she could use. I didn't think she would remember we were only a mile from the hotel and figured that while she was inside I would steal the car. As we pulled over she hesitated for a minute and then said to me in a wicked voice, "Do not try and deceive me. I know your plan."

She told me to drive or she would throw me out of the car. I hesitated for a moment, and all of a sudden she reached over, grabbed my neck, and attempted to choke me. I pushed her away and began to drive as she requested. By that time I was out of ideas. Within moments we reached the hotel and she started to cry and beg for my forgiveness. I knew that was a trick and ordered her not to touch me. I said that I was going to get ice for her drinks. Joanne went into the bathroom in tears.

By that time I felt helpless but knew that I had to survive. I rushed over to the main office and told the nice old lady behind the front desk that my roommate was crazy. I told her of the dowsers' convention and the things that I had seen. I asked her to hide me from Joanne. She sensed how desperate I was and took me into her home in the back of the hotel. She said that she would try to contact a man of God and told me to take it easy. I was not more that twenty yards from the room that Joanne and I were staying in. My luggage was there, but I was willing to leave it behind, because I didn't want to chance going back. I was afraid because I felt that Joanne would find me by reading my mind or tracking me down with her pendulum or something.

I hid myself behind the couch, stayed away from the windows, and remained very quiet and still. I made a collect call to my parents at 10:30 P.M. and told them that they were right. I said that Joanne was very evil and that I had to get home, because I was scared. My father told me to keep my mother posted on where I was. I gave him directions, and he began his seven-hour drive to come and get me.

God to the Rescue

The hotel owner put me in contact with the pastor of a Baptist Church in Vermont. After he heard my story he told me that he would be right over.

When the pastor arrived the things he said began to open my eyes. I had been deceived all the way back to the UFOs and now it was time for my life to change. The hotel owner insisted that we check up on Joanne because of the possible threat to her establishment. The pastor convinced me that I had to face her and that I had to get my luggage back. He said that she was possessed by demons and that the Lord's protection would be on us. We went over to the room and found her passed out cold on the bed. I picked up my luggage and dropped all of the crystals that she had given me on the bed. I wanted nothing to do with this lady or what she stood for. I just wanted to go home and start my life over.

The pastor took me to his home and read to me from the Bible. I felt anger toward him and had violent thoughts, but I knew that he could help me and that the thoughts were not mine. I prayed to the Lord and asked that all of my powers be taken away by him. I repented out loud and repeated prayers said by the pastor. I asked to be saved and to be taken from the hands of Satan and his demons. During that time I felt very sick to my stomach. The pastor said that this was normal, considering what I had gone through. I had seen the movie *The Exorcist* and felt like I was living it. In Jesus' name the pastor demanded the names of any demons that may have been tormenting me, but none spoke up. By the power of the Lord Jesus Christ he commanded them to leave me.

For the first time in weeks, even months, I felt down to earth. I was no longer floating around in a hypnotic trance. I felt the evil powers leave me and the gentle touch of the Lord Jesus Christ come on me. I was born again! I accepted Jesus as my Lord and Savior. I knew that a new life for me had just begun that Friday, September 16, 1988.

My father arrived around 5:00 A.M. on Saturday morning. I was on my way back to New York and a new life. It was gradually getting light but not nearly as fast as the light of the Lord which had come on me earlier that evening. I was tired and worn out, and for the first time in many weeks felt the effects of the lack of sleep. I was happy to be with my father but still very scared and insecure. The Vermont pastor gave me a Bible to read and put me in touch with a local pastor in New York. I knew that he and his church were to become a very important part of my life. I knew that my experiences would be used in helping others become more aware of the spiritual hosts of wickedness that are constantly searching for souls to feed on and ultimately destroy.

A New Understanding

I do not believe that I was ever on board a UFO. The whole sighting-abduction seemed to be very dreamlike even though I was wide awake. I believe that I was somehow spiritually hypnotized at the time of my sighting. The sighting may have been some kind of materialization or transformation of energy induced by demonic forces. The UFO has been photographed by other witnesses and seen by thousands, so there had to be something out there. Once I gave up my free will to resist the manifestation and decided to accept it, I was open for the spiritual hypnosis that led to some kind of subconscious movie being played out in my mind. This movie now became reinforced when I visited the New Age hypnotist and further gave up my free will to the forces at work.

As the days went by, I played right into the hands of Satan, and other aspects of the occult were more easily introduced and accepted. I was in contact with familiar spirits. I used divining rods and crystals to increase the manifestation of the supernatural powers that were inhabiting my body. I was blacking out for hours at a time allowing my body to be controlled by demonic forces. I was simply a human puppet willfully handing over my strings to an unknown force that claimed to be the universal power of "light and love."

Eventually God had to leave me with a decision. He lifted the satanic veil that was blinding me by exposing the true nature of the demons at work within Joanne. By God's grace I was given the chance to turn my life over to Jesus Christ and to ask him for help and forgiveness for my detestable actions.

Questions or comments concerning the subject matter of this book should be addressed to:

William M. Alnor
Eastern Christian Outreach
P.O. Box 11322
Philadelphia, PA 19137

Please enclose a self-addressed, stamped envelope.
Write if you would like to be on the mailing list to receive our ministry's *Christian Sentinel* newsletter.

Notes

Introduction

1. Nolan Walters, "UFO Beliefs Cited in Desertion Case," *Philadelphia Inquirer,* 16 July 1990: 5A.

2. Carl Sagan, "UFOs: The Extraterrestrial and Other Hypotheses," *UFOs—A Scientific Debate*, eds. Sagan and Thornton Page (New York: Norton, 1972), 272.

3. Brad Steiger, *The Fellowship* (New York: Ballantine, 1989), 161.

4. Ibid., 67.

5. Ibid., 67–68.

6. Tara Gravel, "Interview with David Jacobs, Ph.D." Temple University journalism paper, 6 December 1990.

7. Cited in John Weldon with Zola Levitt, *What on Earth Is Happening?* (Irvine, Calif.: Harvest House, 1975), 99.

8. The MJ-12 theory is one of the hottest things in UFOlogy right now. It maintains that President Harry Truman created a secret UFO working group called Majestic 12 to handle an alien disk that allegedly crashed near Roswell, New Mexico, in 1947 and to work with aliens in a long-term cooperative agreement. Purported leaked government documents were released, including one signed by Truman. However, UFO skeptic Philip J. Klass exposed it as a hoax (see the 27 September 1987, *Philadelphia Inquirer*) and in the Winter 1990 issue of the *Skeptical Inquirer* Klass showed how Truman's signature had been lifted from another document.

9. John Wiley, "Phenomena, Comment and Notes," *The Smithsonian,* January 1983: 24.

10. Frank Rossi, "A Perennial Prankster's Not-So Stories," *Philadelphia Inquirer,* 12 December 1990: 1E, 7E.

Chapter 1
Armageddon and the 144,000

1. See 1 Kings 18 and 19 for the story of Elijah on Mount Carmel and his flight from Jezebel.

2. The late Dr. Allan Hynek, the most influential figure in modern UFOlogy, created designations for UFO sightings. A close encounter of the first kind is a sighting of

a UFO at close range; the second kind is a close sighting that leaves physical evidence of a landing; a third kind is a close sighting that includes seeing a humanoid creature by the spacecraft; the fourth kind is an abduction by the UFO.

3. Hal Lindsey, *The Late Great Planet Earth* (New York: Bantam, 1981), 152–53.

4. 2 Thessalonians 2:4.

5. See also Jeremiah 30:7; Joel 2:11; Zephaniah 1:14; Malachi 4:5.

6. William Alnor, "UFO Cults Are Flourishing in New Age Circles" *Christian Research Journal* (Summer 1990): 5.

7. "Star-Borne Has Moved!" *The Starry Messenger,* September 1990: 3.

8. *11:11—The Opening of the Doorway* (Charlottesville, Va.: Star-Borne Unlimited, 1990), 6.

9. Solara Antara Amaa-ra, "11:11 The Opening of the Doorway" *The Starry Messenger* (Sept. 1990): 18.

10. Meg Sullivan, "New Age Will Dawn In August, Seers Say, And Malibu Is Ready," *Wall Street Journal,* 23 June, 1987. See also José Argüelles, *The Mayan Factor* (Santa Fe: Bear & Co, 1987).

11. Mark Cotta Vaz, *Spirit in the Land,* (New York: Signet, 1988), 15.

12. Solara Antara Amaa-ra, Lecture, Whole Life Expo, New York, 26 Oct. 1990.

13. Solara, *The Star-Borne: A Remembrance for the Awakened Ones,* 2d ed. (Charlottesville, Va.: Star-Borne Unlimited, 1990), 59.

14. Brad Steiger, *Gods of Aquarius* (New York: Berkley, 1983), 115. (Book 3 of The Star series). Other books in the series include *The Star People, Revelation: The Divine Fire,* and *Reflections from an Angel's Eye.*

15. Ibid., 116.

16. Brad Steiger, *The Fellowship* (New York: Ballantine, 1989), 180.

17. Ibid., 180–81.

18. Steiger, *Gods,* 115–116.

19. Ibid., 116.

20. Steiger, *Fellowship,* 187.

21. Ibid., 189.

22. Doug Groothuis, *Unmasking the New Age* (Downers Grove: InterVarsity, 1986), 18.

23. Ibid., 19.

24. Steiger, *Fellowship,* 185–86.

25. Triton, *The Magic of Space,* ed. John Hay (Larchmont, N.Y.: Triad Publishing, 1962).

Chapter 2
The Second Coming According to the Space Brothers

1. Sandra Mitchell, "The Crop Circle Mystery," The International Fortean Organization, Fortfest '90 conference, McLean, Va., 10 Nov. 1990. Mitchell and her colleague, Andrew E. Rothovius, who had been in England investigating the crop circles mystery, presented lectures on the phenomenon.

2. Ibid., Rothovius' speech.

3. Maria Goodavage, "Circles in the Fields Inspire Talk of UFOs," *USA Today,* 15 Nov. 1990, 6A.

4. Dava Sobal, "Field of Dreams?" *Omni,* December 1990: 122. This article, quoting a British crop circle expert, points out that Army researchers "got film footage of an orange light in the sky moving slowly to the east, dipping down to ground level, and then picking up speed" before leaving the area. Several circles appeared in the path of the light.

5. Goodavage, 6A.

6. "Visitors from Outer Space," *Share International News* (Fall 1990): 2.

7. William Alnor, "The Christ Has Presented His Credentials to the Media, New Age Organization Says," *Christian Research Journal* (Summer 1990): 35.

8. Ibid.

9. Ibid.

10. Ibid.

11. Rick Branch, "Is the Maitreya the Second Coming of Christ?" *Watchman Expositor* 8 (Nov. 3, 1991): 6.

12. Ibid.

13. Benjamin Creme, *The Reappearance of the Christ and the Masters of Wisdom* (Hollywood, Calif.: The Tara Center, 1980). Cited by Branch, ibid.

14. Ron Rhodes, *The Counterfeit Christ of the New Age Movement* (Grand Rapids: Baker, 1990), 121.

15. Rhodes' book, pages 119–129, contains an excellent discussion of the four prongs of Theosophy.

16. Rudolf Steiner, *The Four Sacrifices of Christ* (Spring Valley, N.Y.: Anthroposophic Press, 1944), 20.

17. Goldman, Stuart, unpublished manuscript on Whitley Strieber on file, cited in Alnor, "UFO Cults . . ."

18. Steiger, *Gods,* 39–40.

19. Steiger, *Fellowship,* 50.

20. Winfield S. Brownell, *UFOs: Key to Earth's Destiny!* (Lytle Creek, Calif.: Legion of Light, 1980), 73–82.

21. Ibid., 78–81.

22. Ibid., 78.

23. David Spangler, *Links with Space* (Marina Del Rey, Calif.: DeVorss, 1976), 13.

24. Ibid., 28.

25. Raphael, *The Starseed Transmissions*, ed. Kenneth X. Carey (Kansas City: Uni-Sun, 1987), 1–2.

26. Ibid., 1.

27. Ibid., 2.

28. Ibid., 22.

29. Ibid., 16.

30. Ibid.

31. Ibid., 66.

32. Ibid.

33. Steiger, *Gods*, 115.

34. Ibid., 115–16.

35. Douglas Curran, *In Advance of the Landing: Folk Concepts of Outer Space* (New York: Abbeville Press, 1985), 38–39.

36. Ibid., 75.

37. Ibid., 33.

38. Ibid.

39. Mike Granberry, "Cultists Dwell on Their Past Lives," *Akron* (Ohio) *Beacon Journal*, 3 Oct. 1986, D3. Granberry is a staff writer for the *Los Angeles Times*, the publication that originated the story of Norman.

40. William M. Alnor, *Soothsayers of the Second Advent* (Old Tappan, N.J.: Fleming H. Revell, 1989), 29.

41. Robb Fulcher, "Story of Spacemen Broadcast by Man," *The* (Portland) *Oregonian*, 8 May 1984, B2. The story originated from *United Press International*.

42. Ibid.

43. Ibid.

44. David Tucker, "3 Hours on a UFO," *The Dekalb News/Sun*, 18 Sept. 1985, 1B.

45. Brownell, 42.

46. Ibid.

47. Ashtar Command, *Project: World Evacuation*, compiled by Tuella (Salt Lake City: Guardian Action International, 1982), x–xi.

48. Whitley Strieber, *Transformation: the Breakthrough* (New York: Avon, 1989), 22.

49. Raphael, 37.

50. Brad Steiger, "Starseeds & Starpeople—Have They Arrived from Other Planets?" *UFO Universe*, Sept. 1988: 66.

51. Steiger, *Fellowship*, 27–28.

52. James J. Brookes, *Maranatha or the Lord Cometh* (St. Louis: Edward Bredell, 1878), 81.

Chapter 3
The Second Coming According to Jesus

1. R.C. Sproul, *Reason to Believe* (Grand Rapids: Zondervan, 1982), 32–34.

2. D. James Kennedy, *Why I Believe* (Waco: Word, 1980), 106-07. There are many books on the historical evidence of the resurrection. Some of the more popular include Josh McDowell's *Evidence that Demands a Verdict* (vol. 1 rev. ed.) (San Bernardino, Calif.: Here's Life, 1979) and his shorter treatment, *More Than a Carpenter* (Wheaton: Tyndale, 1980). Kennedy also quotes some older books such as T. W. Fawthrop's *The Stones Cry Out*, Simon Greenleaf's *The Testimony of the Evangelists*, and others.

3. Robert G. Clouse, ed. *The Meaning of the Millennium: Four Views*, (Downer's Grove: InterVarsity, 1977). The four views are historic premillennialism, dispensational premillennialism, postmillennialism, and amillennialism. Of the four, the first two views are probably the most popular today, while the third view is the least popular.

4. *The New International Dictionary of the Bible*, gen. ed. Merrill C. Tenney; rev. ed. J. D. Douglas (Grand Rapids: Zondervan, 1987), 207.

5. Alnor, "The Christ . . .", *Christian Research Journal* (Summer 1990): 35.

6. Alnor, *Soothsayers*, 47–48.

7. See also the following verse, which is a poetic discription of the new age: "And he shall judge among many people, and rebuke strong nations afar off; and they shall beat their swords into plowshares, and their spears into pruning hooks; nation shall not lift up a sword against nation, neither shall they learn war any more" (Micah 4:3 KJV).

8. According to one major school of prophecy, this verse could refer to the rapture. Nevertheless, it still portrays the physical appearance of Jesus Christ.

9. Alnor, *Soothsayers*, 47.

10. Walter Martin, "UFOs," Rock Fellowship Church, Fresno, California, 14 June 1987.

11. One of the most notable exceptions is the case of William Cooper, who in a few short years has become a popular speaker at New Age conventions. Cooper says the United States government working in conjunction with the "grays" may be trying to overthrow the world and sell humankind into slavery. Cooper, though a powerful speaker, is short on facts. In late 1990 and in 1991 the *MUFON UFO Journal*, probably the most influential (and semiscientific) voice in the UFO community, published two articles and a letter to the editor critical of Cooper, his fact gathering, and his sanity (*MUFON UFO Journal*, 103 Oldtowne Rd., Seguin, Tex. 78155-4099).

12. Steiger, *Fellowship*, 50.

13. Steiger, *Gods*, 122.

14. Elliott Miller, *A Crash Course on the New Age* (Grand Rapids: Baker Book House, 1989), 155.

15. "Channeling: Share the Spirit," prod. Vicki Sufian, *West 57th Street*, NBC, KYW-TV, Philadelphia, 27 June, 1987.

16. Miller, 158.

Chapter 4
The Modern Myth Becomes a New Religion

1. Curran, 13.

2. Jacques Vallee, *Messengers of Deception* (Berkeley: And/Or Press, 1979), 9.

3. Cited in Curran, 11.

4. Philip J. Imbrogno, "Close Encounters of the Tristate Kind," *Spotlight* (February 1990): 39.

5. Cited in Curran, 14.

6. See Jacques Vallee, *Anatomy of a Phenomenon* (Chicago: Henry Regnery, 1985), 47. The book was later released in an Ace paperback.

7. Jaime H. Shandera and William L. Moore, "3 Hours That Shook the Press," *MUFON UFO Journal* (September 1990): 7.

8. "The government lied," proclaims the cover of the 1989 book, *Majestic*, by Whitley Strieber (New York: Berkley, 1990) that talks about the Roswell affair and the recovery of four dead aliens at the site. The many accounts differ over what may have happened at Roswell. Some say the government fears a public panic if they reveal that the world is being visited on a regular basis by aliens. But in my opinion, UFOlogist John Keel's explanation may be closer to the truth when he states the recovered materials could have been the remains of a Japanese fugo balloon released during World War II. Keel is skeptical of all the new books coming out today about the Roswell incident, partly because of the hundreds of witnesses who have suddenly appeared to talk about it.

9. Curran, 14.

10. Gary Kinder, *Light Years* (New York: Atlantic Monthly, 1987) 137.

11. Ibid., 137–39.

12. Brad Steiger with Alfred Bielek and Sherry Hanson Steiger, *The Philadelphia Experiment & Other UFO Conspiracies* (New Brunswick, N.J.: Inner Light, 1990), 19.

13. David Wimbish, *Something's Going on Out There* (Old Tappan, N.J.: Fleming H. Revell, 1990), 41–43.

14. Brad Steiger, *The UFO Abductors* (New York: Berkley, 1988), 69.

15. Philip J. Klass, "The Condon UFO Study: A Trick or a Conspiracy?" *The Skeptical Inquirer* (Summer 1986): 330.

16. Philip J. Klass, "Many UFOs Are Identified as Plasmas," *Aviation Week and Space Technology* (Oct. 3, 1966): 54.

17. In the 1980s UFO-and-space expert and skeptic James Oberg also got into the act with his offer of one thousand dollars to the defense fund of anyone facing prosecution for revealing alien corpses, hidden saucers, or UFO secrets.

18. Philip J. Klass, "The Condon UFO Study . . .," 328.

19. James Oberg, "Space Encounters," *The Omni Book of the Paranormal & the Mind*, ed. Owen Davies (New York: Kensington, 1983), 107–13.

20. Front page exposés on the UFO cult in the *San Francisco Chronicle* (Nov. 1, 1975) and the *Sacramento Bee* (Nov. 22, 1975) were two examples.

21. "'88 Update: The UFO Two and Their Crew." This four-page paper dated October 1988 was sent to Dr. J. Gordon Melton, director of the Institute for the Study of American Religion. A letter from an anonymous follower of the sect was enclosed. The paper is on file at Dr. Melton's office at the University of California, Santa Barbara.

22. Curran, 21.

23. "Vallee Visits Soviet Union." Interview. *UFO* 5 (1990): 16.

24. Rita DeMontis, "Is There a UFO Coverup?" *Toronto Sun*, 20 Aug. 1988: 42.

25. Howard Blum, interview, National Public Radio, KCRW, Los Angeles, 10 Oct. 1990.

26. Ibid.

27. Curran, 23.

28. According to an Oct. 15, 1989 Reuters dispatch, witnesses to the alleged landing were found to be elusive.

29. William Alnor, "In the Soviet Union, a Growing Psychic-Occult Revival," *Christian Research Journal* (Winter/Spring 1990): 5–6.

30. Tom Walker, "Belgian Scientists Seriously Pursue a Triangular UFO," *Wall Street Journal*, 10 Oct. 1990: 1.

31. Pamela Constable, "Brazilian Cult Blends Jesus, Flying Saucers, Clairvoyance," *The Register* (Orange County, California), 6 April 1985: E13.

32. Tom Wolfe, foreword, *In Advance of the Landing: Folk Concepts of Outer Space*, by Douglas Curran (New York: Abbeville Press, 1985).

Chapter 5
New Age Channelers Owe a Lot to UFOs

1. J. Z. Knight, *A State of Mind, My Story* (New York: Warner, 1987), 103–04.

2. Paul Kurtz, "Spiritualists, Mediums, and Psychics: Some Evidence of Fraud," *A Skeptic's Handbook of Parapsychology*, ed. Paul Kurtz (Buffalo: Prometheus, 1985), 209.

3. J. Gordon Melton and George Eberhart, *The Flying Saucer Contactee Movement: 1950-1990* (Santa Barbara: Santa Barbara Centre for Humanistic Studies, 1990), iii.

4. Ibid., 4.

5. Ibid.

6. James W. Moseley, "Some New Facts about 'Flying Saucers Have Landed,'" *Saucer News* (Oct. 1957): 6.

7. Melton and Eberhart, 4.

8. The July 1989 edition of the *Rainmaker News* of Florida saluted Adamski "who more than once was taken up in spacecraft and visited other planets."

9. Fred Steckling, president of the foundation, has continued the work of Adamski by producing a book, which contains contrived pictures, titled *Alien Bases on the Moon*. GAF International, P.O. Box 1722, Vista, CA 92083.

10. Curran, 79.

11. Ibid., 79–81.

12. "The Aetherius Society: A Brief Introduction" (The Aetherius Society, 1989).

13. Frank Stranges, "Coming of the Space Guardians," National New Age & "Truth about UFOs" Conference, San Diego, 16 March 1991.

14. Brownell, 156–57.

15. Melton and Eberhart, 25.

16. Kurtz, 211.

17. Cited in Jon Klimo, *Channeling* (Los Angeles: Jeremy Tarcher, 1987), 5–6.

18. Klimo, 5–6.

19. Ibid., 14–15.

20. Ibid., 4–5.

21. Steiger, *Gods*, 114–15.

22. Miller, *Crash Course*, 143.

23. Ibid.

24. Ruth Montgomery, *Aliens among Us* (New York: Ballantine, 1986), 4.

25. Ibid., 2–3.

26. Ibid., 3.

27. Florence Graves, "Searching for the Truth: Ruth Montgomery Investigates Life, Death, and the Hereafter," *New Age Journal* (January/February 1987): 24–26.

28. Wimbish, 66–67.

29. Graves, 26.

30. Wimbish, 63.

31. Graves, 26.

32. Montgomery, 223–24.

33. Ibid., 224.

34. Graves, 26–27.

35. "Bill Cox, Globetrotting Researcher to Reveal . . .Amazing Powers of the Spacemen," *Inner Light* 19, 1990: 8.

36. Goldman, Stuart, unpublished manuscript on Whitley Strieber on file, cited in Alnor, "UFO Cults . . .", 4.

37. *Extraterrestrial Earth Mission: We Are One* (Sedona, Ariz.: Earth Mission).

38. Strieber, *Transformation*, 252.

39. Ibid., 232.

40. Steiger, *UFO Abductors,* 11–12.

41. Telephone interview with Barbara Schutte on Feb. 28, 1991.

Chapter 6
Communion, MacLaine, and Occult Myths

1. Whitley Strieber, *Communion* (New York: Beech Tree, 1987), 26.

2. Ed Conroy, *Report on Communion* (New York: William Morrow, 1989), 24.

3. Strieber, *Communion*, 28–30.

4. Ibid., 28.

5. Goldman, Stuart, unpublished manuscript on Whitley Strieber on file, cited in Alnor, "UFO Cults . . . ," 7.

6. Strieber, *Communion*, 57.

7. Ibid., 126.

8. Ibid., 83.

9. Ibid., 131.

10. Ibid., 277.

11. Ibid., 280.

12. Strieber, *Transformation*, 209.

13. Ibid., 79.

14. Ibid.

15. Ibid., 69.

16. Ibid., 36. Also note on page 240, Strieber redefines the term *demon* and makes it appear as if it is a positive force or being. He claims that the word *demon* is derived from the Greek term *daimon,* and its meaning is similar to the term *soul.* He writes that that part of the person, the soul, could become transformed, and that tradition indicates that daimon transformed would return to earth to give knowledge to others.

17. Ibid., 251.

18. Ibid., 242–43.

19. Ibid., 260.

20. Alnor, "UFO Cults . . .", 5.

21. Goldman, 10.

22. Alnor, "UFO Cults . . .", 5.

23. Conroy, 25.

24. Dennis Stacy, "Dis-Communion?" *MUFON UFO Journal* (July 1991): 11.

25. Tal Brooke, "Alien Mesages on the Big Screen," *Spiritual Counterfeits* Project Journal (Double Issue—Vols. 18:1, 2, 1992): 60.

26. Klimo, 42.

27. Shirley MacLaine, *Out on a Limb* (New York: Bantam, 1983), rack edition, 354.

28. Cited in Antonio Huneeus, "Shirley MacLaine's Extraterrestrial Connection," *UFO Universe* (Sept. 1988): 33.

29. Ibid., 32.

30. Ibid., 52.

31. Ibid.

32. Paul Zweig, "Talking to the Dead and Other Amusements," *New York Times Book Review* (Oct. 5, 1980): 11.

33. L. Sprague de Camp, *Lost Continents* (New York: Dover, 1970), 54.

34. Zweig, 11, 48.

35. de Camp, 57–58.

36. Steiger, *Gods*, 134.

37. Klimo, 177.

38. de Camp, 56. Blavatsky had a colorful view of the Lemurians. According to de Camp she thought they were apelike and egg-laying. Some of them had four arms and some had an eye in the back of their heads. Their downfall was the discovery of sex.

39. "Lemuria." *Encyclopedia of Occultism & Parapsychology*, ed. Leslie Shepard 1 (Detroit: Gale, 1978), 515–16.

40. de Camp, 53–54.

41. Eric Pement, "Don't Touch that Dial! The New Age Practice of Channeling" *Cornerstone* (Nov. 28, 1989). Pement defines Akashic Records as "a scribal form of the Universal Mind, containing all the history of the universe." Certain occultists claim they can read these records.

42. de Camp, 76–77.

43. Pement, "Channeling . . ."

44. Doris Agee, "Edgar Cayce on ESP," *The Edgar Cayce Collection*, ed. Hugh L. Cayce (New York: Bonanza, 1986), 410.

45. Edgar Cayce readings 364–6, 274–17, 294–185, 39–3 on file at the Christian Research Institute in Irvine, Calif.

46. Karla Poewe-Hexham and Irving Hexham, "The 'Evidence' for Atlantis: Addressing New Age Apologetics," *Christian Research Journal* (Summer 1989): 17.

47. de Camp, 57–58.

48. Poewe-Hexham and Hexham, "The 'Evidence' for Atlantis . . .": 17.

49. Klimo, 23.

50. Susan M. Watkins, *Conversations with Seth* (Englewood Cliffs: Prentice Hall, 1980), 132. See also Jane Roberts, *The "Unknown" Reality: A Seth Book*, vol. 2, notes and intro. by Robert Butts (Englewood Cliffs: Prentice Hall, 1979), 754–56.

51. Spangler, 16–17.

52. Triton, *The Magic of Space,* ed. John May (Larchmont, N.Y.: Triad Publishing, 1962), 66.

Chapter 7
Is Hollywood Setting Us Up for the Next Generation?

1. Steiger, *Gods . . .* , 126–29.

2. Ibid., 132.

3. *The Truth about UFOs and ETs,* videotape, narrated by Brad Steiger with Francie Steiger (Atlan Productions, 1982; 1989 Goodtimes Home Video, 1989).

4. Steiger, *Gods . . .* , 129.

5. *The Truth about UFOs and ETs,* videotape.

6. Mark Albrecht, "Close Encounters of the Third Kind," *Spiritual Counterfeits Project Newsletter* (Jan.–Feb. 1978).

7. Steiger, *Gods . . .* , 133.

8. Brad Steiger, *The Seed* (New York: Berkley, 1983), 91–93, 95.

9. Steiger, *Gods...,* 133.

10. Ibid., 132–33.

11. Rene Echevarria, "Transfigurations," *Star Trek: The Next Generation*, Synopsis by Patrick D. O'Neill. Presented in *Star Trek: The Next Generation Magazine* (90–91 season): 14 48–51.

12. Steiger, *Gods . . .* , 158–62.

13. Woodrow Nichols and Brooks Alexander, "The Modern Prometheus: Science Fiction and the New Consciousness," *UFOs: Is Science Fiction Coming True? SCP Journal* (Aug. 1977) 2: 3–4.

14. Ibid., 8.

15. Ibid.

16. Ibid.

17. Fred Bell, Workshop, Whole Life Expo, New York, Oct. 27, 1990.

18. Jacques Vallee, *Confrontations: A Scientist's Search for Alien Contact* (New York: Ballantine, 1990), 17.

19. Ibid. 20.

Chapter 8
Evil Lurks

1. "Molech, Moloch," *The New International Dictionary of the Bible*, pictorial edition (Grand Rapids: Zondervan, 1987), 667.

2. "Baal," Ibid., 113.

3. Ibid. Also, F. Duane Lindsey's commentary on Judges in *The Bible Knowledge Commentary*, Old Testament, ed. John F. Walvoord and Roy Zuck (Wheaton, Ill.: Scripture Press, 1985), 383, discusses Hadad and talks about the "many local varieties of the worship of Baal. He mentions Baal of Peor (Num. 25:3), Baal Gad (Josh. 11:17), Baal-Berith (Judg. 9:4), and Baal-Zebub (2 Kings 1:2).

4. Ibid., "Baal-zebub," 115. See 2 Kings 1:2,3,6,16; Matt. 10:25; 12:24, 27; Mark 3:22; Luke 11:15, 18–19.

5. F. Duane Lindsey, "Judges," 383.

6. "Chemosh," *The New International Dictionary of the Bible*, 200–01.

7. "Molech," *Davis Dictionary of the Bible*, 4th rev., ed. John D. Davis (Old Tappan, N.J.: Fleming H. Revell, 1977), 532.

8. F. Duane Lindsey, 383.

9. Thomas L. Constable, "1 Kings," *The Bible Knowledge Commentary*, 508.

10. "Ashtoreth," *New International Dictionary of the Bible*, 101.

11. Thomas Constable, "2 Kings," *The Bible Knowledge Commentary*, 583.

12. *Boyd's Bible Handbook* (Eugene, Oreg.: Harvest House, 1983), 93–94. Amos 5:26 in the King James Version: "But ye have borne the tabernacle of your Moloch and Chiun your images, the star of your god, which ye made to yourselves." *The New International Dictionary of the Bible* states that Chiun was "possibly Saturn as god, but the meaning of the Hebrew word is uncertain."

13. Donald R. Sunukjian, "Amos," *The Bible Knowledge Commentary*, 1442.

14. Brownell, 34–35. Cited from Van Tassel's book, *I Rode a Flying Saucer* (Los Angeles: New Age, 1952).

15. Clifford Wilson, *UFOs and Their Mission Impossible* (New York: New American Library, 1974), 95, 168, 178–88.

16. John A. Keel, *UFOs: Operation Trojan Horse* (New York: G. P. Putnam & Sons, 1970), 230. Cited by Wimbish, 83.

17. Anton S. LeVey, *The Satanic Bible* (New York: Avon, 1969), 144–46.

18. Johanna Michaelsen, *Like Lambs to the Slaughter: Your Child and the Occult* (Eugene, Oreg.: Harvest House, 1989), 312–13.

19. Ibid., 313.

20. When Elijah had his confrontation with the 450 prophets of Baal (1 Kings 18 & 19) he also requested that 400 prophets of Ashtoreth show up at the altar as well. Scripture indicates that he slaughtered the prophets of Baal, but it is silent as to whether the Ashtoreth prophets were also slain.

21. One can examine ancient Asherah poles in various museums.

22. Curran, 81.

23. Ibid.

24. *Proceedings of the College of Universal Wisdom Inc.*, 8 (no. 4): 4. *Proceedings* was the official publication of Van Tassel's organization. Among the items published in them were the messages from the space brothers.

25. Ibid. For more information on Pyramidology, see my last book, *Soothsayers of the Second Advent.* Chapter 18 exposes many date-setting errors committed by pyramidologists. I noted that "all Great Pyramid speculation seems to be one of the most futile and diabolical tail-chasing and time-wasting efforts a Christian can be involved with in these last days."

26. Ibid.

27. Ashtar Command, *Project: World Evacuation*, compiled by Tuella (Salt Lake City: Guardian Action, International, 1982), introduction.

28. "What is the 'Ashtar Command?'" undated pamphlet produced by the Ashtar Command.

29. "Operation Deliverance," speech by Universarium Foundation founder Zelrun Karsleigh, July 30, 1976. Cited in Brownell, 164–65.

30. Ibid., 165.

31. T. James, *Spacemen: Friends and Foes*, part 1 (Los Angeles: Understanding New Age Publishing Co., 1956), 2–5.

32. Ibid., 8, 11, 13, 17.

33. Valdamar Valerian, *Matrix II* (Stone Mountain, Ga.: Arcturus Books, 1989), 10–11.

34. Wimbish, 92.

35. Ashtar, *New World Order: Prophecies from Space* (New Brunswick, N.J.: Inner Light, 1990), 5.

36. Ibid., 141.

37. Ibid.

38. Commander X, "Aliens & Atlanteans of Mount Shasta," *UFO Review*, no. 32.

39. Michaelsen, 309.

40. Ashtar, 96.

41. Ibid., 33. God cast Lucifer, "the morning star" from heaven (in Isaiah) because he thought too highly of himself and rebelled against God. "You said in your heart, 'I will ascend to heaven; I will raise my throne above the stars of God: I will sit enthroned on the mount of assembly, on the utmost heights of the sacred mountain. I will ascend above the tops of the clouds; I will make myself like the Most High'" (Isa. 14:13, 14).

42. David Spangler, *Reflections on the Christ* (Moray, Scotland: Findhorn Publications, 1978, 3d ed., 1981), 45. Cited by Michaelsen.

43. Ernest L. Norman, *The True Life of Jesus of Nazareth: The Confessions of St. Paul* (El Cajon, Calif.: Unarius, 1969).

44. "That Rare, Unique, Treasured Commodity, Good News! Satan or the Anti-Christ Has Now Been Overcome!!" undated Unarius pamphlet: 1.

45. Ibid., 2. This statement is even more blasphemous when one considers that it equates the name *Jaweh*, which is the same phonetically as *Yaweh,* believed to be the holy Hebrew name for God by Bible scholars, with Satan.

46. Conroy, 276.

47. Conroy also brings up this possibility on page 282 and adds that UFOlogists do not discuss this idea in print very often.

48. Lynn G. Catoe, *UFOs and Related Subjects: An Annotated Bibliography* (prepared for the USAF Office of Scientific Research), cited in the *SCP Journal*, Aug. 1977, vol. 1, no. 2.

49. Colin Wilson, *Aleister Crowley: The Nature of the Beast* (Wellingborough, England: Aquarian Press, 1988), 69.

50. Jon Trott, "About the Devil's Business," *Cornerstone* 13 (Issue 93): 8. Despite this declaration, Crowley also took on the name Baphomet, a Luciferian designation, called on the name of Beelzebub for protection, and once started going by the name Chioi Khan, which is Hebrew for the Beast. See Wilson, 70, 75.

51. Wilson on p. 50 defines occult magic as "basically the development of a 'psychic faculty' which enables a person to see below the surface of the normal reality."

52. Conroy, 282.

53. Aleister Crowley, *The Book of Lies* (York Beach, Maine: Samuel Weiser, 1913, first paperback ed. 1980), 6. Crowley is quoted as saying, "My association with Free Masonry was therefore destined to be more fertile than almost any other study."

54. Wilson, 20–22, 64.

55. Bob Larson, *Satanism: The Seduction of America's Youth* (Nashville: Thomas Nelson, 1989), 153.

56. John Frattarola, "America's Best Kept Secret," *Passport* (Oct.–Nov. 1986): 4.

57. Wilson, 71.

58. Aleister Crowley, *The Book of the Law* (York Beach, Maine: Samuel Weiser, 1976), 5.

59. Kenneth Grant, *Outside the Circles of Time* (London: Frederick Muller, 1980), 18 & jacket cover.

60. Conroy, 277.

61. Ibid., 283.

62. Steiger, *Gods*, 237. Some UFOlogists also cite Robert K. Temple, *The Sirius Mystery* (New York: St. Martins), 1976. It theorizes that the Dogon tribes of Africa were visited by reptilians from Sirius centuries ago.

63. Wilson, 158–59.

64. Conroy, 283.

65. Crowley, *Law*, 7.

66. Ibid., 9.

67. Conroy, 282.

68. Cited by Larson, 157.

69. Wilson, 73.

70. Wilson, 81–82.

71. Bob Larson, *Larson's New Book of Cults* (Wheaton: Tyndale, 1989), 194.

Chapter 9
Channeling Fallible Gods

1. I did not participate in the two-hour long session. Each person was expected to talk directly to the space being that had taken over Short's body for advice. I simply passed, and observed, tape recording the entire session.

2. Short-Korton apparently has a history of telling people to move. See page 124 in Curran.

3. Edwin A. Blum, "John," *The Bible Knowledge Commentary*, New Testament, 312.

4. Ibid.

5. Robert C. Girard, *Arcturus Book Service, Catalogue 1991–6, June*, commentary, 4. Mr. Girard can be reached at P.O. Box 831383, Stone Mountain, Ga. 30083-0023. I talked with Mr. Girard on the phone about his view of Jesus. He affirmed the quotation, and went into more detail about Jesus. He claimed Christ was responsible for almost all the wars of humankind since the first century. However, he claimed Jesus was misunderstood by his followers, who went astray when they began to worship him.

6. Robert Short, "Channeling the Space Brothers" *National New Age & "Truth About UFOs" Conference*, Workshop, San Diego, March 16, 1991.

7. Robert Short, "World Predictions—2000 & Beyond," *National New Age & "Truth About UFOs" Conference*, speech,. San Diego, March 15, 1991.

8. For a bibliographic list of UFO book titles that tell of the 1950s scene see Melton and Eberhart's *The Flying Saucer Contactee Movement: 1950–1990,* available from the Santa Barbara Centre for Humanistic Studies, Box 91611, Santa Barbara, CA 93190-1611.

9. Short, "Channeling . . ."

10. Joshua Strickland, *There Are Aliens on Earth! Encounters* (New York: Grosset & Dunlap, 1979), 31–33.

11. Hal Wilcox, *Zemkla: Interplanetary Avatar* (Los Angeles: Galaxy, 1966), 33.

12. Brownell, 87–90.

13. John Jess, *Who's Flying the UFOs?* (Wheaton, Ill.: Chapel of the Air, 1966), 10.

14. James A. Harder, "Information or Misinformation?" *MUFON Journal* (Nov. 1990): 11.

15. Huneeus, 52.

Chapter 10
A Swiss Man Meets a Different Jesus Back in Time

1. The gathering was Fortfest '90, an annual conference sponsored by the International Fortean Organization (P.O. Box 367, Arlington, VA 22210-0367). The group is named for author Charles Fort (1874–1932) who often wrote about strange and unexplained phenomena. Forteans are very interested in the UFO phenomenon. They have not taken an official position on it, however.

2. Dennis Stacy, "New Books," *MUFON UFO Journal* (Feb. 1987): 11.

3. Gary Kinder, *Light Years* (New York: *Atlantic Monthly,* 1987), 224–25.

4. Ibid., 225.

5. Ibid., 218.

6. Eduard "Billy" Meier, "My Youth," *Contact: Erra to Terra* (Oct. 1989): 10.

7. Kinder, 79.

8. Ibid., 80.

9. For two excellent books dealing what should be a deathblow to the idea that Jesus traveled to India, see Ron Rhodes' *The Counterfeit Christ of the New Age Movement*; and *Revealing the New Age Jesus,* by Douglas Groothuis (Downers Grove, Ill.: InterVarsity, 1990). However, as we have seen in this book, most New Agers probably won't pay much attention to the facts. They want to believe Jesus was an occultist and that he learned it in India.

10. Kinder, 82.

11. Ibid., 84.

12. Ibid., 201.

13. Lee J. Elder and Thomas K. Welch, *UFO . . . Contact from the Pleiades,* vol. 1, rev. ed., text by Wendelle C. Stevens (Phoenix: Genesis III, 1980), 71.

14. Kinder, 150.

15. Ibid., 263.

16. Ibid., 231.

17. Ibid., 99.

18. Ibid., 208.

19. Ibid., 58.

20. Ibid., 112–14.

21. Ibid., 62.

22. J. Randolph Winters, "A Search for Truth," *Contact: Erra to Terra* (Oct. 1989): 21.

23. J. Randolph Winters, "The Pleiades Project, Program of Events," special two-day seminar, undated, 93.

24. Ibid., 94, 95.

25. Ibid.

26. Ibid., 94.

27. Ibid., 95.

28. Ibid., 94–97.

29. Elder and Welch, 64–70.

30. "The Pleiades Project," 95.

31. Joseph Gudel, Robert Bowman and Dan Schlesinger, "Reincarnation—Did the Church Suppress it?" *Christian Research Journal* (Summer 1987): 8–12. See also Stephen F. Cannon's excellent article, "No Ma'am . . . That's Not History! Shirley MacLaine, Reincarnation and Scholastic Dishonesty," *Personal Freedom Outreach Journal* (Jan.–March 1990): 8–10.

32. Diane Tessman, "A Message to Earth from Space Brother Tibus," *UFO Review* (no. 32): 28.

33. Fred Bell, workshop, Whole Life Expo, New York, Oct. 27, 1990.

34. Randall Sullivan, "Aetherius Society: Sending Prayers to Jesus on Venus," *Los Angeles Herald Examiner,* 1 Aug. 1983, B6.

35. John W. Dean, *Flying Saucers Close Up* (Clarksburg, W. Va.: Saucerian, 1970), 141.

36. Rhodes, 37.

37. Brownell, 60, 61.

38. Ibid., 204–207.

39. Sandra Michael, Body of Light, 5663 Balboa Ave. #257, San Diego, CA 92111.

40. "Hussein—Not as Bad as Western Media Says," *Share International News* (Fall 1990): 1. This message from Maitreya was reported on Sept. 9, 1990.

41. Jane Palzere, one of the authors of *The Jesus Letters,* claims Peale endorsed the book and did not rescind his endorsement. Peale's administrative assistant, however, wrote me and said Peale made a mistake in endorsing the book many years ago without fully reading it. He does not endorse the New Age movement, she wrote.

42. Jane Palzere, Anna Brown, *The Jesus Letters* (Newington, Ct.: Janna Press, 1979), 28, 29, 35, 51.

43. Ibid., 63.

44. Alnor, "UFO Cults . . .", 6–7.

45. Rael, *The Message Given to Me by Extraterrestrials* (Tokyo: Raelian Foundation, 1986), 84.

46. Rael, *Let's Welcome our Fathers from Space* (Tokyo: Raelian Foundation, 1987), 92, 95, 96.

47. Alnor, "UFO Cults . . .", 6.

48. Raelian Movement workshop, Whole Life Expo, New York, Oct. 27, 1990.

49. Andre Pinconneault, guide coordinator for the Raelian movement in North America. Informational form letter dated Sept. 7, 1990.

50. Vallee, Messengers, 144.

Chapter 11
Ancient Tall Tales from the Ruler of the Air

1. Strieber, *Transformation*, 252.

2. Steiger, *Gods*, 18, 125.

3. See Philip J. Imbrogno's, "Close Encounters of the Tristate Kind," in *Spotlight*, February 1990, which covers the New Jersey, New York, and Connecticut areas.

4. Strieber, *Communion*, 284.

5. Telephone interview with Barbara Schutte on Feb. 28, 1991.

6. Robert S. Ellwood, Jr., *Words of the World's Religions* (Englewood Cliffs, N.J.: Prentice-Hall, 1977), 201–02.

7. "Japanese UFO and Space Symposium," *MUFON UFO Journal* (May 1991): 12.

8. A.C. Bhaktivedanta Swami Prabhupada, *Bhagavad-Gita As It Is* (New York: MacMillan, 1972). In a foreword to the book by Edward C. Dimock, he notes that Prabhupada's translation and commentary were original, and different from certain others. "In this translation the Western reader has the unique opportunity of seeing how a Krishna devotee interprets his own texts."

9. John Weldon with Zola Levitt, UFO's: *What on Earth Is Happening?* (Irvine, Calif.: Harvest House, 1975), 23.

10. Steiger, *Fellowship*, 104.

11. "The Inca-Shaman-UFO Connection," *UFO Review* (No. 33, 1991): 26.

12. Vallee, *Anatomy*, 1.

13. Ibid., 3.

14. Ibid., 4.

15. Ibid., 3.

16. Richard G. Wittmann, "Flying Saucers or Flying Shields," *The Classical Journal* 63 (No. 5, 1968): 223–24.

17. Vallee, *Anatomy*, 6.

18. Ibid.

19. Weldon and Levitt, *UFO's . . .* , 25.

20. W. R. Drake, "Spacemen in the Middle Ages," F.S.R., X (May, 1964): 11–13, quoted in Jacques Vallee's *Anatomy of a Phenomenon*, 5.

21. Weldon and Levitt, *UFO's . . .* , 25,

22. Vallee, *Anatomy*, 7.

23. Letter from Shirley A. Riemenschneider, *Time*, 9 Oct. 1989, 16. Riemenschneider's letter, however, notes that fairy rings are caused by a fungus. They can also be a round area in which many mushrooms thrive.

24. Strieber, *Communion*, 244. (Strieber was referring to the research of Budd Hopkins, one of his former associates mentioned prominently in *Communion* who claimed in his 1987 book *Intruders* that aliens, for unknown reasons—possibly sinister—were

genetically manipulating human women by impregnating them with part alien babies, then removing the fetuses from their bodies a short time later and raising the offspring themselves.)

25. Ibid., 248.

26. Rossell H. Robbins, *The Encyclopedia of Witchcraft and Demonology* (New York: Crown, 1959), 254.

27. Ibid., 255, 258–59.

28. Vallee, *Messengers* . . . , 13.

29. William M. Alnor, "Mormon Church Secretly Alters Its Temple Rituals," *Christian Research Journal* (Summer 1990): 6.

30. Walter R. Martin, *The Kingdom of the Cults* (Minneapolis: Bethany, 1985), rev. and expanded ed., 170, 172.

31. Ibid., 172.

32. James Walker, "Truths that Transform," national radio show from D. James Kennedy's Coral Ridge Presbyterian Church, Ft. Lauderdale, Fla., Oct. 22, 1990.

33. Wimbish, 98.

34. Vallee, *Messengers*, 192.

35. Grant, jacket cover and 50.

36. "Cult of the Month—Scientology: Pandora's Box," *Cornerstone* (Chicago) (issue 31, 1976): 11, 16, 23.

37. Ibid.

38. Ibid., 11.

39. "Scientology," Spiritual Counterfeits Project fact sheet (Box 4308, Berkeley, CA 94704).

40. Richard Behar, "The Thriving Cult of Greed and Power," *Time*, 6 May 1991, 51–53.

41. Ralph Lee Smith, "Scientology—Menace to Mental Health," *Today's Health*, Dec. 1968, 38. Cited by Walter Martin in *The Kingdom of the Cults*, rev. 1985 ed., 346.

42. Behar, 51–53.

43. Vallee, *Messengers* . . . , 19.

44. Ibid., 18.

45. Ibid., 21.

46. Alnor, "UFO Cults . . .", 5.

47. Martin Gardner, "Notes of a Fringe-Watcher," *Skeptical Inquirer* 16 (Fall 1991): 227–28. This article and a previous one in the Spring 1991 issue is interesting in that it explores the idea that Kellogg and Dr. William Sadler, both prominent Seventh Day Adventists at one time, may have incorporated some Adventist doctrine into the *Urantia Book*.

48. Alnor, "*UFO Cults* . . .", 5. For a detailed Christian critique of the *Urantia Book* I heartily recommend obtaining Dean Halverson's article, "Urantia . . . the Brotherhood, the Book," which was published in the Spiritual Counterfeits Project's August 1981 newsletter (P.O. Box 2418, Berkeley, CA 94702).

49. Martin Gardner, "Notes of a Fringe-Watcher," *Skeptical Inquirer*, Winter 1990, 124.

50. Gardner, Spring 1991, 124.

51. Gardner, Winter 1990, 126.

Chapter 12
The False Origin of the Species

1. Gene M. Phillips, "Insights into the Ancient Astronauts Theory," *MUFON 1991 International UFO Symposium Proceedings* (Sequin, TX: MUFON, 1991) 82.

2. According to Sitchin's biographical sheet published on p. 14 of the *1991 MUFON Symposium Proceedings,* he was a "leading journalist and editor in Israel for many years, he now lives and writes in New York. He is a member of the Israel Exploration Society, the American Oriental Society, and the Middle East Studies Association of North America.

3. Indeed his books only contain two references to Christ. In *The Stairway to Heaven,* p. 72, he says tradition indicates that during the Christ child's flight to Egypt his family rested by a shrine that depicted a spaceship. And in *The Wars of Gods and Men,* pp. 223–24, he mentions that the ancient Sumerian religion has a parallel story of an alien being entombed alive in the Great Pyramid (only to escape later), which is a parallel to the New Testament story of Christ's resurrection.

4. Clifford Wilson, *The Chariots Still Crash* (New York: Signet, 1976), 7–8.

5. Ibid., 8.

6. Timothy Ferris, "All that Glitters Is Not God," *Rolling Stone*, 30 Jan. 1975: 45.

7. Cited in "Scholars Submit New Arguments to Shred Space 'Chariots' Theory." CARIS tract, Santa Ana, Calif.

8. Ibid.

9. Wilson, *The Chariots . . .* , 5.

10. Ferris, 45.

11. Von Daniken manuscript on file at the Christian Research Institute, Irvine, Calif.

12. Wilson, *The Chariots . . .* , 146–47.

13. de Camp, 55.

14. Ibid., 55.

15. Ibid., 57–58.

16. Vallee, *Messengers . . .* , 235.

17. Gerhard R. Steinhauser, *Jesus Christ: Heir to the Astronauts* (New York: Simon and Schuster, 1976) pocket edition, 11, 32, 57, 59.

18. Irwin Ginsburgh, *First Man, Then, Adam* (New York: Simon and Schuster, 1975), 89, 93, 97, 101. This was also demonstrated in an old *Twilight Zone* episode where a lone surviving human who crash-landed his spaceship on a deserted planet found a blonde woman and named her Eve.

19. Marc Dem, *The Lost Tribes from Outer Space* (New York: Bantam, 1977), 24, 33, 35, 179, 181, 185.

20. R.L. Dione, *Is God Supernatural?* (New York: Bantam, 1976), 1, 68, 85, 86.

21. R.L. Dione, *God Drives a Flying Saucer* (New York: Bantam, 1973), 100.

22. Neil Freer, *Breaking the Godspell* (Phoenix: Falcon, 1990), 118.

23. Ibid., 42.

24. Ibid., 6.

25. Zecharia Sitchin, *The Wars of Gods and Men* (New York: Avon, 1985), 345–49.

26. Zecharia Sitchin, *The 12th Planet* (New York: Avon, 1978), 370.

27. Arnold B. Rhodes, *The Mighty Acts of God* (Richmond, Va.: CLC, 1964), 29.

28. I. D. E. Thomas, *The Omega Conspiracy* (Herndon, Va: Growth, 1986), 104.

29. Ibid., 232.

30. "Giants," *The New International Dictionary of the Bible*, 387.

31. Wilson, *The Chariots* . . . , 152-53.

32. Ibid., 153.

33. Freer, 107–14.

34. Neil Freer, "Beyond the New Age." Workshop question-and-answer time. Whole Life Expo, New York, Oct. 27, 1990.

Chapter 13
Tail Chasing with Wolves

1. Frank E. Stranges workshop, "The Mastership Seminar," National New Age & "Truth about UFOs" Conference, San Diego, March 17, 1991. I did not participate in Stranges' unbiblical prayer or ceremony.

2. Frank E. Stranges, *My Friend from Beyond Earth* (Van Nuys, Calif.: International Evangelism Crusades, 1981), rev. ed., 20–21.

3. Ibid., 22.

4. "UFO: Friend, Foe or Fantasy," Christian Research Institute tract, 20–21.

5. Frank E. Stranges, *The Stranger at the Pentagon* (Van Nuys, Calif.: International Evangelism Crusades, 1967), v. See also page 14 in the same book where a statement was made that an earthling who visited Venus had no difficulty adjusting, with "the atmosphere being basically the same as on the Earth."

6. Ibid., 1.

7. Valiant Thor, *Outwitting Tomorrow* (Van Nuys, Calif.: International Evangelism Crusades, 1978), 11–32. For a thorough refutation of Great Pyramid theology, please see my book, *Soothsayers of the Second Advent.*

8. Stranges, *Stranger*, 14.

9. In Genesis 11 all humankind was one group with one language and was involved in a huge building project called the Tower of Babel. God confused their language and "scattered them over the face of the whole earth" (Gen. 11:9).

10. Stranges, *My Friend*, back cover.

11. Stranges, *Stranger*, back cover.

12. One early biography on the back cover of *Stranger* said Stranges "attended Eastern Bible College and North Central Bible College," while another account of him in a newspaper article said he received "doctor of psychology and philosophy degrees from Faith Bible College and Theological Seminary in Ft. Lauderdale, Fla." In the back cover of *My Friend* he also claims to have a doctor of theology degree and a "Doctor of International Law degree from Union University" along with holding many, many law enforcement awards. I am investigating Stranges's degrees.

13. International Evangelism Crusades/International Theological Seminary Catalogue, 1984, 14.

14. Ibid., 29–33.

15. Recently I wrote the seminary for information and received no response. At the San Diego conference I asked Stranges's wife, who was manning the I.E.C. book table, whether the seminary still existed. "Oh no," she said, adding that they recently closed it. Two minutes later I asked Stranges, whom I sat next to during a good portion of the conference, whether his seminary still existed. "Oh yes!" he said. "We're fully accredited, and we now have seventeen satellite campuses all over America."

16. International Evangelism Crusades/International Theological Seminary Catalogue, 1984, 32.

17. Russell Chandler, *Understanding the New Age* (Dallas: Word, 1988), 357.

18. Frank E. Stranges lecture, "Coming of the Space Guardians," National New Age & "Truth about UFOs" Conference, San Diego, March 16, 1991.

19. Barry H. Downing, *The Bible and Flying Saucers* (New York: Berkley, 1989), 220.

20. Ibid., 14.

21. Ibid., 16.

22. William Alnor, "Conference for Cults Ministries Focuses on 'New Age' Issues," *Eternity,* May 1985, 14 (see statement on the New Age movement).

23. "UFO: Friend, Foe or Fantasy," Christian Research Institute tract, 14.

24. Downing, *The Bible...,* xiii.

25. Ibid., xxi–xxii.

26. Barry Downing, "E.T. Contact: the Religious Dimension," *MUFON 1990 International UFO Symposium Proceedings* (Seguin, Texas: MUFON, 1990), 55.

27. Curran notes that Betty Andreasson Luca claims that when aliens visited her she offered them the family Bible and they gave her a slim book, the contents of which, they said, would be revealed to her in time. They then took her inside their ship and performed a painful operation on her and told her that humankind was on the verge of destroying itself. Then one of them, whom Betty surmised was Jesus, called her his chosen one.

28. Barry Downing, "E.T. Contact . . .", 58.

29. Ibid., 47.

30. Ibid., 49.

31. Ibid., 50.

32. Ibid., 54.

33. Vallee, *Anatomy,* 3.

34. Walter Martin, "UFOs," Rock Fellowship Church, Fresno, California, 14 June 1987.

35. G. Cope Schellhorn, *Extraterrestrials in Biblical Prophecy* (Madison, Wis.: Horus House, 1990), 247.

36. Ibid., 375.

37. Barry Downing, "E.T. Contact . . .", 57.

38. John F. Walvoord, "Revelation," *The Bible Knowledge Commentary,* New Testament, 945.

39. Brownell, 29.

40. "Panel discussion on hoaxes," The International Fortean Organization, Fortfest '90 conference, McLean, Va., Nov. 10, 1990.

41. Barbara Schutte, "Do you know about UFOs and ETs?" tract.

42. Steiger, *The Fellowship,* 90–91.

43. "Indian Lore," *Rain*Maker Newsletter,* July 1989: 4.

44. Sean Devney, "Ed Conroy Reports on Communion," *UFO Universe,* May 1990: 15.

45. Ibid.

46. Klimo, 164–65.

47. Ibid., 166.

48. Vallee, *Messengers,* 62.

49. Curran, 88–95.

50. Sandra Mitchell, "The Crop Circle Mystery," The International Fortean Organization, Fortfest '90 conference, McLean, Va., Nov. 10, 1990.

51. "The Mysterious Crop Circle Formations of England Now Decoded," undated press release, Crypto-Phenomena Museum. (P.O. Box 2534, Malibu, CA 90265).

52. Vallee, *Anatomy . . .* , 206.

Chapter 14
Extraterrestrial Life and the Parallel Universe

1. Lee Siegel, "New Radio Receiver Expands Search for Extraterrestrial Life," Associated Press, *Orange County Register*, 13 Oct. 1990: A11.

2. Ibid.

3. John Holmes, "Ears Open for Otherwordly Signals," *Insight*, 17 Aug. 1987, 52–53.

4. Jim Detjen, "Star Search: The Discoverer of Pluto is Honored," *Philadelphia Inquirer*, 18 Oct. 1990: 1B.

5. Robert Jastrow and Malcolm H. Thompson, *Astronomy: Fundamentals and Frontiers* (New York: John Wiley & Sons, 1972), 384. Since writing this astronomy textbook, Jastrow has become even more liberal over the chances for there being intelligent extraterrestrial life, even suggesting that advanced extraterrestrial life may take the form of spirits. See Dave Hunt and T. A. McMahon, *America: The Sorcerer's New Apprentice* (Eugene, Oreg.: Harvest House, 1988), 17.

6. Wimbish, 181.

7. J. Allen Hynek and Jacques Vallee, *The Edge of Reality* (Chicago: Henry Regnery Company, 1975), xii–xiii.

8. Mark Albrecht and Brooks Alexander, "UFOs: Is Science Fiction Coming True?" *SCP Journal* 1 (Aug. 1977): 21–22.

9. Weldon and Levitt, 95.

10. Ibid., 161.

11. Strieber, *Transformation*, pp. 201–02.

12. Albrecht and Alexander, 20.

13. Steiger, *The Fellowship*, 192.

14. Hunt and McMahon, 255.

Appendix: Pursued by Aliens

1. This testimony has been adapted with permission from the booklet, *UFO's and the New Age Movement: Satanic Deception Exposed*, 1991 rev. ed. To reach Mr. Gianguzzi, contact the author.

2. The individual's real name was not used so as to protect her privacy.

Scripture Index

Genesis

Book of   177, 200
1:26   163
2:17   238
3:5   110, 157, 210
6   109, 201, 207, 211
6:4   212
11:1–9   239

Exodus

7:9   12
8:7   239
8:18   240
20:16   70
22:18   241
23:24   140

Leviticus

19:31   241
20:6   241
20:27   241

Numbers

21:29   137

Deuteronomy

4:2   214
4:19   160
12:3   140
16:21   140
17:1–5   160
18:9–11   160
18:9–12   127

18:9–12, 15   93
18:10–12   241
18:20–22   94

Judges

2:13   140
11:24   137

1 Samuel

28:6   241

1 Kings

11:2, 3, 5, 7   137

2 Kings

2:11   22
17:16–17   160
21:3–5   134
21:6   134
22:1–23:30   138
23:4   138
23:5   160

1 Chronicles

10:13   241
10:13–14   93
17:12–14   62

2 Chronicles

2:5–6   224
33:6   241

Job

Book of   220
9:9   167
38:7   217
38:31   167

Psalms

Book of   177
2   63
16:9–10   63
21:4   63
22   62
22:18   63
23   153
41:9   62
46:10   34
82:1, 8   157
82:1, 6   157
82:2–7   157
102:16   24

Isaiah

2:4   33, 218
2:6   241
5:20   146, 210
7:14   62
8:19   241
8:19–20   93, 127
9:6   63
11:1   62
11:4, 6, 8–9   33
14:12–15   145
35:5–6   62
40:3   62

285

Subject Index

288